Special Thanks To

Sarah Morgan, Production

Lori Darlington, Technical Editor

Carol Grace, Copy Editor

Nancy Davis, Cary Norsworthy, and Mimi Heft at Peachpit Press

Julie Stodola and Shaun Parkinson, and other helpful folks at Sausage Software

David Fugate, Waterside Productions

Julie Parker, Morale Booster

Richard Grace, Ever-Lovin' Hubby

Puddy, Big Fat Cat

VISUAL QUICKSTART GUIDE

HotDog Pro

FOR WINDOWS

ELISABETH PARKER

Peachpit Press

Visual Quickstart Guide

HotDog Pro for Windows

Elisabeth Parker

Peachpit Press
1249 Eighth Street
Berkeley, CA 94710
(510) 524-2178
(510) 524-2221 (fax)

Find us on the World Wide Web at: *http://www.peachpit.com*

Peachpit Press is a division of Addison Wesley Longman

ISBN: 0-201-69667-3

0 9 8 7 6 5 4 3 2 1

Printed and bound in the United States of America

CONTENTS

TABLE OF CONTENTS

Chapter 4 Creating a Web Page 43

HotDog 101: An Introduction

Maybe you've decided it's about time you set up a Web site for your business (or just for personal enjoyment). Or maybe you already have a Web site, but you'd like to do more with it. Either way, you'll love HotDog Pro. It's user friendly and full of great features. HotDog Pro helps you create Web pages with cutting edge features for business and fun, keep your Web site organized, check your spelling and links, maintain a list of HTML tags that you can add to, ensure that your pages download quickly, preview pages, and more. *The HotDog Pro Visual QuickStart Guide* takes a task-oriented approach to get you up and running fast.

What You Need to Get Started

To start using HotDog Pro, you need Windows 95, a 100 MhZ processor or better (you can get by on less, but some of the advanced features may work more slowly), 8 MB of RAM (memory), sufficient free disk space (HotDog Pro with SuperToolz takes up a little more than 22 MB of disk space), an Internet account and WebSite, and of course, HotDog Pro. You can get HotDog Pro by downloading it from Sausage Software's Web site at *www.sausage.com*.

Why Use HotDog Pro?

Why use HotDot Pro? Simple. It's easy, it's fast, and it's feature-packed. HotDog Pro's user-friendliness gets beginners up and running quickly, while its speed and flexibility enable professionals to create Web sites with cutting-edge content. With HotDog Pro, as shown in Figure 1, you can work the way you want to work, not the way some software company wants you to work. It gives you complete control over your Web pages, help when you need it, and support for the latest innovations on the Web. And best of all, HotDog Pro works with what you already have. You don't need a Rambo computer or to have your Internet service provider (ISP) install software on their server in order for your Web site to work properly once you upload it.

Figure 1. HotDog Pro application window with **Rover** Web page preview, source code, and list of Web site files displayed.

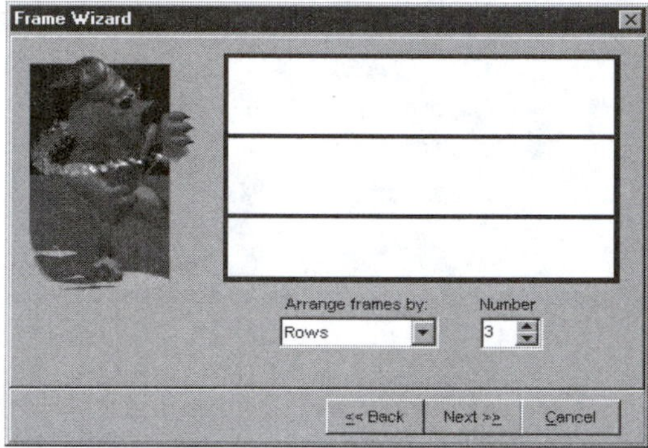

Figure 2. Wizards, like HotDog Pro's **Frame Wizard**, guide you through complex tasks.

Features that make HotDog Pro Easy

- **User-friendly interface:** Toolbar buttons, the **Resource Manager**, **SuperToolz**, and Wizards make creating, formatting, uploading, and maintaining Web pages a snap.
- **Wizards:** Wizards guide you through the more difficult tasks, like setting up pages with tables, forms, and frames. The **Frame Wizard** is shown in Figure 2.
- **Plenty of help:** HotDog Pro comes with a glossary of terms, an HTML reference, and a searchable Help system. Tooltips appear to explain toolbar buttons and Web page elements. You can also launch tutorials from the splash screen (shown in Figure 3) that appears when you launch HotDog Pro.
- **Error Checking:** HotDog Pro helps you check the accuracy of your spelling, links, and HTML syntax. You can also use the **BandWidth Buster** to determine how long your pages will take for visitors to download.

Figure 3. Need an HTML or Internet crash course? Next time you start up HotDog Pro, click one of the options on the splash screen when it appears.

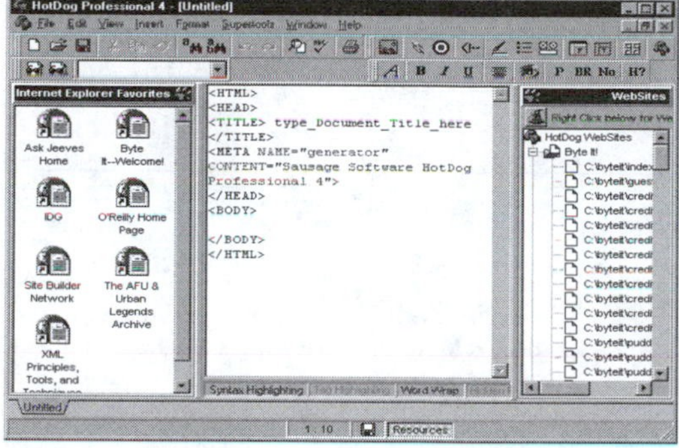

Figure 4. Hot Dog Pro application window with HTML source code and Resource Manager window panes displayed.

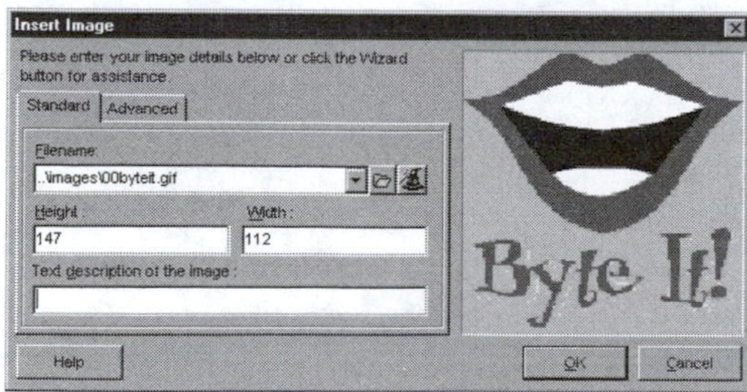

Figure 5. HotDog Pro's easy dialog boxes guide you through tasks, such as inserting images.

It's fast

- **Work more quickly:** Text editors are faster than graphical applications because you can work directly with HTML source code, shown in the center pane of the application window of Figure 4.
- **Resources at your fingertips:** You can keep files and other resources easily accessible. HotDog Pro lets you display lists of local files, Internet Favorites and Netscape Bookmarks, HTML tags, and more in the resource window panes (shown to the right and left of Figure 4).
- **Instant HTML Code:** You can do lots of neat stuff without memorizing or entering tedious HTML code. Dialog boxes and Wizards (like the **Insert Image** dialog box shown in Figure 5) prompt you for information, then HotDog Pro enters all the grunt code for you.

It's feature-packed

- **Bells and Whistles:** Easy-to-use tools, like the **Java Animator** shown in Figure 6, help you design gee-whiz pages with Java animations, JavaScript scripts, tables, frames, image maps, electronic forms, style sheets, and more.
- **Support for Online Businesses:** You can set up your site to charge digital micropayments for content with the **InfoSeller**; create channels with the **Channel Wizard**; apply Internet ratings to your pages and reassure your target audience that your content is appropriate with **SafeSurf** (shown in Figure 7); and more.
- **Site Management:** The **WebSites Manager** makes it easy to keep track of your Web site content and upload pages and other material to your server.

- **Error-checking:** HotDog Pro's **Link Verifier**, spell checking, and **Bandwidth Buster** help you avoid the pitfalls of Web publishing. In addition, HotDog Pro highlights possible HTML syntax errors, depending on which version of HTML you specify.
- **No Memorizing:** The **Resource Manager** helps you display lists of things that are hard to remember, like HTML tags, special characters, Netscape Bookmarks, Internet Explorer Favorites, and local files. You can drag items from these lists and drop them into your Web page document.
- **Rover Page Preview:** Use HotDog Pro's built-in **Rover** feature, as shown in Figure 8, to preview your pages, or preview pages in your favorite Web browser.
- **Help with Repetitive Tasks:** You can create templates for pages with repeating elements, and the **MultiFile Find and Replace** feature (shown in Figure 9) lets you apply changes to multiple pages throughout your Web site. The **Resource Manager** also lets you drag and drop items from lists to create links and insert page elements.
- **Automatic Uploading and Downloading:** To ensure that what's on your computer corresponds with what's on your server, HotDog Pro makes uploading and downloading files from your Web site a simple task.
- **Flexibility:** You can add new HTML tags to HotDog Pro's list, display lists and other resources when you need them and hide them when you don't (that's why HotDog Pro doesn't always look the same in the illustrations shown throughout the book), customize HotDog Pro's preferences, set up multiple Web site projects with the **WebSites Manager**, and more.

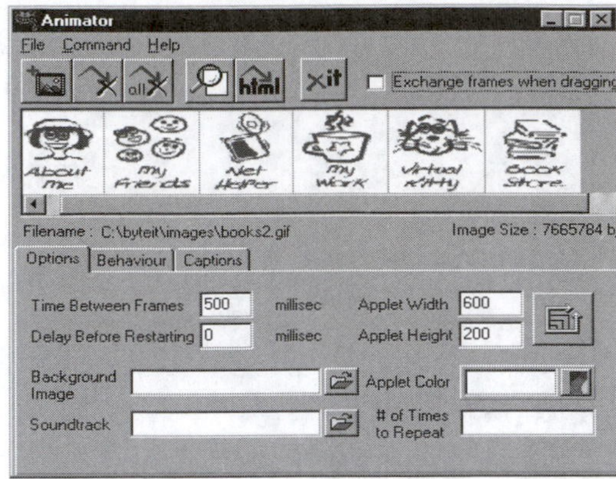

Figure 6. Tools like the **Java Animator** make it easy to add exciting, cutting-edge content to your pages.

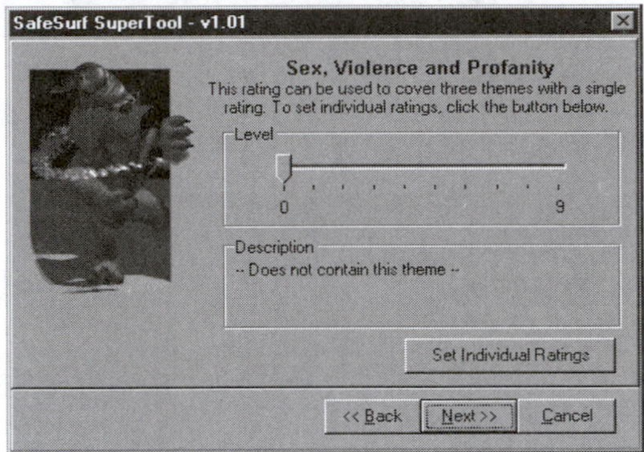

Figure 7. Tools like **SafeSurf** help you do business on the Web. **SafeSurf** lets you rate your content, so your viewers can judge whether it's appropriate for themselves or their children.

FEATURES

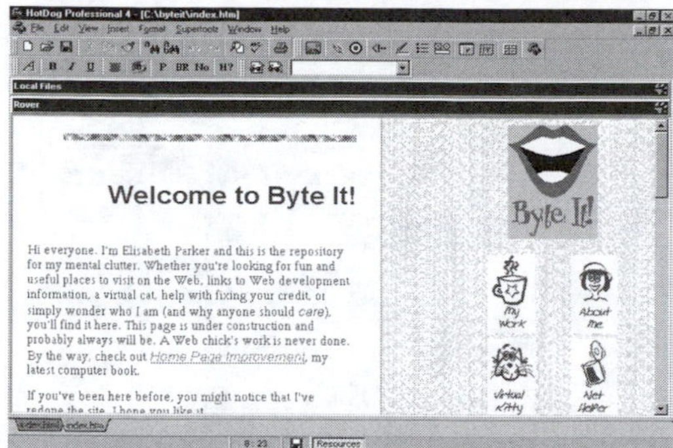

Figure 8. You can preview your pages with the **Rover**, HotDog Pro's convenient built-in browser.

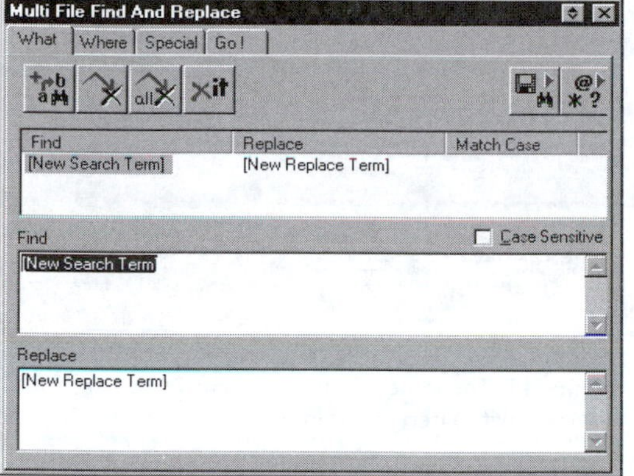

Figure 9. Tools like **MultiFile Find and Replace** help you work faster by eliminating repetitive tasks.

Why Buy this Book?

Who actually *likes* reading computer books? Not me. Fortunately, you won't have to do too much reading. I wrote the *HotDog Pro Visual QuickStart Guide* for people who like to learn by doing. Whether you're new to HotDog Pro or new to Web publishing in general, this book gets you up and running fast. The *HotDog Pro Visual QuickStart Guide* takes a practical hands-on approach and has lots of illustrations so you can spend less time reading and more time developing your Web site. The book's layout is also designed to help you find information quickly when you need it (you can also look up topics in the index). Best of all, Peachpit Press has also priced this book affordably so that breaking into Web publishing doesn't mean breaking your piggy bank.

I should also mention that at the time of this writing, there were no other books about HotDog Pro. But never fear, I'll do my best to tell you everything you need to know. Please visit my Web site at *www.byteit.com/HDPvqs/* for HotDog Pro-related updates. You can also email me at *eparker@byteit.com*.

What's a Web Page?

A Web page is a HyperText Markup Language (HTML) document. What's the difference between an HTML document and a regular word processing document? Not much. An HTML document is a plain text document (with no bolded text or any other formatting) with the .HTML or .HTM file name extensions. Each document consists of your text, along with special HTML codes that tell Web browsers like Internet Explorer and Netscape Navigator how to format text, where to display images, when text and images should function as links, when JavaScript scripts should run, and how to launch CGI scripts, Java Applets, and other associated files stored on the server.

HTML documents don't look too exciting until you view them in a Web browser. It's just a lot of text with weird-looking codes. Figure 10 shows an HTML document displayed in the HotDog Pro application window. Figure 11 shows the same HTML document (Web page) displayed in Internet Explorer.

So where does HotDog Pro fit into the scenario? It provides you with toolbars, lists, resources, wizards, and other tools to generate these HTML documents, so you don't have to memorize and enter all this stuff yourself.

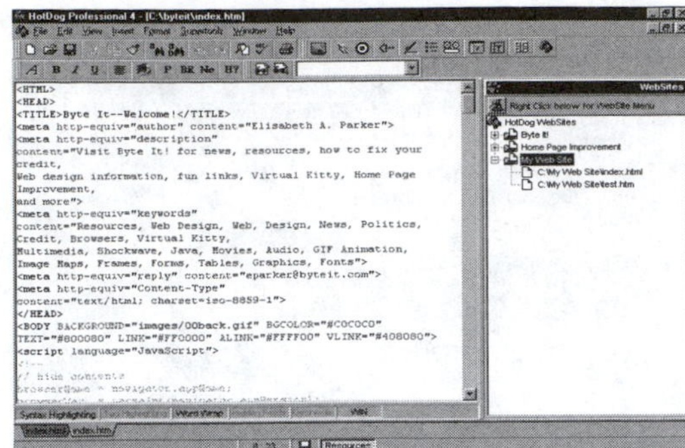

Figure 10. HTML document shown in the HotDog Pro application window.

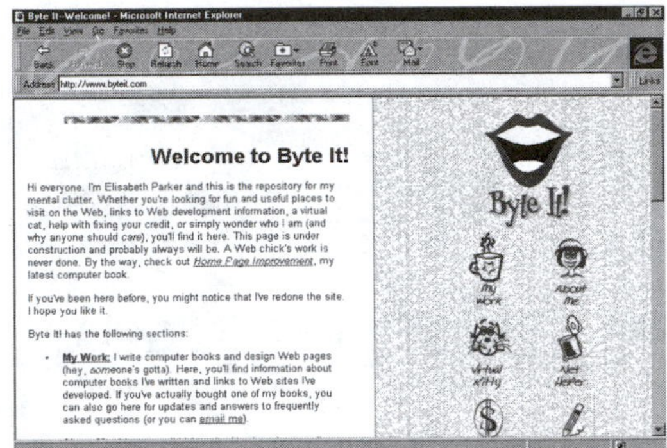

Figure 11. The same HTML document (Web page) displayed with Internet Explorer.

What Web Pages Are Made Of

- **Text:** HTML documents include your text—all of the things you want to say on your Web page. You can type your text in the HotDog Pro work area as you would type text in a word processing document. You can then use HotDog Pro's toolbar buttons to format your text.
- **HTML tags:** HTML tags are the codes that tell Web browsers how to load your Web pages. You can apply formats and links to text by selecting toolbar buttons or dragging items from HotDog Pro's list of HTML tags. Or you can insert tables, forms, and other page elements by placing your cursor in the area of the document where you want the element to appear and clicking the appropriate toolbar button.
- **HTML source code:** The entire contents of your HTML document, including your HTML tags, text, and JavaScript scripts, is called *HTML source code.* Table 1 gives a close-up of the source code for some of the text displayed in Figure 11.
- **JavaScript Scripts:** JavaScript code that runs in a Web page is entered directly in the HTML document in which it appears. HotDog Pro's **JavaScript Tools** (shown in Figure 12) help you apply JavaScript scripts

Source Code for Figure 11 Web Page

THE SOURCE CODE	WHAT IT MEANS
<H1 ALIGN="Right">Welcome to Byte It!</H1>	Enclosed text displays as level 1 heading and aligns to the right.
<P ALIGN="Right">Hi everyone. I'm Elisabeth Parker and this is the repository for my mental clutter...</P>	Enclosed text displays as an individual paragraph that aligns to the right.
By the way, check out my <A HREF="HDPVQS/index.html">HotDog Pro Visual Quickstart Guide</A>	Enclosed text displays as a link. When clicked on, the specified document loads.

Table 1. HTML source code for some of the text displayed in Figure 11.

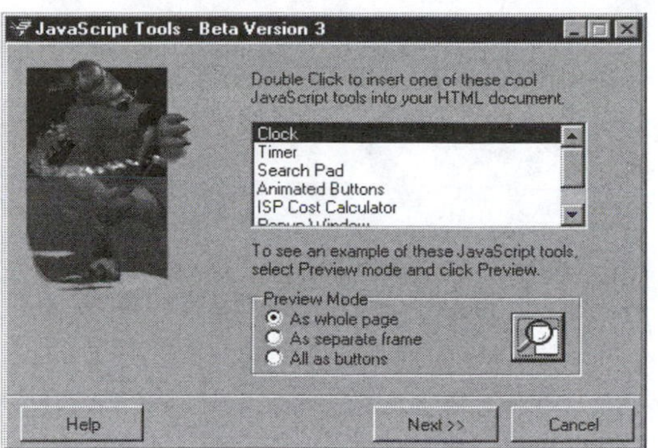

Figure 12. JavaScript Tools make it easy to add JavaScript scripts to your Web pages.

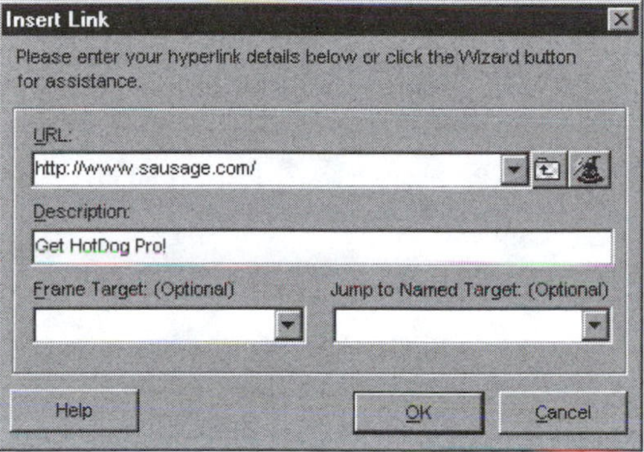

Figure 13. The **Insert Link** dialog box makes it easy to launch the **Insert Link Wizard** and make links.

to your HTML document (you don't need to know JavaScript to use **JavaScript Tools**). You can also copy JavaScript code from other HTML documents (with the author's permission of course), paste them into your HTML document, and make edits with HotDog Pro's **JavaScript Language Editor** (if you know a little JavaScript).

- **Associated Files:** Objects like images appear to be part of a Web page when viewed in a Web browser. But that's all an illusion. Associated files are stored separately from the actual Web document. They are also sometimes referred to as external files. HTML codes in the document tell Web browsers how to load these files. HotDog Pro makes it easy for you to enter the right codes.
- **Links:** Think links! They're what make the Web interactive. Links are indicated by visual cues like underlined text or images that look like they want the viewer to do something with them. When you click a link, something happens. HotDog Pro's **Insert Link** dialog box appears (shown in Figure 13) and the **Insert Link Wizard** makes linking easy. You can jump visitors to other Web pages or Web sites; invite them to send you email; help them launch a multimedia file; and more.

What's a Web site?

A Web site is an individual or organization's entire collection of Web pages and associated files. One Web site can contain many other Web sites within it. When you decide to set up a Web site, your ISP, office, school, or other type of organization that hosts the server you use creates a directory for you (*directory*, by the way, is Web-speak for *folder*). The main document in this directory is the *index* page—which you must name **index.html** or **index.htm**.

Putting It All Together

HotDog Pro helps you through all of the stages of building your Web site, from creating the first HTML document to uploading your content to the server and keeping your site running properly. The steps listed in the following section provide a quick overview of how to build a Web site with HotDog Pro.

To build a Web site

1. Create a Web site and your first HTML document with HotDog Pro's **WebSite Manager** (you can also add an existing site to the **WebSite Manager**).
2. Type what you want to say in your HTML documents (you can also copy and paste text from your word processing files).
3. Format your text, make links, and add images. You can also use HotDog Pro's tools to add fun bells and whistles and advanced capabilities to your Web site.
4. Add more pages if you want.
5. Preview your page in HotDog Pro's **Rover**, or in your favorite Web browser.
6. Use HotDog Pro's tools to check your spelling, links, and HTML syntax. You can also use the **BandWidth Buster** to make sure your pages won't take too long to download.
7. Upload pages and associated files to your Web server with the **WebSite Manager**.

You'll learn how to do all of these things as you read the book.

1

Setting Up

You've heard great things about HotDog Pro. But where can you get the program? It doesn't come as a packaged CD-ROM that you can pick up at the local computer store. Instead, you have to download HotDog Pro from Sausage Software's Web site at www.sausage.com.

HotDog Pro even has a system for purchasing and registering your software online. Getting software online at any time of the day or night from the comfort of your home or office is quite convenient. But since you might not be used to doing things this way, this chapter takes you through the process of downloading, installing, and registering HotDog Pro. You'll also learn how to download and install HotDog Pro's SuperToolz with the **AutoDownloader**. SuperToolz are special add-ons that let you do more exciting things with your Web site.

Getting HotDog Pro

HotDog Pro costs $99.95, but you can download and use it free of charge for the 14-day trial period. The program automatically disables itself when the free trial period expires.

To get HotDog Pro

1. Go to Sausage Software's Web site at *www.sausage.com*.
2. When the Web site appears, as shown in Figure 1, select the latest version of HotDog from the pull-down list and click the **Go!** Button. Web sites change all the time, so Sausage Software's page may not look *exactly* like Figure 1.
3. Follow Sausage Software's download instructions and click the link to the installer file.
4. When the **Save As** dialog box appears, as shown in Figure 2, browse for the folder you want to download the HotDog Pro installer file into.
5. Take a break and have a snack. The HotDog Pro installer file is 5,577 KB and takes about 40 minutes to an hour to download, depending on the speed of your connection.

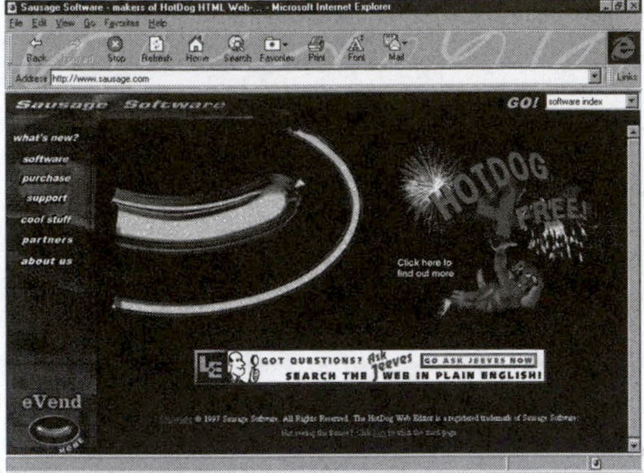

Figure 1. To get HotDog Pro 4.0, go to Sausage Software's Web page at *www.sausage.com*, and follow the instructions.

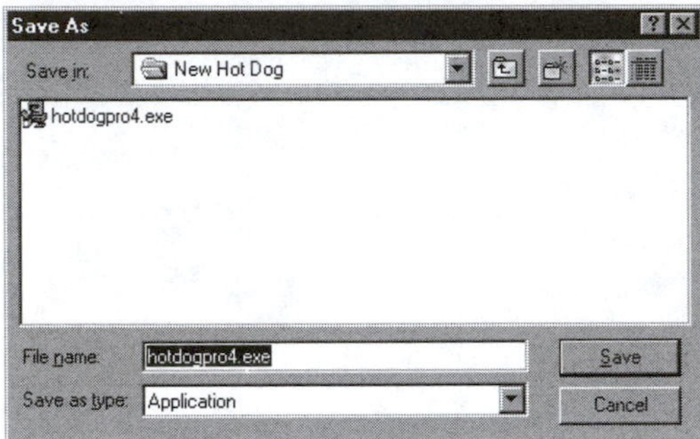

Figure 2. When you click the link to the HotDog Pro installer file, the **Save As** dialog box appears.

✔ Tip

- When you save a file you're about to download, the file's name appears in the **Save As** dialog box's **File name** text field. The currently selected folder appears in the **Save in** pull-down list window. Don't forget the name of the file or what folder you saved the file to!

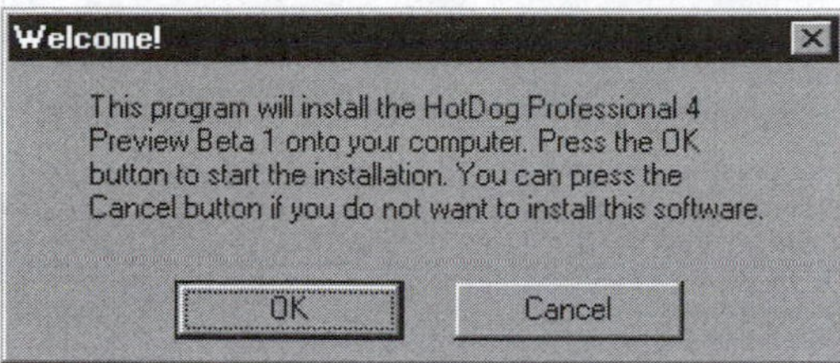

Figure 3. When you launch the installer, the **Welcome!** dialog box appears.

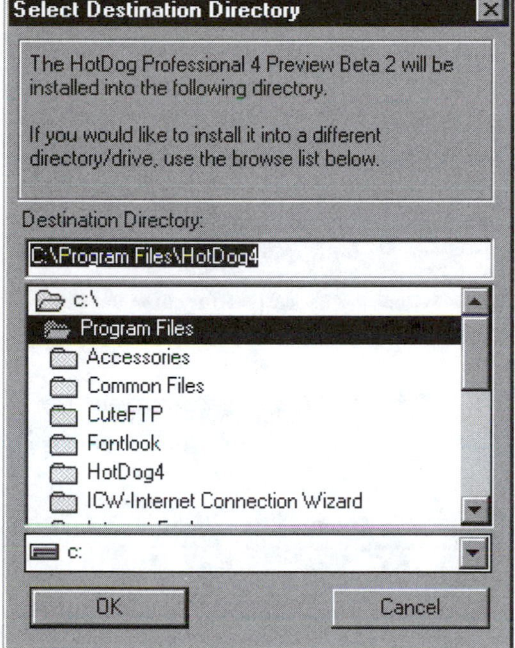

Figure 4. The **Select Destination Directory** dialog box asks where to install HotDog Pro.

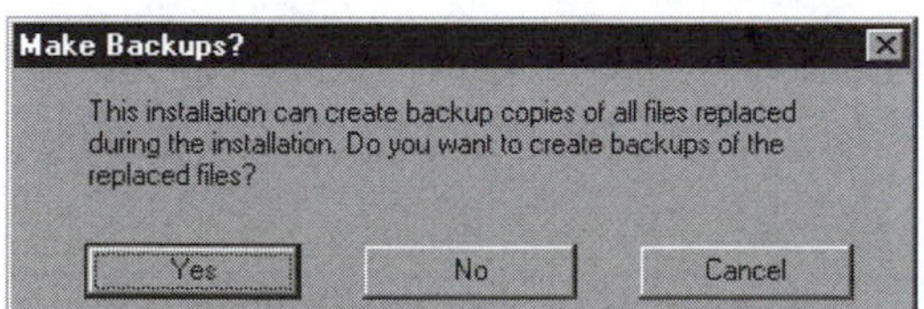

Figure 5. The **Make Backups?** dialog box asks if you'd like to back up your files.

Installing HotDog Pro

Once you finish downloading HotDog Pro, you can disconnect from the Internet and install the program. HotDog Pro consists of two parts: the main application and SuperToolz. SuperToolz are special add-ons that help you add advanced features to your Web site. Because the HotDog Pro main application is so large, you need to download and install them separately with the AutoDownloader. This section and the ones immediately following tell you how to install and purchase, register, or trial the main application. The "Introducing SuperToolz" and "Getting Your SuperToolz" sections later in this chapter tell you more about SuperToolz and how to download and install them.

To install HotDog Pro

1. Locate and double-click the **HotDog Pro** executable file to launch the setup program.
2. When the **Welcome!** dialog box appears (it looks similar to the one shown in Figure 3), click the **OK** button.
3. When the **Select Destination Directory** dialog box appears, as shown in Figure 4, tell the setup program where to put HotDog Pro. To avoid future complications, I recommend that you click **OK** to confirm the default destination directory, C:\Program Files\HotDog4.
4. When the **Make Backups?** dialog box appears, as shown in Figure 5, click the **Yes** button to make back up copies of system files that may get replaced during installation. Replacing system files with more recent versions shouldn't effect your computer's performance negatively.
   But it's a good idea to copy the old ones just in case.

5. When the **Select Backup Directory** dialog box appears, as shown in Figure 6, click OK to copy the files to the default destination directory, C:\Program Files\HotDog4\BACKUP.
6. When the **Installing** dialog box appears, as shown in Figure 7, wait for the setup program to finish copying files.
7. When the **Installing Windows Internet Pack** dialog box appears, click **Yes** if you do not have Internet Explorer version 3.0 or above installed on your system. If you already have Internet Explorer version 3.0 or higher installed, click **No**.
8. When the **Add to Start Menu?** dialog box appears, click the **Yes** button. This adds HotDog Pro to your start menu so you can access the application more easily.
9. When the HotDog Pro **Successfully Installed** dialog box appears, click the **OK** button.

That's it! You're done. Now you can purchase HotDog Pro, register it, or just try it out.

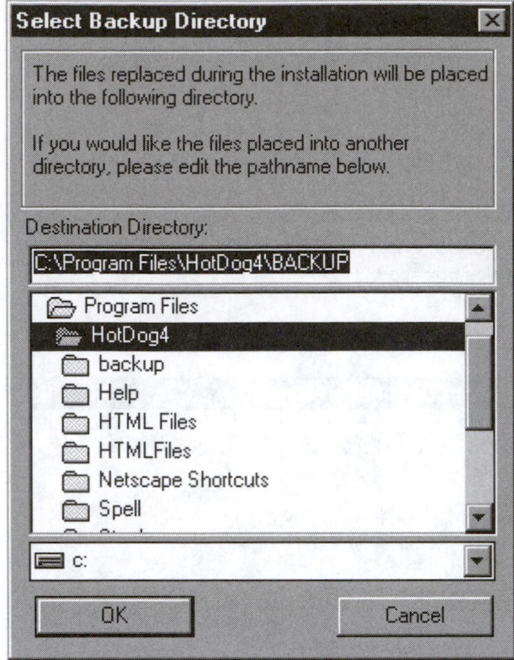

Figure 6. Choose a backup directory from the **Select Backup Directory** dialog box.

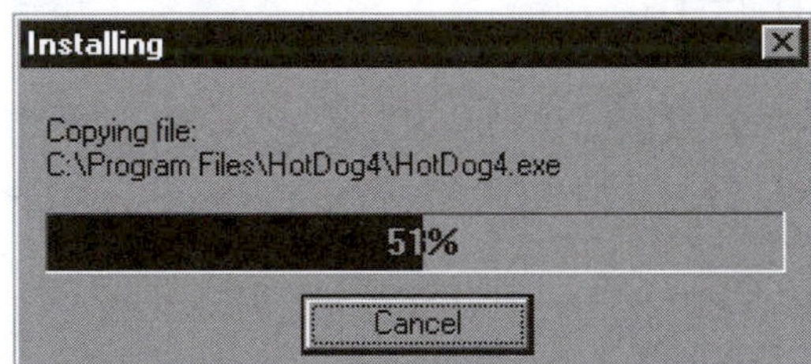

Figure 7. The **Installing** dialog box tells you that the HotDog Pro is being installed.

✔ Tips

- The easiest and fastest way to purchase and register HotDog Pro is by using the CISM.
- Check Sausage Software's Web site for special offers before purchasing with the CISM or by fax. Sometimes you can only take advantage of special offers by purchasing HotDog Pro via Sausage Software's Web site.

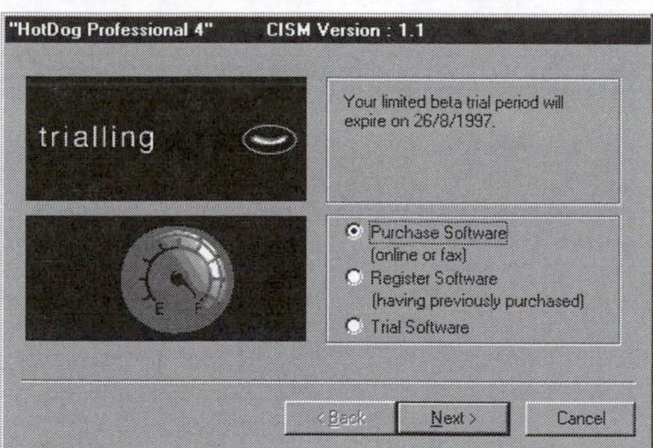

Figure 8. The **CISM—trialling** dialog box appears when you launch HotDog Pro until you purchase and register your software.

Copying Your Order and Registration Information

To keep your order and registration number handy, you can copy them into a text file. You need this information in order to register some of your SuperToolz.

To copy your order number and registration key to a text file

1. Register or purchase HotDog Pro.
2. When the **CISM—Your purchase has been approved by eVend** dialog box appears with your order number and registration key, select your order number from the **Order No.** text box.
3. Copy the order number using the **CTRL+C** key combination.
4. Open a new text file and paste the order number using the **CTRL+V** key combination.
5. Return to the **CISM—Your purchase has been approved by eVend** dialog box and repeat steps 3-4 to copy the registration key.
6. Save and name your text file.

Registering, Purchasing, or Trialling HotDog Pro

HotDog Pro's Customer Interface Service Module (CISM) makes it easy for you to purchase and register your software. But it takes a little getting used to. If you have more than one computer, make sure that you have HotDog Pro installed on the computer you use most frequently. Unlike with other software programs, you cannot register HotDog Pro on more than one computer.

If you haven't yet purchased and registered HotDog Pro, the **CISM—trialling** dialog box appears, as shown in Figure 8, and offers the following options:

- **Purchase Software (online or fax):** You can purchase and register your software online, or have the CISM generate and print out an order form that you can fax.
- **Register Software (having previously purchased):** When you purchase HotDog Pro through the order form on Sausage Software's Web site or by sending a fax, the people at Sausage Software email you an order number. You can then use the order number to register your copy of HotDog Pro with the CISM.
- **Trial Software:** You can use HotDog Pro on a trial basis for 14 days. The **CISM—trialling** dialog box appears every time you launch the program until you purchase and register it.

✔ Tips

- If you print out your order number and registration keys from the CISM, you may need to switch your printer settings to landscape (horizontal) mode first.
- You can also fax, telephone, or "snail mail" your order.

To purchase Hot Dog Pro with the CISM

1. Connect to the Internet and launch HotDog Pro.
2. When the **CISM—trialling** dialog box appears, as shown in Figure 8, select the **Purchase Software (online or fax)** radio button and click the **Next** button.
3. When the **CISM—please choose your method of purchase** dialog box appears, as shown in Figure 9, click either the **Purchase software online** radio button, or the **Purchase software via fax** radio button.
4. If you choose to purchase your software via fax, click the **Next** button and follow the instructions to print out a form so you can fill in your information and fax it to Sausage Software. You can then register HotDog Pro when your order number comes via email (see the "To register with the CISM" section.
5. If you choose **Purchase software online** (my recommended option), click the **Next** button, follow the instructions and enter your name, email address, credit card number, and other order information as prompted by the dialog boxes.
6. When the CISM approves your purchase and generates your order number and registration key, as shown in Figure 10, click the **Print** button to print out the information so you can have them handy for future reference.
7. Click the **Finish** button to launch your newly purchased and registered copy of HotDog Pro.

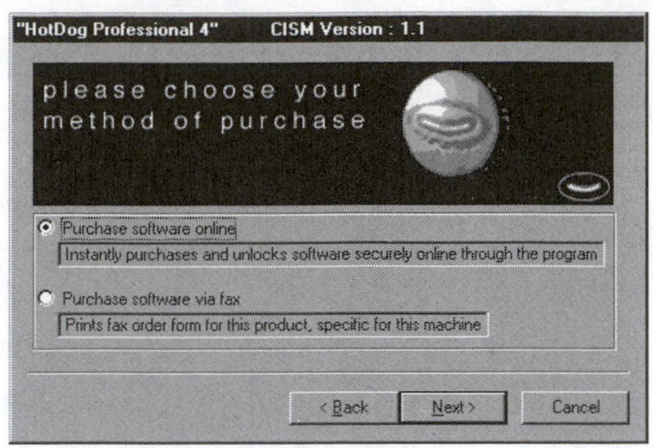

Figure 9. Tell HotDog how you'd like to send your order with the **CISM—please choose your method of purchase** dialog box.

Figure 10. When the server verifies your purchase, the **CISM—your purchase has been approved by eVend** dialog box appears.

✔ Tips

- To purchase or register HotDog Pro online with the CISM, you need to connect to the Internet first.
- I've mentioned *key combinations* a few times, and will continue doing so throughout the book. Key combinations help you do simple things, like copying and pasting text, by pressing two or three keys at the same time.
- If you aren't sure whether you want to purchase HotDog Pro yet, that's OK. You can try it out free of charge for the 14-day trial period.

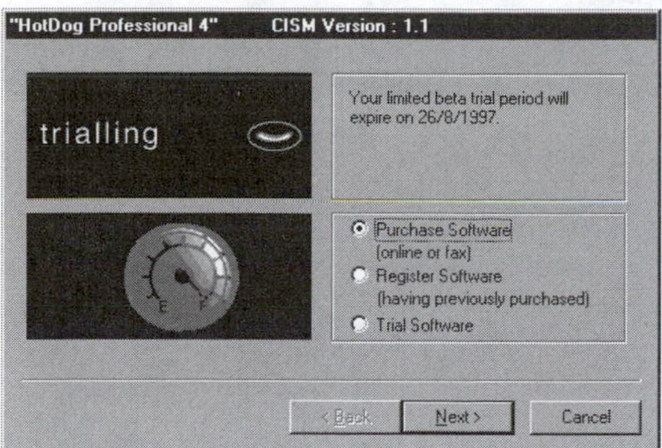

Figure 11. The CISM—trialling dialog box appears when you launch HotDog Pro until you purchase and register the program.

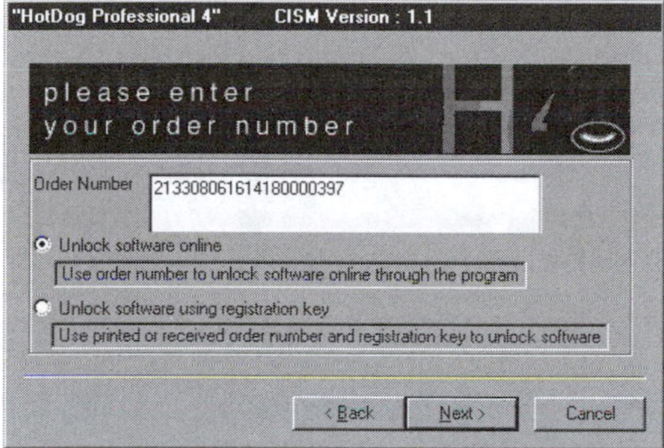

Figure 12. When you choose to register HotDog Pro, the **CISM—please enter your order number** dialog box appears so you can enter your order number.

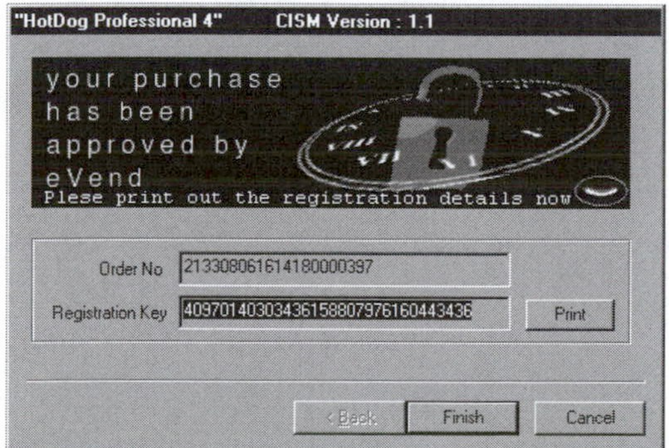

Figure 13. When the server verifies your purchase, the **CISM—your purchase has been approved by eVend** dialog box appears.

To register with the CISM

1. If Sausage Software has sent you an email message with your order number, copy it to your system's clipboard by selecting the order number (without any of the surrounding text) and using the **CTRL+C** key combination.
2. Connect to the Internet and launch HotDog Pro.
3. When the **CISM—trialling** dialog box appears, as shown in Figure 11, click the **Register Software (having previously purchased)** radio button, then click the **Next** button.
4. When the **CISM—please enter your order number** dialog box appears, as shown in Figure 12, use the **CTRL+V** key combination to paste your order number into the **Order Number** text field. If you have a printout of your order number, you can also enter it manually.
5. Select the **Unlock software online** radio button, click the button, and enter your name, email address, and other information when prompted by the **CISM** dialog boxes.
6. Wait a couple of minutes for the CISM to communicate with Sausage Software's server and process your information.
7. When the **CISM—your purchase has been approved by eVend** dialog box appears, as shown in Figure 13, copy your order number and registration key into a text file for future reference, as explained in the "Copying Your Order and Registration Information" section.
8. Print out your order number and registration key by clicking the **Print** button.
9. Click the **Finish** button.

Launching HotDog Pro

Now that you know how to register, purchase, or trial HotDog Pro, let's take a look at it. HotDog Pro even displays a splash screen when you start up the application. From the splash screen, you can choose to go straight to the application window, take a tutorial, or learn more about the Internet or HotDog Pro. In addition, the HotDog Pro application window displays an HTML document with more information.

To launch HotDog Pro

1. Select HotDog Pro from the Programs group on the Start menu.
2. If you haven't yet purchased and registered HotDog Pro yet, the **CISM—trialling** dialog box appears. If it does, choose an option and follow the instructions as explained in the previous sections of this chapter. HotDog Pro starts up when you finish using the CISM.
3. When the splash screen appears, as shown in Figure 14, click **Just Start HotDog** (or you can explore other options first, as explained in the following "Splash screen options" section).
4. When the application window appears with the **Important! Read this...** document displayed, as shown in Figure 15, you can take a peek at HotDog Pro. You can also begin downloading your SuperToolz, as explained in the "Introducing SuperToolz" section).

Figure 14. The HotDog Pro splash screen offers options for learning more about HotDog Pro, starting a tutorial, learning about how the Internet works, or starting the application.

✔ Tips

- If you're new to computers or Web pages, never fear. HotDog Pro is here. By checking out the splash screen options, you can learn everything you need for getting started.
- To close the Read Me file and start working, select **Close** from the **File** menu.

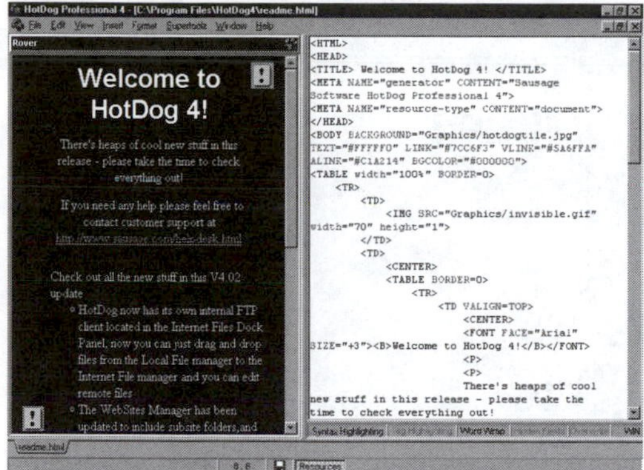

Figure 15. When you first start up HotDog Pro, the application window with a Read Me file displays.

Splash screen options

- **Tell Me About HotDog 4**: Gives you a quick overview of HotDog Pro's features.
- **Start a Tutorial**: Takes you through a useful little HTML crash course.
- **Tell Me About the Internet**: Explains how the Internet, World Wide Web, and Web pages work.
- **Just Start HotDog:** Launches the application.
- **Don't show me this screen again**: Click this checkbox if you're absolutely positive you don't want this screen to display any more.

Introducing SuperToolz

SuperToolz are special HotDog Pro components that help you create gee-whiz Web sites. They work seamlessly with the application, but you have to use the AutoDownloader to get them separately. First, I'll tell you what the SuperToolz are, and then I'll tell you how to get them.

SuperToolz

- **Button Editor:** Resize images and make other minor edits on the fly, instead of launching a separate graphics application, as shown in Figure 16.
- **BandWidth Buster:** Provides detailed information about elements in your Web pages, and how long pages will take for visitors to download, as shown in Figure 17. The **BandWidth Buster** also helps you reduce image sizes to make pages download more quickly.
- **Image Mapper:** Create image maps lickety split.
- **Java Animator:** Assemble cool Java animations—without any programming.
- **JavaScript Language Editor:** If you know a little JavaScript and use it in your Web pages, this tool makes it easier for you to edit and work with your scripts.
- **JavaScript Tools:** Don't know JavaScript? Let JavaScript Tools help you create nifty page gizmos like a clock or animated buttons that change when the user passes their mouse over them.
- **MultiFile Find and Replace:** Saves you lots of time and tedious work by enabling you to search and replace text and HTML tags in multiple documents, as shown in Figure 18.

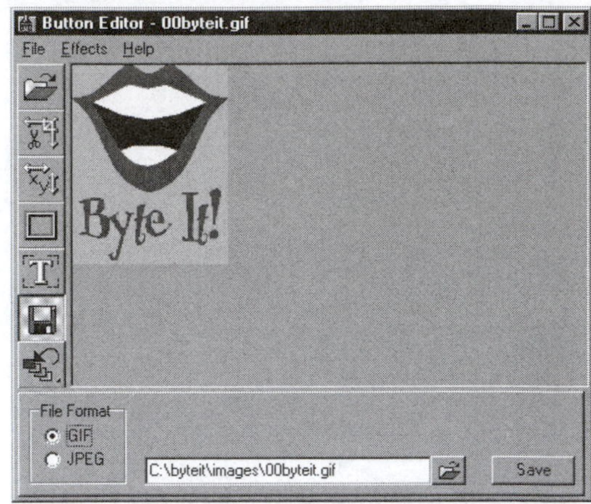

Figure 16. You can make simple changes to images with the SuperToolz **Button Editor**.

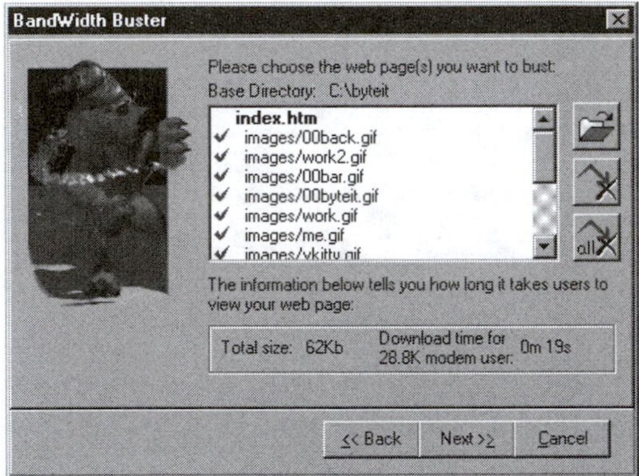

Figure 17. See how long your Web page takes to download with the SuperToolz **BandWidth Buster**.

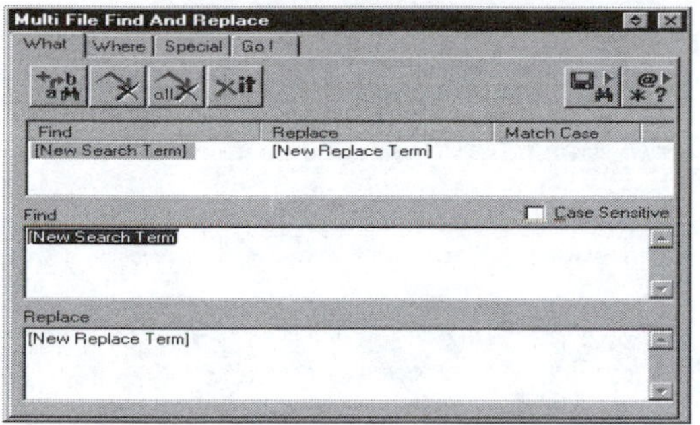

Figure 18. Make changes to multiple documents with SuperToolz **MultiFile Find and Replace.**

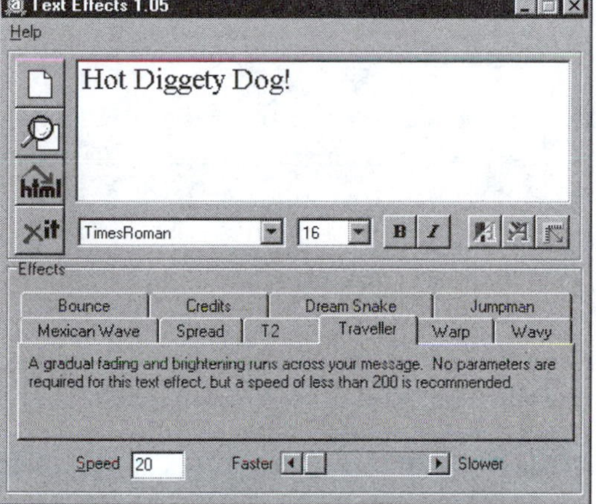

Figure 19. Generate animated text messages with SuperToolz **Text Effects.**

- **Visual Table Editor:** Provides a graphical view of your tables, so you can make edits, add images, and more—without having to struggle with HTML table tags.
- **Text Effects:** Add spiffy-looking animated text effects to your pages with the Text Effects tool, shown in Figure 19.
- **WebSite Downloader:** Go online and download Web page content from your server quickly and easily.
- **InfoSeller:** Sets up your Web site so you can charge digital micropayments for your content.
- **Channel Wizard:** If you update your Web site frequently, you can set it up as a channel that visitors can have automatically downloaded to their computers (both Netscape Communicator 4.0 and Internet Explorer 4.0 support Channels).
- **SafeSurf:** Use **SafeSurf** to rate your Web site content by levels of sex, violence, and language, and incorporate ratings information into your Web pages.
- **LinkExchange:** The Link Exchange (located at *www.linkexchange.com*) is an organization that helps businesses and individuals display banner ads on each other's pages for more exposure. The service is free. The **LinkExchange** SuperTool helps you register and insert the required HTML code in your Web page.
- **RealAudio-Video:** You can convert your sound and video files to real-time streaming RealAudio and RealVideo files that visitors can play back with Progressive Network's RealMedia browser plug-in.

Getting Your SuperToolz

Before you can start using HotDog Pro's SuperToolz, you have to download and install them. Does that sound like a pain? Don't worry. The AutoDownloader makes it easy, and fairly fast too.

To get your SuperToolz

1. Connect to the Internet.
2. Select **Run AutoDownloader** from the **SuperToolz** menu in HotDog Pro's application window.
3. When the **Proxy Server** dialog box appears, click **OK**.
4. When the **AutoDownloader** window appears, as shown in Figure 20, select an item from the list by double-clicking it.
5. Repeat step 4 for each item on the list.
6. When you've selected all of the items you want from the list, click the **Download** button.
7. When the **Downloading Files** dialog box appears, take a break. The SuperToolz can take some time to download.
8. When the AutoDownloader's **Download of SuperToolz Successful!** dialog box appears, click **OK**.

The **AutoDownloader** even installs the SuperToolz for you. To launch one of your SuperToolz, select an item from HotDog Pro's SuperToolz menu. Some SuperToolz need to be registered. If so, the **CISM trialling** dialog box appears, and you can register it as explained in the "To register with the CISM" section of this chapter.

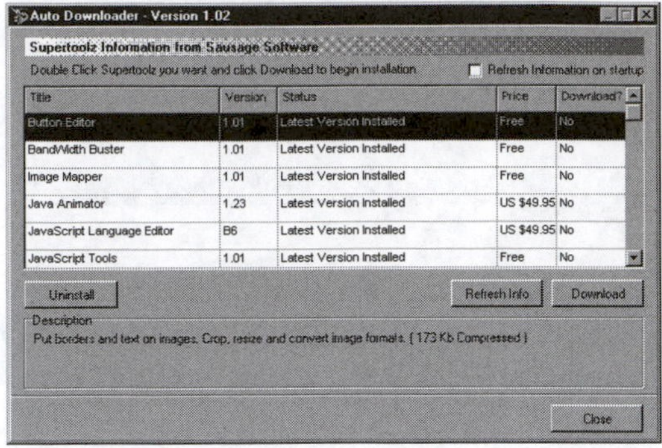

Figure 20. The **AutoDownloader** window displays a list of SuperToolz that you can download.

✔ Tips

- Offices, schools, and other organizations use *proxy servers* for security reasons. The AutoDownloader sometimes won't work with Proxy servers. You can also download SuperToolz from HotDog Pro's Web site and install them individually.
- The AutoDownloader list tells you whether you have the latest version of each SuperTool. Go online, launch the AutoDownloader and click the **Refresh Info** button.

2

GETTING STARTED

Now that you've installed HotDog Pro and the SuperToolz, let's take a look at it. Before you can start working, however, you still need to do a few things. First, I'll explain how to display and work with toolbars and resources—HotDog Pro's tools for building Web sites by pointing and clicking. This chapter also tells you how to customize the application's preferences and how to specify HTML filters. Preferences are settings that tell the application how to display and run. You can change them to make working with HotDog Pro easier and faster. HTML Filters tell HotDog Pro which version of HTML you want to use. You can also specify which browser or browsers you want your site to be compatible with.

A Quick Look at HotDog Pro

You may have noticed that HotDog Pro's application window doesn't always look the same in all the pictures shown in this book. No, you're not imagining things. The application window looks different depending on what toolbars and resources you choose to display and where you choose to display them. Figure 1 shows the HotDog Pro application window with the title bar, menu bar, toolbars, document window pane, and resource window panes.

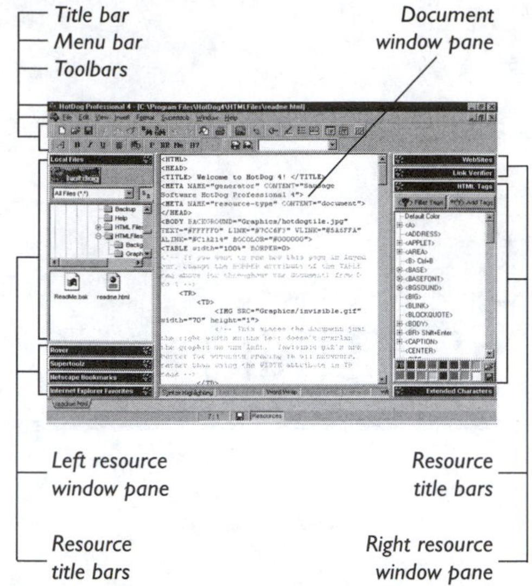

Figure 1. HotDog Pro application window with title bar, menu bar, toolbars, document window pane, and resource window panes displayed.

Application window elements

- **Title bar:** The title bar appears at the top of the application window and displays the directory path and HTML document name of the file you're currently working on.
- **Menu bar:** The menu bar appears below the title bar. When you select menu bar items, menus display so you can select options.
- **Toolbars:** HotDog Pro comes with four different toolbars. You can choose which ones to display by selecting them from the **View** menu. You can also move toolbars around to different positions in the application window, so they don't get in your way while you're working.
- **Document window pane:** Displays the current HTML document you're working on with the text and HTML source code. You can resize the document window pane to make it wider or more narrow.
- **Resource window panes:** Resources are lists of links, images, Web sites, HTML codes, special characters and other Web page and Web site elements. When you select a resource from the **View** menu, the list of items appears in a window pane to the left or right of the document. You can then drag and drop items from the window pane into your HTML document.

✔ Tips

- The HotDog Pro welcoming page shown in Figures 6-8 is previewed in **Rover**, a HotDog Pro resource. We'll talk more about displaying resources later in this chapter.
- HotDog Pro helps you remember things with tooltips. When you pass your cursor over toolbar buttons and other application window elements, tooltips appear and tell you what each thing does.
- If you get stuck, don't panic. Just go to the **Help** menu and look up the topic you need help with.
- When you have several resources open at once, the most recently selected one appears in front. You can access other selected resources by clicking the resource title bars.

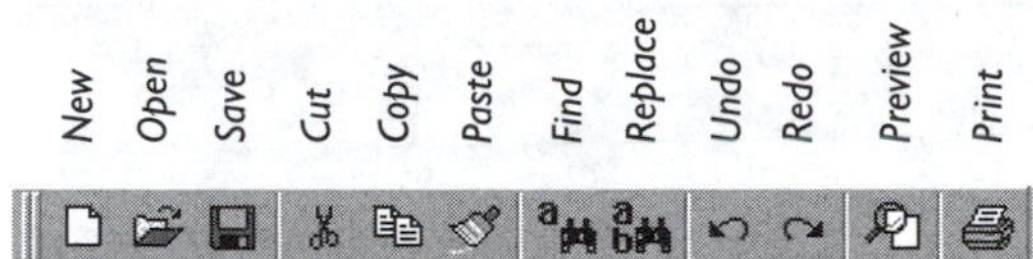

Figure 2. Use the **Standard** toolbar for basic tasks.

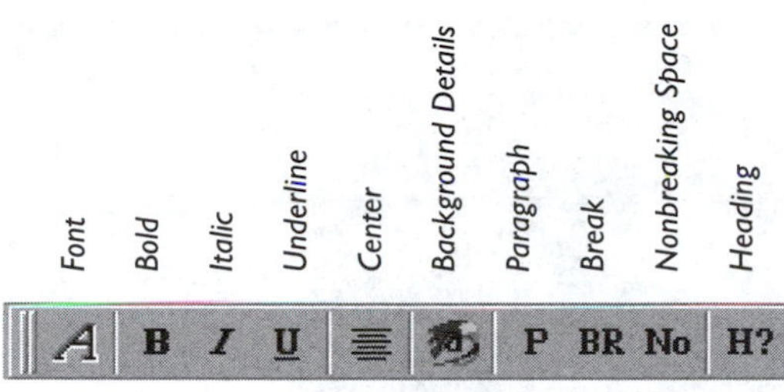

Figure 3. Use the **Format** toolbar to format text.

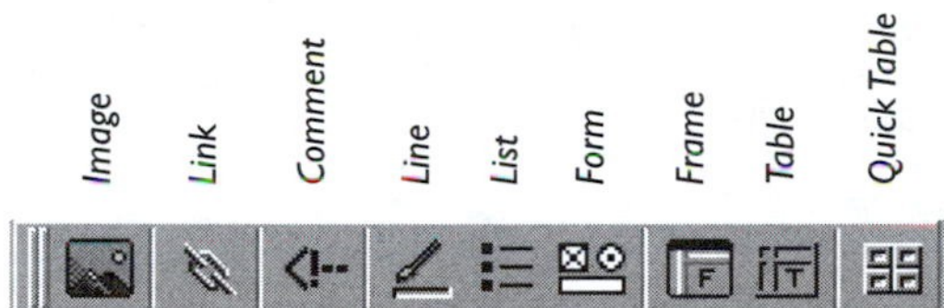

Figure 4. Use the **Insert** toolbar to insert images, links, and other objects into your Web pages.

Figure 5. You can apply styles to your Web pages with the **CSS Style Sheets** toolbar.

Displaying the Toolbars

When you launch HotDog Pro for the first time, the application window seems to be missing something. Why? Because you haven't displayed the toolbars yet. The people at Sausage Software understand that we all work differently. Some of us have small computer screens and need to have as few things cluttering the application window as possible. They designed HotDog Pro's toolbars so you can move them around, and decide when you want to display or hide them. This section tells you how to work with the toolbars.

Toolbars

- **Standard toolbar:** For basic tasks, such as creating, opening, and saving HTML documents, as shown in Figure 2.
- **Format toolbar:** For applying fonts, text styles, colors, and other formats to text, as shown in Figure 3.
- **Insert toolbar:** For inserting objects, such as images, links, forms, and tables, as shown in Figure 4.
- **CSS Style Sheets toolbar:** For applying cascading style sheets (CSS) to your documents, as shown in Figure 5. Style sheets help you automate text formatting, as explained in Chapter 12.

To display a toolbar

1. Select **Toolbars** from the **View** menu.
2. When the cascading menu appears, as shown in Figure 6, select a toolbar from the list.
3. To display additional toolbars, repeat steps 1 and 2.

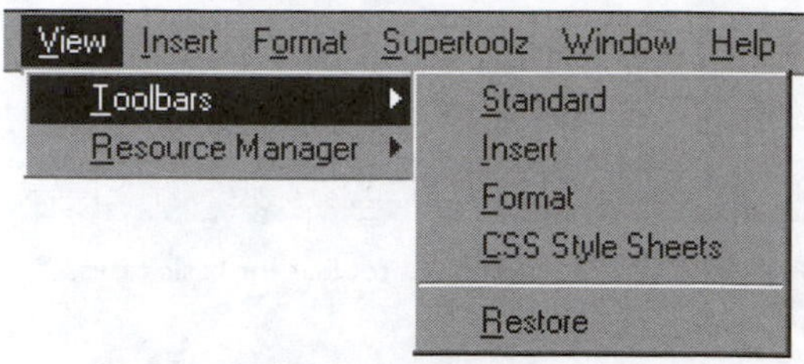

Figure 6. To display a toolbar, select **Toolbars** from the **View** menu and choose a toolbar from the cascading list.

The Standard toolbar automatically positions itself on the upper-left side of the application window beneath the Menu bar. The other toolbars appear as floating toolbars in the application window as shown in Figure 7. You can move them to a different position, or anchor them beneath the menu bar, as explained in the following task list, "To anchor a toolbar."

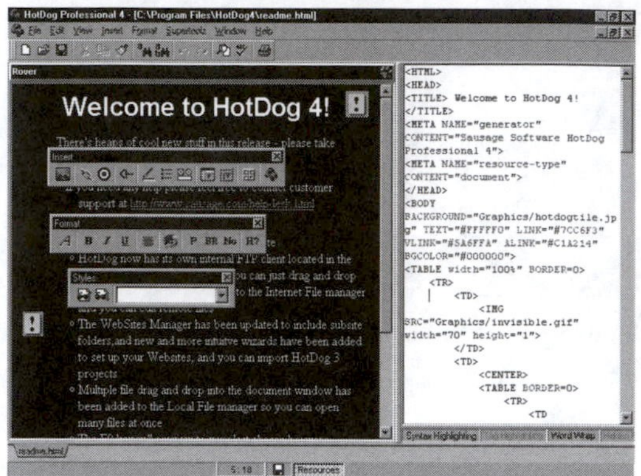

Figure 7. The **Standard** toolbar automatically anchors itself beneath the menu bar. The others first appear as floating toolbars that you can reposition.

To anchor a toolbar

1. Select the toolbar you want to anchor by clicking on the toolbar's title bar (the black bar with the toolbar's name).
2. Hold down your mouse button and drag it towards the menu bar. The toolbar disappears and looks like a gray rectangular outline when you drag it, as shown in Figure 8.
3. When you're finished dragging the toolbar towards the menu bar and the rectangle becomes narrower, release the mouse button.

To reposition a toolbar

1. Select the toolbar you want to reposition by clicking on the toolbar's selection bar (the double line on the left side of the toolbar).
2. Hold down your mouse button and drag the toolbar to the desired location in the application window.

✔ Tips

- You can also anchor toolbars to the bottom of the application window, or between the document and resource window panes (toolbars can also orient vertically).
- Toolbars can float anywhere on your computer screen—even when you move them outside of the HotDog Pro application window.
- You can also display toolbars by clicking on a toolbar with the right mouse button and selecting an item from the pop-up list.
- A check mark next to a toolbar list item indicates that the toolbar is displayed.

Figure 8. When you drag a toolbar to a new location, it appears as a gray rectangle while you drag it.

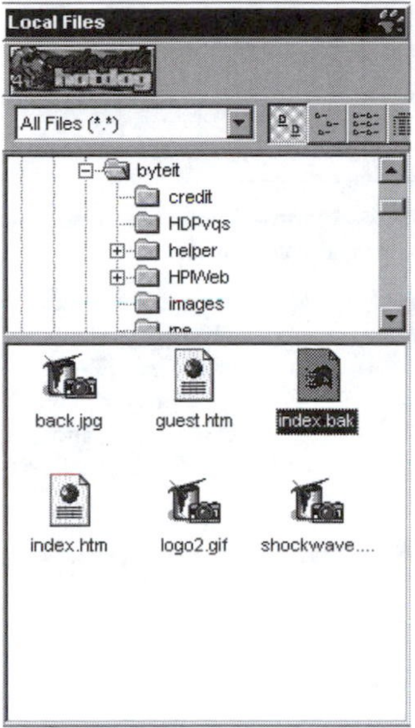

Figure 9. The **Local Files** resource displays a list of files on your computer.

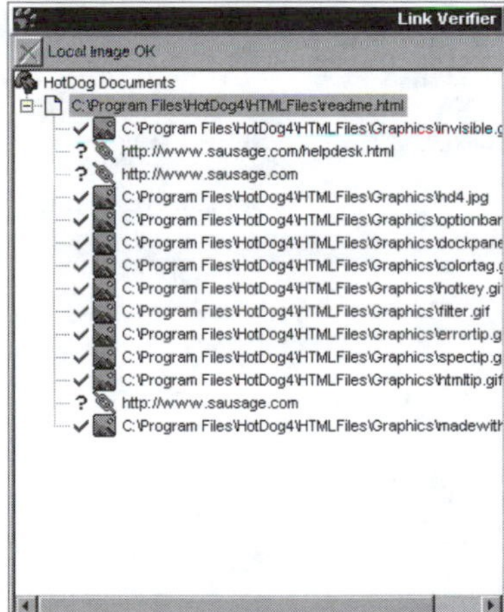

Figure 10. The **Link Verifier** helps you check your links and external files in the current document.

Displaying Resources with the Resource Manager

HotDog Pro's **Resource** Manager helps you keep track of your Web pages and elements (like images and links) that you either put in your pages or plan to put in your pages. This sure makes building Web sites a lot easier. This section first tells you what resources are available and then tells you how to display your resources so you can use them.

Resources

- **Local Files Manager:** Displays a list of the folders on your computer, and files contained in the currently selected folder, as shown in Figure 9.
- **Rover:** Displays a preview of the current HTML document as a Web page (as shown earlier in this chapter). For more about previewing pages, see Chapter 16.
- **Link Verifier:** Displays a list of links and external files (like images and Java applets) contained in the current document and tells you whether they work or not, as shown in Figure 10. For more about verifying your links, see Chapter 16.
- **WebSites Manager:** Displays a list of Web sites that you've created, and a list of the files contained in each Web site, as shown in Figure 11. Once you create a Web site and import your files into the WebSites Manager (as discussed in Chapters 3 and 15), HotDog Pro also helps you automatically upload pages (as discussed in Chapter 17).
- **HTML Tags Manager:** Displays a complete list of HTML tags that you can drag and drop into your HTML document, as shown in Figure 12.

- **SuperToolz:** Displays available SuperToolz so you can launch them, as shown in Figure 13. SuperToolz are discussed throughout the book. For a list of SuperToolz and brief descriptions of what each one does, see Chapter 1.
- **Extended Characters:** Displays a list of special characters that you can drag and drop into your HTML document, as shown in Figure 14 and explained in Chapter 4.
- **Netscape Bookmarks:** Displays a complete list of your Netscape folders and bookmarks so you can drag and drop links to your favorite Web sites, as discussed in Chapter 6.
- **Internet Favorites:** Displays a complete list of Internet Explorer Favorites, so you can drag and drop links to your favorite Web sites, as shown in Figure 15 and explained in Chapter 6.

To display a resource

1. Select **Resource Manager** from the **View** menu.
2. Choose a resource from the cascading menu, as shown in Figure 16.
3. When the resource appears in the left or right hand resource window pane, you can repeat steps 1 and 2 to display additional resources.

✔ Tips

- You can also display the **Resource Manager** list by clicking on a currently displayed resource's title bar with the right mouse button and selecting an item from the pop-up list.
- A check mark next to an item on the **Resource Manager** list indicates that the resource is currently displayed.

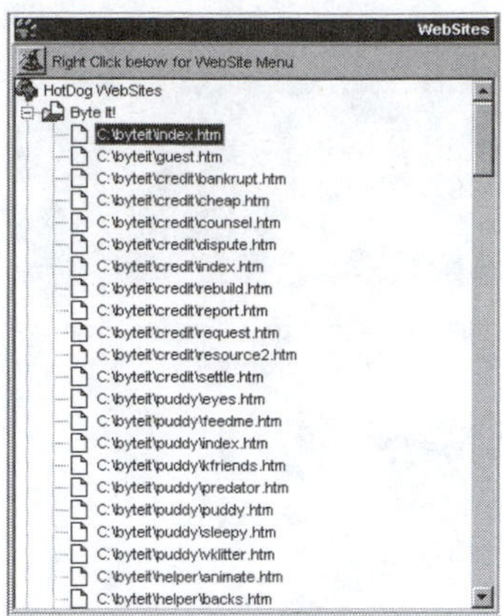

Figure 11. The **WebSites Manager** helps you keep track of Web site content and upload files.

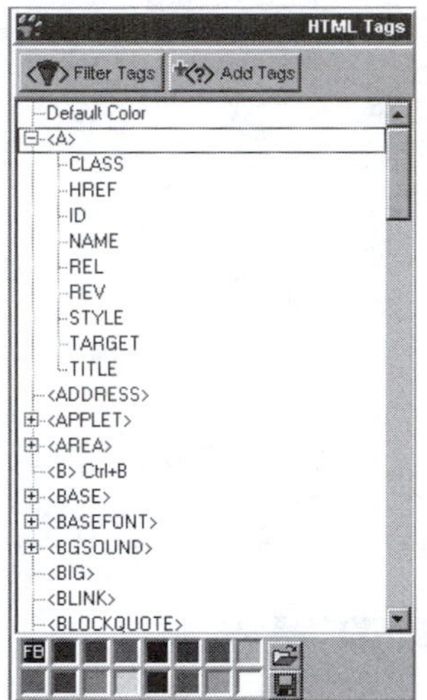

Figure 12. No more memorizing HTML codes! The **HTML Tags** Manager makes it easy to drag and drop HTML tags into your document.

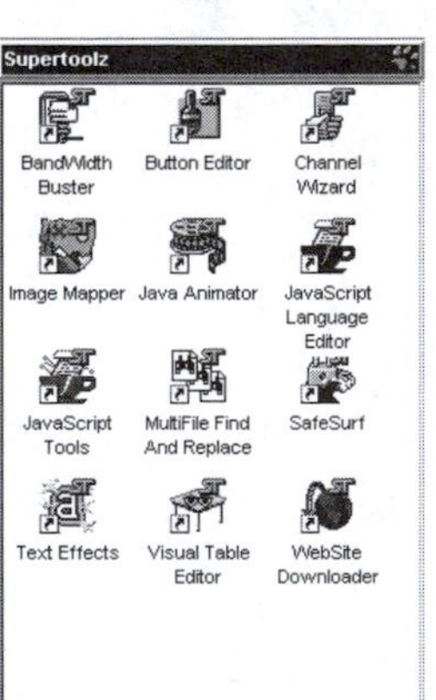

Figure 13. You can display a list of **SuperToolz** so you can view and launch them more easily.

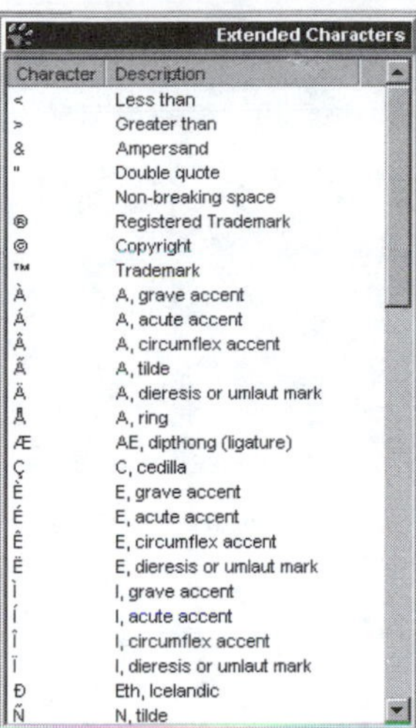

Figure 14. Web browsers won't display special characters, such as copyright symbols and foreign characters with accents correctly unless you enter the correct HTML codes. The **Extended Characters** Manager makes dragging and dropping special characters into your document easy.

Figure 15 The **Internet Favorites** resource makes it easy to drag and drop links to your favorite Web sites. HotDog Pro imports them from Internet Explorer.

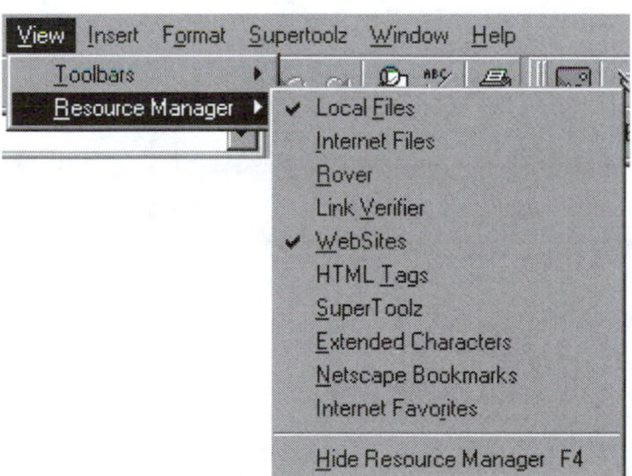

Figure 16. To display a resource, select **Resource Manager** from the **View** menu and choose a resource from the cascading menu.

Customizing HotDog in the Preferences dialog box

As you become more familiar with HotDog Pro, you can customize it to your liking through the **Preferences** dialog boxes. Preferences are default settings that tell an application how to display and run. You can change these settings any time you like. The following sections explain HotDog Pro's **Preferences** dialog boxs and what all the settings mean. You can either read this and edit your preferences now, or come back to this later when you're ready to make changes.

To edit Preferences

1. Select **Preferences** from the **Edit** menu.
2. When the Preferences dialog box appears (the default selection is **General** Preferences), as shown in Figure 17, select a category from the list on the left.
3. When the options for the preferences category appear on the right side of the Preferences dialog box, you can edit your settings. I explain the ten categories of preferences in the following sections.

✔ Tips

- **Local Files**, **Rover, SuperToolz**, **Netscape Bookmarks**, and **Internet Favorites** display in the left-hand resource window pane. The **WebSites** Manager, **Link Verifier**, **HTML Tags** Manager, and **Extended Characters** list appear in the right-hand resource window pane.
- The resource title bars and the most recently selected resource for each resource window pane display in front, with other resources layered below it. To display a different resources list, click the appropriate title bar.

General Preferences

The **General** Preferences dialog box, as shown in Figure 17, contains basic options for working with HotDog Pro—such as whether or not to save files automatically after a specified number of minutes.

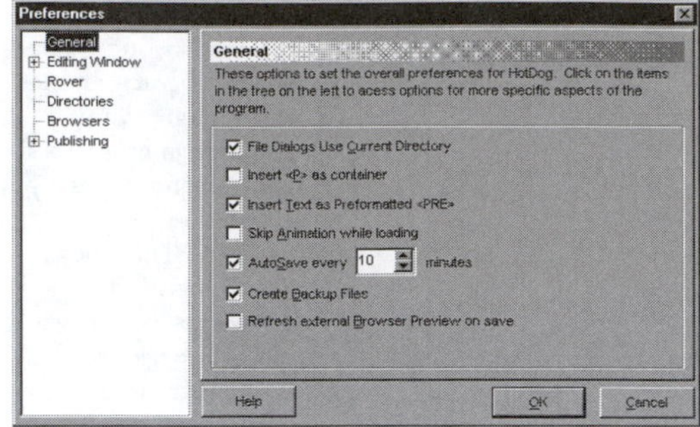

Figure 17. You can select basic options from the **General** Preferences dialog box.

To set General Preferences

1. Select **Preferences** from the edit menu and select the **General** item from the list when the **Preferences** dialog box appears.
2. Select the **File Dialogs Use Current Directory** checkbox to save files to and open files from the folder that the file you're currently working on is located in. Or deselect the checkbox to save to a default directory (which you can specify in the **Directory Preferences** dialog box).
3. Select the **Insert <P> as container** checkbox to automatically insert a closing **</P>** tag when you insert a **<P>** tag. Or deselect the checkbox to leave out the closing **</P>** tag.
4. Select the **Insert Text as Preformatted <PRE>** checkbox to automatically preformat text and preserve spacing attributes.
5. Select the **Skip Animation while loading** checkbox to launch HotDog Pro more quickly. This gets rid of that cool (but slow) animation of the dog waving that appears when you launch HotDog Pro. Or leave the checkbox deselected if you like having the HotDog Pro character wave to you.
6. Select the **AutoSave every __ minutes** checkbox and select a number of minutes from the scrolling list to save the current document automatically at the intervals you specify. Or deselect the checkbox to disable HotDog Pro's AutoSave feature.

✔ Tips

- You can resize the resource window panes by clicking the border adjacent to the document window pane and dragging it to the left or the right.
- As with all Windows 95 applications, when you open and save files with HotDog Pro, a dialog box appears and displays a list of files and folders with a folder selected. You can save a lot of time browsing for folders by selecting the **File Dialogs Use Current Directory** checkbox.
- The HTML **<P>** tag specifies that a new paragraph begins and that an extra space should appear between the new paragraph and the text or page element above it. Closing tags are optional for **<P>** tags, but some people prefer to close them any way.
- Web browsers do not display spaces and tabs in your text unless you use the **<PRE>** preformatting tag. If your text formatting relies heavily on tabs and spacing, you should select the **Insert Text as Preformatted <Pre>** checkbox.
- The **AutoSave every __ minutes** option helps you avoid losing your work.
- The **Create Backup Files** option saves copies of the document you're currently editing. If you don't like your changes, you can open the backup copy and start over. A backup file has the same name as its corresponding HTML document, with the .BAK file name extension.

7. Select the **Create Backup Files** checkbox to make a backup copy of the document you're currently editing. Or deselect the checkbox to disable the backup feature.
8. Select **Refresh external Browser Preview on save** to automatically load a fresh copy of your page in your browser when you save your pages. Or deselect the checkbox to disable this feature.
9. Click **OK** to save your changes or click **Cancel** to revert to the previous settings.

Editing Window Preferences

The **Editing Window** Preferences dialog box, as shown in Figure 18, lets you tell HotDog Pro how to display, handle, and print your HTML document so you can enter, edit, and print text more easily.

To set Editing Window Preferences

1. Select **Preferences** from the **Edit** menu, then select **Editing Window** from the category list when the Preferences dialog box appears.
2. Select the **Drag 'n' Drop Text Editing** checkbox so you can select text and drag it to other locations on your page.
3. Select the **Show Hidden Fields** checkbox if you want extra spaces, carriage returns, and tabs to display in your document.
4. Select the **Smooth Scrolling** checkbox to scroll through your document more quickly.
5. Select the **Auto Indent** checkbox to automatically place your cursor directly below the first character in the previous line of text when you press the Enter key.
6. Select the **Word Wrap** checkbox to automatically wrap text so it doesn't extend beyond the document window's viewing area.
7. Select the **Show Print Margin** checkbox to display your document with a print margin (the amount of space specified for the margins if you print out the page).
8. Select a number from the **Tab Size** scrolling list to change the tab measurement.

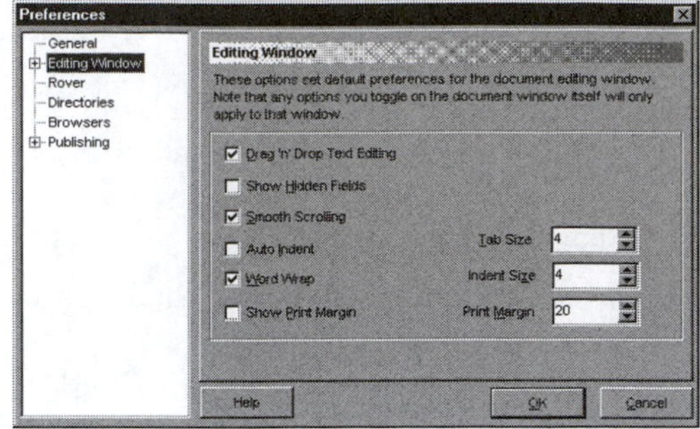

Figure 18. You can select options for how HotDog Pro displays, handles, and prints text in the **Editing Window** Preferences dialog box.

EDITING WINDOW PREFERENCES

✔ Tip

- You can only use HotDog Pro to edit plain (unformatted) text files, like HTML documents, CGI scripts, Java applet files, and cascading style sheet (CSS) documents.

9. Select a number from the **Indent Size** scrolling list to change the indent measurement.
10. Select a number from the **Print Margin** scrolling list to change the print margin measurement.
11. Click **OK** to save your changes or **Cancel** to revert to the previous settings.

Appearance Preferences

You can choose how you want text to appear in your document window by specifying a font and font size in the **Appearance** Preferences dialog box, as shown in Figure 19, so you can view your work more easily.

To set Appearance Preferences

1. Select **Preferences** from the **Edit** menu, then select **Appearance** from the category list when the Preferences dialog box appears.
2. Select the font you wish to display from the **Editor Font** pull-down list.
3. Select the font size you wish to display from the **Size** pull-down list.
4. You can preview how your text will appear in the **Sample** box.
5. Click **OK** to save your changes or click **Cancel** to revert to the previous settings.

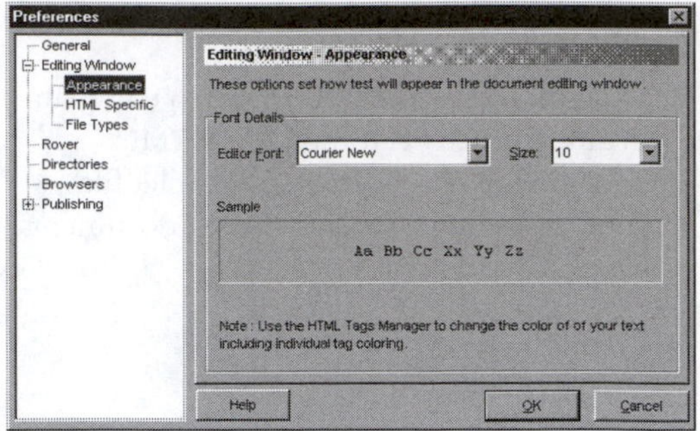

Figure 19. You can choose which font style and size you wish to display when working with HTML documents in the **Appearance** Preferences.

✔ Tips

- If you don't see the **Appearance, HTML Specific**, and **File Types** items on the Preferences dialog box category list, click the + sign next to the **Editing Window** list item.
- Your **Editing Window—Appearance** selections will not effect the appearance of your Web pages—they only determine how text appears on the screen while you're working with HTML documents.

APPEARANCE PREFERENCES

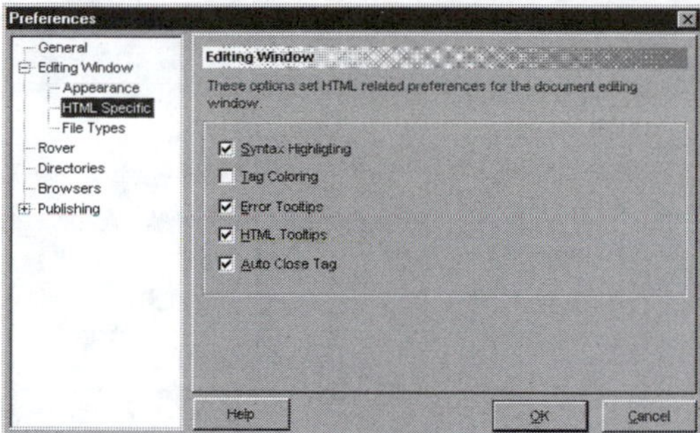

Figure 20. You can specify settings for how HTML codes display in your document in the **HTML Specific** Preferences dialog box.

✔ Tip

- Choosing to display error and HTML tooltips helps you learn HTML more quickly, but can also slow down HotDog Pro's performance slightly. If you don't want to display tooltips, leave the **Error Tooltips** and **HTML Tooltips** checkboxes deselected.

HTML Specific Preferences

The **HTML Specific** Preferences, as shown in Figure 20, let you specify how you want HTML codes to appear while working in your Web page documents. For example, you can tell HotDog Pro to highlight possible HTML errors, and have HTML codes appear in a different color from your regular text to make them easier to locate.

To set HTML Specific Preferences

1. Select **Preferences** from the **File** menu, then select **HTML Specific** from the list.
2. Select the **Syntax Highlighting** checkbox to highlight possible errors in your HTML code.
3. Select the **Tag Coloring** checkbox to display HTML codes in a different color from the rest of your text.
4. Select the **Error Tooltips** checkbox to display an explanatory message about highlighted HTML errors in your document when you pass your cursor over them.
5. Select the **HTML Tooltips** checkbox to display explanatory messages about HTML codes in your document when you pass your cursor over them.
6. Select the **Auto Close Tag** checkbox to automatically close tags when you enter them.
7. Click **OK** to save your changes or **Cancel** to revert back to the previous settings.

File Types Preferences

The **File Types** Preferences, as shown in Figure 21, tell HotDog Pro how to handle various text file types that you may come across. File types are indicated by file name extensions, such as .HTML or .HTM for HTML documents. You can use HotDog Pro to work with many other types of text files besides HTML documents. For example, you may want to open a plain text file (.TXT) saved from a word processing document and make some quick edits before converting it to an HTML document.

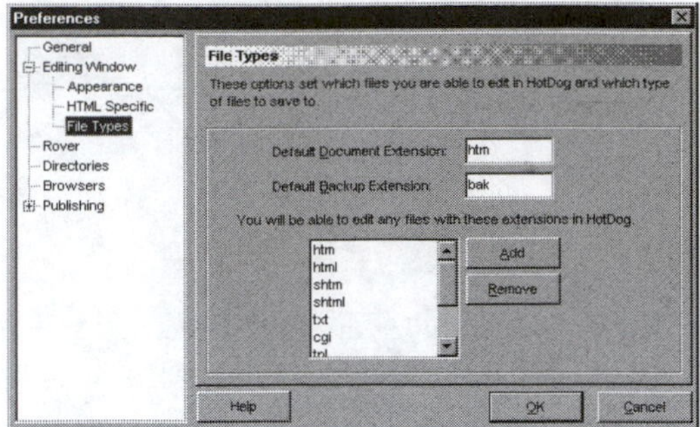

Figure 21. You can tell HotDog Pro how to handle various text files in the **File Types** Preferences dialog box.

To set File Types Preferences

1. Select **Preferences** from the **Edit** menu and select the **File Types** item from the category list when the Preferences dialog box appears.
2. Enter your preferred HTML document extension (either **html** or **htm**) in the **Default Document Extension** text box.
3. Leave the **bak** file name extension for backup files entered in the **Default Backup Extension** text field as is.
4. The scrolling list displays text file extensions that you can open in HotDog Pro. To add a new file extension to the list, click the **Add** button.
5. If you need to remove a file extension from the list, click the **Remove** button.
6. Click **OK** to save your changes or click **Cancel** to restore the previous settings.

✔ Tips

- UNIX servers (most Web servers run UNIX) are case sensitive. Windows 95 isn't. This "mywebpage.html" and "mywebpage.HTML", are completely different documents on a UNIX server! It's important to remember whether you used upper- or lowercase letters to specify the default file name extension in the **File Types** Preferences dialog box's **Default Document Extension** text field. Otherwise, links to pages within your Web site may not work when you upload pages to your server.
- What's the difference between the **.HTML** and **.HTM** file name extensions for Web page documents? They both mean the same thing. Windows 3.x computers can only use file name extensions with three letters. So, if you exchange files regularly with a Windows 3.x user, use the **.HTM** file name extension. Otherwise, use the **.HTML** file name extensions.

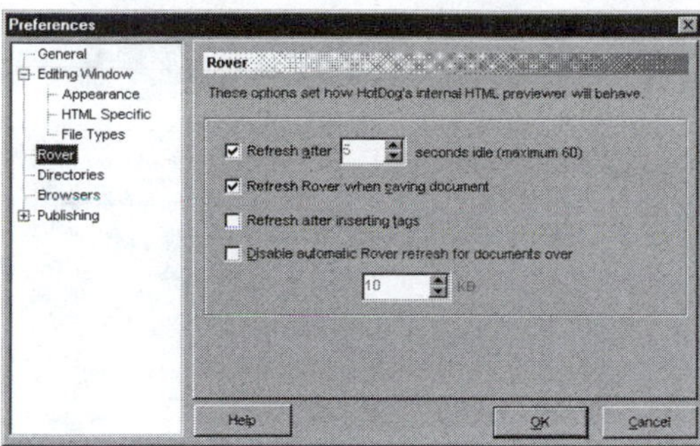

Figure 22. You can specify how often Rover refreshes your page preview in the **Rover** Preferences dialog box.

✔ Tips

- Selecting the **Refresh after inserting tags** checkbox may slow down HotDog Pro's performance.
- Automatically refreshing documents over 10 KB (including images) with **Rover** can also slow down HotDog Pro's performance.

Rover Preferences

When you select **Rover** from the **Resource Manager**, you can preview your Web pages as you would in a regular Web browser. You can specify how frequently **Rover** refreshes its display in the **Rover** Preferences dialog box, as shown in Figure 22. HTML document changes do not appear until **Rover** refreshes. **Rover** settings only apply when **Rover** is activated. Chapter 16 talks about previewing your pages with **Rover** in greater detail.

To set Rover Preferences

1. Select **Preferences** from the Edit menu, then select **Rover** from the category list when the Preferences dialog box appears.
2. Select a number of seconds from the **Refresh after _ seconds idle (maximum 60)** text box.
3. To tell Rover to load a fresh version of your Web page each time you save your document, select the **Refresh Rover when saving document** checkbox.
4. To tell Rover to load a fresh version of your Web page each time you insert a new HTML tag, select the **Refresh after inserting tags** checkbox.
5. If you don't want Rover to automatically refresh documents over a certain size, select the **Disable automatic Rover refresh for documents over _ KB** checkbox, and select a number of KB (Kilobytes) from the scrolling list.
6. Click **OK** to save your changes, or click **Cancel** to revert to the previous settings.

Directories Preferences

HotDog Pro's **Directories** Preferences dialog box, as shown in Figure 23, lets you specify default directories for storing documents, templates, and images. You should specify the directories that you most frequently work with as your default directories.

To set Directories Preferences

1. Select **Preferences** from the **Edit** menu and select **Directories** when the Preferences dialog box appears.
2. Specify a default directory to store your Web page documents in by entering a directory path in the **Documents** text field. Or you can click the folder icon to browse for a directory.
3. Specify a default directory to store your Web page templates in by entering a directory path in the **Templates** text field. Or you can click the folder icon to browse for a directory.
4. Specify a default directory to store your Web page images in by entering a directory path in the **Graphic Images** text field. Or you can click the folder icon to browse for a directory.
5. Click **OK** to save your changes, or click **Cancel** to restore the previous settings.

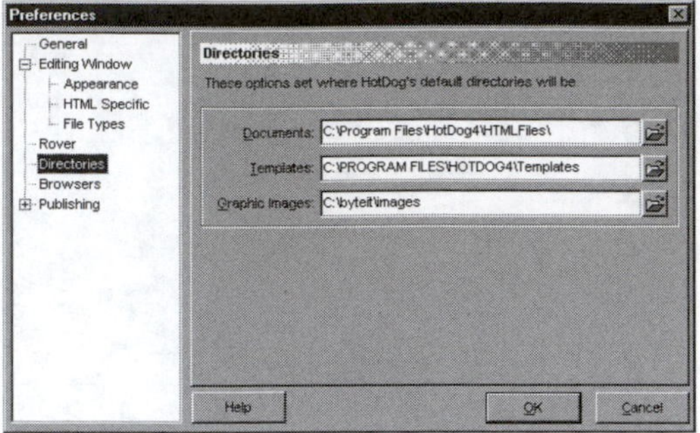

Figure 23. You can specify default directories for storing documents, templates, and images in the **Directories** Preferences dialog box.

✔ Tips

- "Directories" and "folders" mean the same thing.
- You can add as many browsers as you like to the Web Browser list. When you choose to preview pages with a browser (as explained in Chapter 16), a dialog box appears and asks which browser you want to use.
- If you have trouble locating your browser, click the button with the binoculars icon, and HotDog Pro will find it for you.

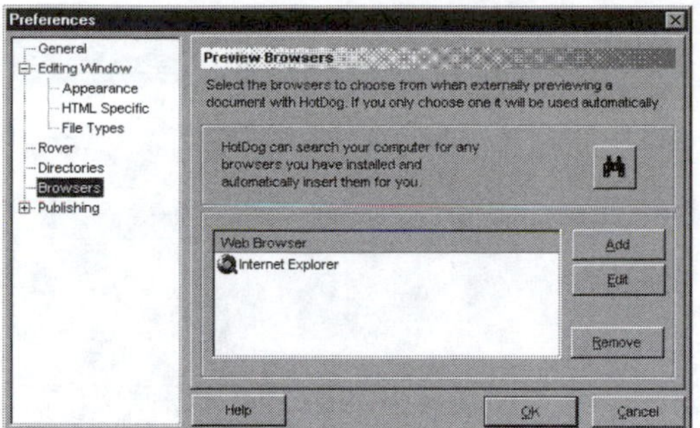

Figure 24. You can add browsers for externally previewing pages through the **Preview Browsers** Preferences dialog box.

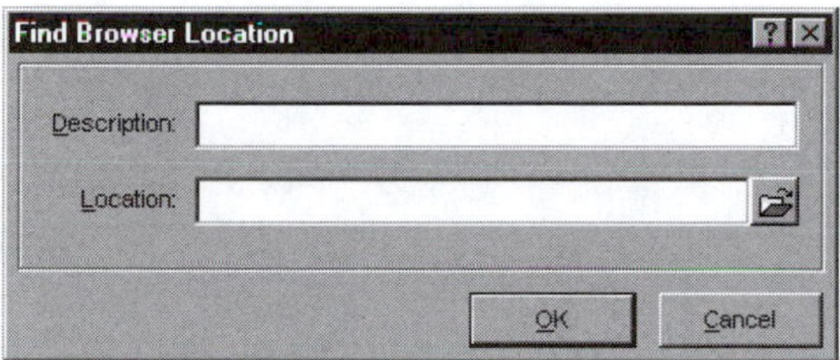

Figure 25. Enter the name of your browser and the directory path to the application file in the **Find Browser Location** dialog box.

Preview Browser Preferences

Rover is a great tool for getting a quick glance of your Web page, but you should also preview your pages with Internet Explorer, Netscape Navigator, or both before uploading them to your Web server. You can list your browsers in the **Preview Browsers** Preferences dialog box, as shown in Figure 24, so HotDog can launch them when you need to preview your pages externally.

To set Browser Preferences

1. Select **Preferences** from the **Edit** menu, then select **Browsers** from the category list when the Preferences dialog box appears.
2. Click the **Add** button.
3. When the **Find Browser Location** dialog box appears, as shown in Figure 25, enter the name of your browser in the **Description** text field.
4. Enter the directory path to the application file in the **Location** text field, or click the folder icon to browse for the application file.
5. Click **OK** to return to the **Preview Browsers** dialog box. Browsers appear as items on the **Web Browser** list.
6. You can add additional browsers to the list by repeating steps 2-5; select an item from the list and click the **Edit** button to edit browser properties; or select an item from the list and click the **Remove** button to remove a browser from the list.
7. When you're finished, click **OK**, or click **Cancel** to restore the previous settings.

Publishing Preferences

While publishing pages to your server, you can have HotDog Pro automatically make some changes to your HTML documents. You can specify these changes in the **Publishing** Preferences dialog box shown in Figure 26.

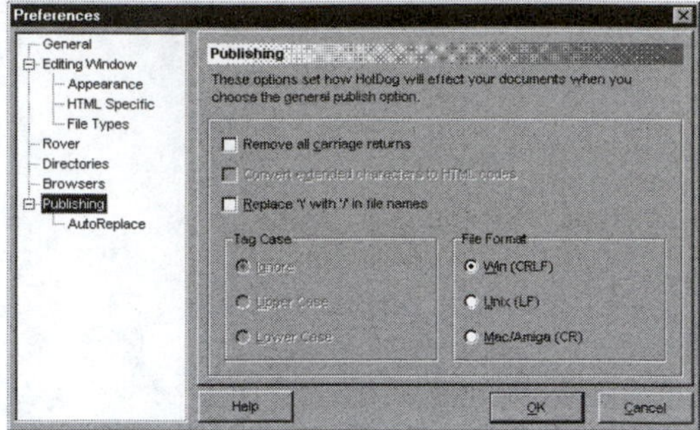

Figure 26. You can specify page elements that you want HotDog Pro to automatically change in the **Publishing** Preferences dialog box.

To set Publishing Preferences

1. Select **Preferences** from the **Edit** menu, then select **Publishing** from the category list when the Preferences dialog box appears.
2. You can tell HotDog Pro to delete all of the carriage returns from your document by selecting the **Remove all carriage returns** checkbox (I do not know why anyone would need to do this).
3. Select the **Convert extended characters to HTML codes** checkbox to ensure that any special characters (like & ampersands) are converted to the correct HTML codes so they display correctly.
4. Select the **Replace '\' with '/' in file names** checkbox to ensure that directory paths to files are specified correctly (directory paths on your computer are entered with \ back slashes, while directory paths on servers are specified with / forward slashes).
5. You can choose to change all HTML codes to either upper- or lowercase letters by clicking one of the **Tag Case** radio buttons. Or you can choose the **Ignore** radio button to leave your tags as they are.
6. You can select a radio button from the **File Format** options to format your document for a Windows NT, Unix, or Macintosh server.
7. Click **OK** to save your changes or click **Cancel** to restore the previous settings.

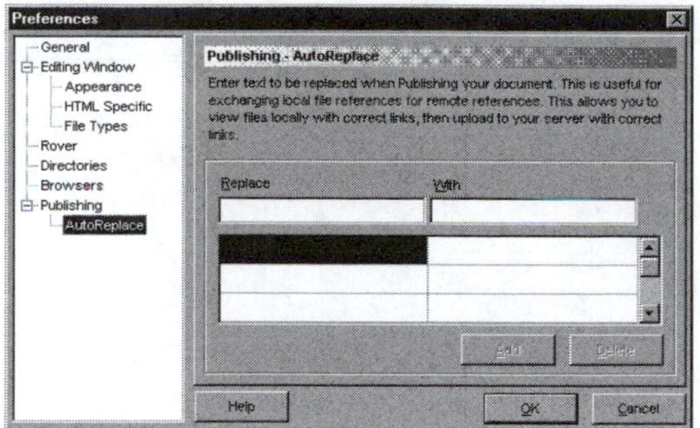

Figure 27. You can specify additional text and characters to be automatically replaced in the **Publishing—AutoReplace** Preferences dialog box.

Publishing—AutoReplace

The **Publishing—AutoReplace** dialog box, as shown in Figure 27, enables you to specify additional text and characters that you want to have HotDog Pro automatically replace in your HTML documents.

To set Publishing—AutoReplace Preferences

1. Select **Preferences** from the **Edit** menu, then select **AutoReplace** from the category list when the **Preferences** dialog box appears.
2. Enter the text or characters you wish to automatically replace in the **Replace** text field (for example, a local file directory path like **C:\mywebpage\images**).
3. Enter the text or characters you wish to automatically replace in the **With** text field (for example, a remote file directory path like **images/**)
4. Click the **Add** button to add your AutoReplace item to the list.
5. You can add more items by repeating steps 2–4.
6. You can remove items from the list by selecting an item and clicking the **Delete** button.
7. Click **OK** to save your changes, or click **Cancel** to restore the previous settings.

Specifying HTML Filters

While building your Web site, you should consider browser compatibility issues. Newer browsers can display the latest versions of HTML, but many people still use older versions of Netscape Navigator and Internet Explorer. It's hard to keep track of all these different browsers and versions of HTML. Especially when you're trying to figure out if that cool page layout will display correctly for visitors using different versions of Netscape Navigator and Internet Explorer.

Never Fear. HotDog Pro's HTML filters can help. You can choose which HTML specifications you wish to conform to and which browsers you want your code to be compatible with. If you enter codes that don't conform to the HTML and browser specifications you've selected, HotDog Pro highlights the codes as errors to warn you that some people may not be able to view your pages the way you intended.

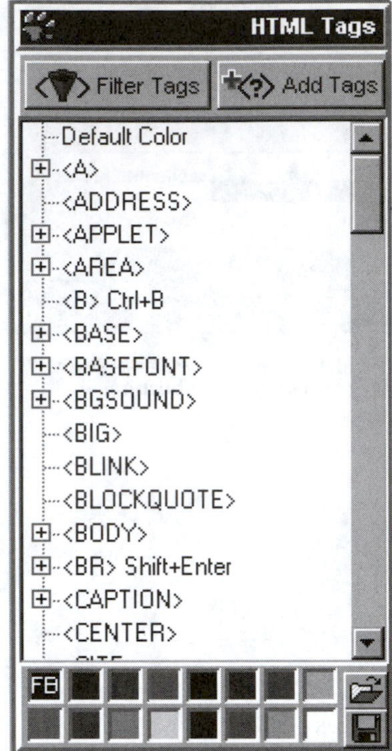

Figure 28. To specify HTML filters, first display the **HTML Tags Manager** in the resource window pane, the click the **Filter Tags** button.

To specify HTML Filters

1. Display the HTML Tags Manager by selecting **Resources** from the **View** menu, then choosing **HTML Tags** from the cascading menu.
2. When the HTML Tags Manager displays in the Resource window pane, as shown in Figure 28, click the **Filter Tags** button.
3. When the **Filter Tags** dialog box appears, as shown in Figure 29, select an HTML version from the **HTML Specifications** list.
4. Select any additional features you want HotDog Pro to support from the **Miscellaneous/User Defined** list (you should at least select the **JavaScript Events** checkbox, since HotDog Pro can help you write some nifty scripts).

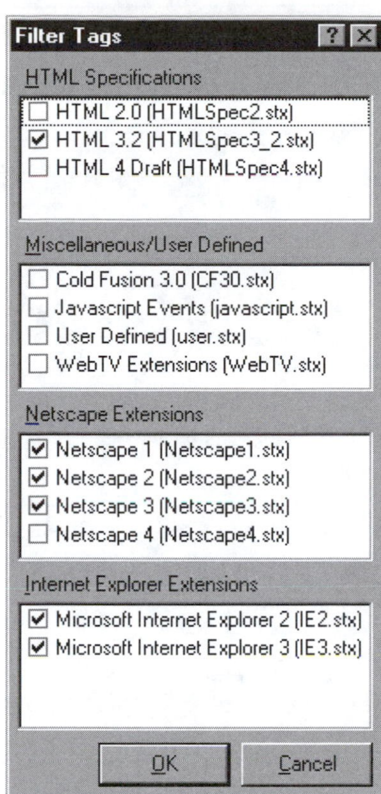

Figure 29. You can choose which HTML versions and browsers to support by selecting items from the **HTML Filters** dialog box.

5. Choose which versions of Netscape Navigator you want your pages to support by selecting items from the **Netscape Extensions** list.

6. Choose which versions of Internet Explorer you wish to support by selecting items from the **Internet Explorer Extensions** list.

7. Click **OK** to save your changes, or click **Cancel** to restore the previous settings.

3

SETTING UP YOUR WEB SITE

This chapter takes you through the basics of setting up your Web site. But yikes! That's a big job. Where does a person begin? Creating Web sites and keeping track of HTML documents and associated files used to be a major hassle. But HotDog Pro's **WebSites** Manager makes it easy. You can either create a new Web site from scratch or import files from an existing site. Thanks to the **WebSite Downloader**, you can even download an existing Web site straight from the server. This chapter gets you started with setting up a new Web site with the **WebSites** Manager, downloading a site from an existing server, and importing files from an existing Web site into the **WebSites** Manager. To learn about the **WebSites** Manager's advanced features, see Chapter 15, which tells you how to keep track of material on your Web site.

The WebSites Manager

The **WebSites** Manager is a list of Web sites that you create. You can then import HTML documents, images, and associated files into your HotDog Pro WebSite. The **WebSites Manager** displays them in a list that makes it easy to remember where files are located. You can even drag and drop files straight into the HTML document you're working on. The **WebSites** Manager also makes uploading and downloading files a lot easier than it used to be. Whether you want to upload an entire Web site, or just the files you've most recently edited, the **WebSites** Manager automates the process. Chapter 17 tells you how to upload your Web site with the **WebSites** Manager.

To display the WebSites Manager

1. Select **Resource Manager** from the **View** menu.
2. When the cascading list appears, as shown in Figure 1, select **WebSites**.

When the **WebSites** Manager appears in the right resource window pane, as shown in Figure 2, you can create a new Web site or work with an existing Web site that you've created in the **WebSites** Manager.

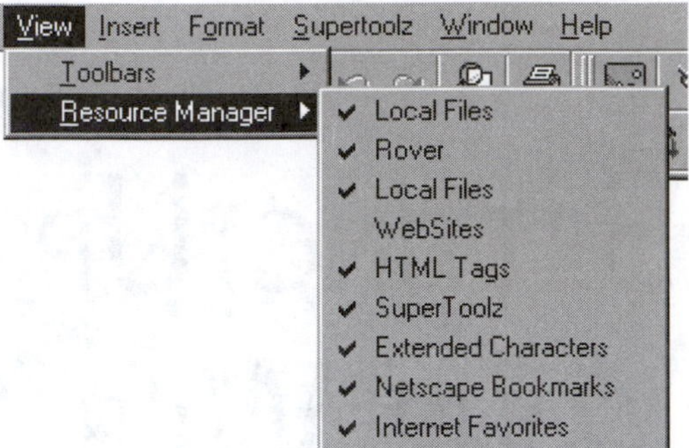

Figure 1. To display the **WebSites** Manager, select it from the **Resource Manager** list.

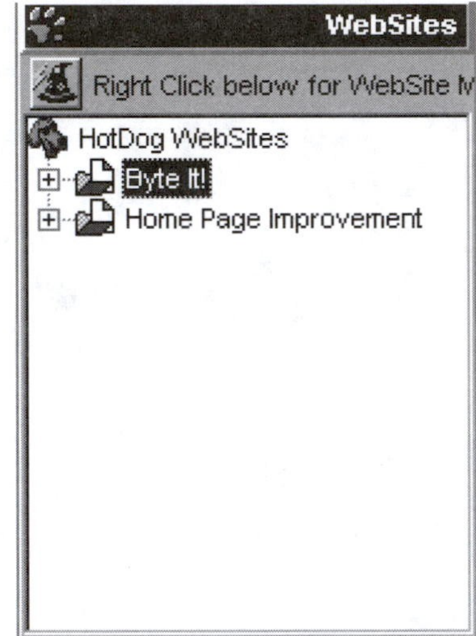

Figure 2. The **WebSites** Manager appears in the right resource window pane.

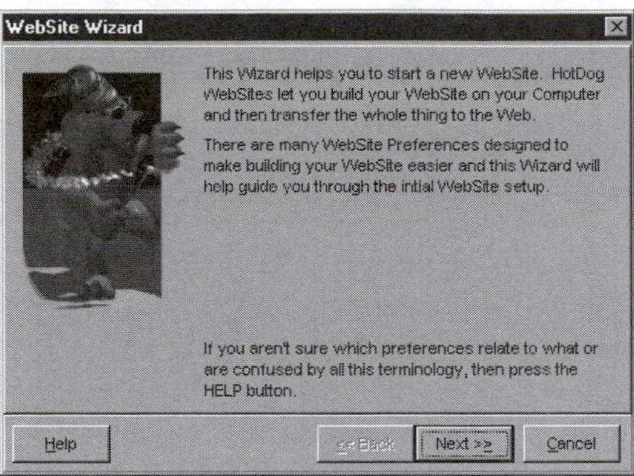

Figure 3. The **WebSite Wizard** takes you through the steps of creating a new HotDog Pro WebSite and guides you with easy-to-follow instructions.

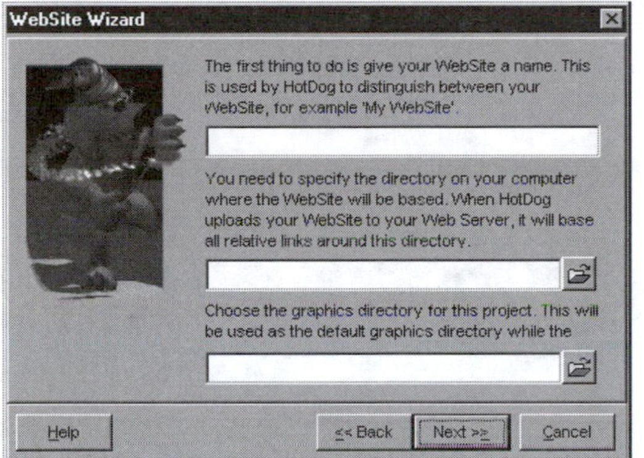

Figure 4. The second **WebSite Wizard** dialog box asks you to name your Web site and specify directories for your HTML documents and images.

Starting a New WebSite

Whether you already have a Web site, or you're starting from scratch, you should first create a HotDog Pro WebSite. Sure you can skip this chapter and use the **Local Files** resource display (as mentioned in the last chapter) to work with your pages. But the **WebSites** Manager makes things a lot easier when you're ready to upload your pages. If you work with more than one Web site, the **WebSites** Manager also makes it easy to access and keep track of them all.

To start a new WebSite with the WebSite Wizard

1. Create a folder for your Web site, then create a folder for your images inside your Web site folder (you can call it anything you want, but people generally name it **images**).
2. Return to the HotDog Pro application window and display the **WebSites** Manager, as explained in the previous section.
3. Click the **Wizard** icon (it looks like a little wizard hat).
4. When the **WebSite Wizard** dialog box appears, as shown in Figure 3, click the **Next** button.
   - **A.** When the second **WebSite Wizard** dialog box appears, as shown in Figure 4, enter a name for your Web site in the first text field (at the top of the dialog box).
   - **B.** In the second text field, enter a directory path to your Web site folder (directory) or click the folder icon to browse for a folder. When you click the folder icon, the **Choose Directory** dialog box appears, as shown in Figure 5, so you can browse for your directory.

C. In the third text field, enter a directory path to the folder you wish to store your images in or click the folder icon to browse for a folder. When you're finished naming your Web site and specifying your directory paths, click the **Next** button.

5. When the third **WebSite Wizard** dialog box appears, as shown in Figure 6, enter your Web server's ftp address in the **Web Server:** text field, and enter your Web site directory in the **Directory:** text field.

   A. Enter your user name in the **User Name:** text field and your password in the **Password:** text field, then click the **Next** button.

6. When the fourth **WebSite Wizard** dialog box appears, as shown in Figure 7, tell HotDog Pro how to handle file uploads that may overwrite existing files on the server, then click the **Next** button.

7. When the fifth **WebSite Wizard** dialog box appears, as shown in Figure 8, click the **Finish** button to create your new Web site, or click the **Cancel** button if you decide not to create a new Web site. You can also click the **Back** button to make quick changes to your settings. When you create a new WebSite, it appears as an item in the **WebSites Manager** list.

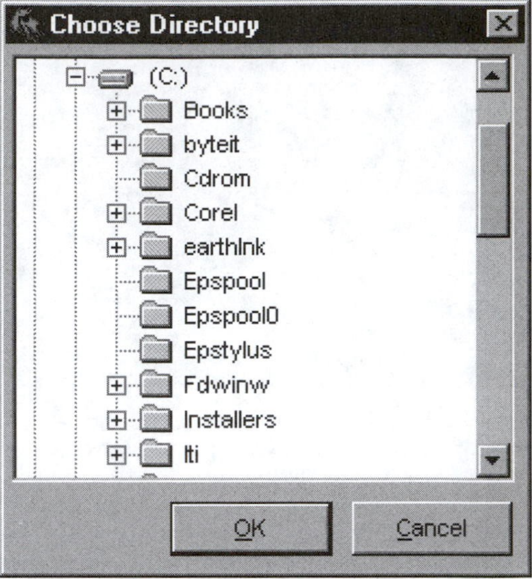

Figure 5. The **Choose Directory** dialog box helps you find the folders for your Web site and your images.

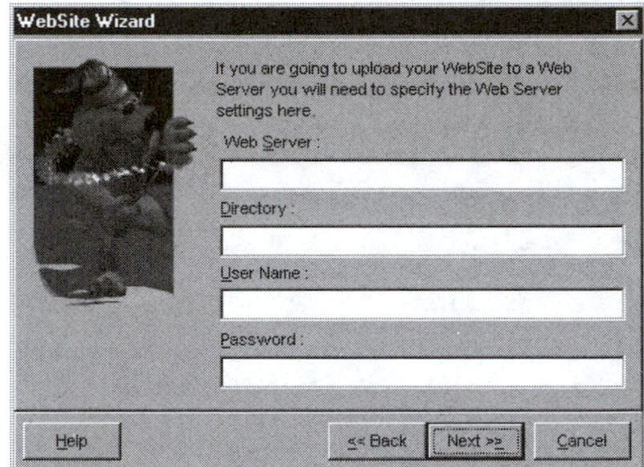

Figure 6. The third **WebSite Wizard** dialog box prompts you for your server information so the **WebSites** Manager can help you upload page.

THE WEBSITE WIZARD

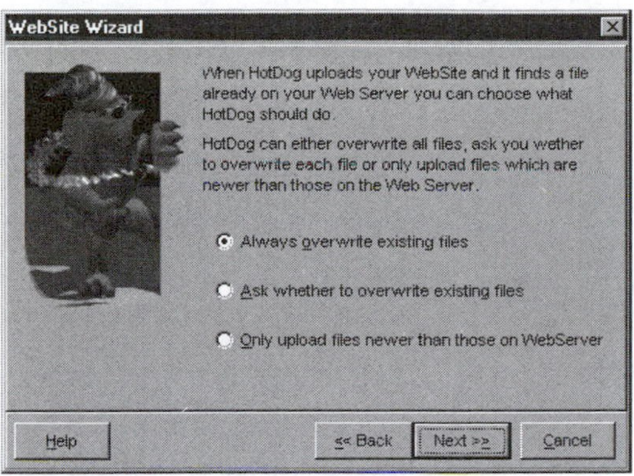

Figure 7. The fourth **WebSite Wizard** dialog box lets you specify how the **WebSites** Manager should handle uploading files that may overwrite existing files on the server (updated pages, for example).

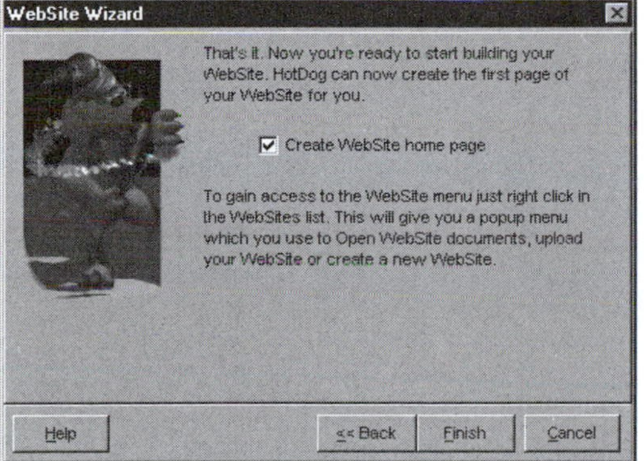

Figure 8. When the fifth **WebSite Wizard** dialog box appears, click the **Finish** button.

✔ Tips

- The first page on your Web site *must* be named **index** with the .html or .htm file name extension (as in, **index.html**).
- When you create a new HotDog Pro WebSite, the **WebSite Wizard** automatically creates an index page for you and displays it in the application window's document window pane so you can start working.
- If you already have a Web site and want to create a HotDog Pro WebSite so you can use the **WebSites** Manager's helpful features, make sure to first copy your existing index document to another folder. Otherwise the **WebSite Wizard** writes over your index page when it creates one, and we certainly wouldn't want that to happen! You can then move your original index page back into your Web folder.
- If you already have a Web site, check your folder after using the **WebSite Wizard** to make sure you don't have two index pages. This happened to me because my index file is named **index.htm** and the **WebSite Wizard** created another one called **index.html**! When you have more than one index page on a Web site, it causes lots of trouble.

Downloading a Web site from a Server with the Website Downloader

Let's say you created a Web site at work or school, and now you'd like to work on it a little more at home. With HotDog Pro, that's no problem. The **Website Downloader** makes it easy to download entire Web sites from a server to your computer.

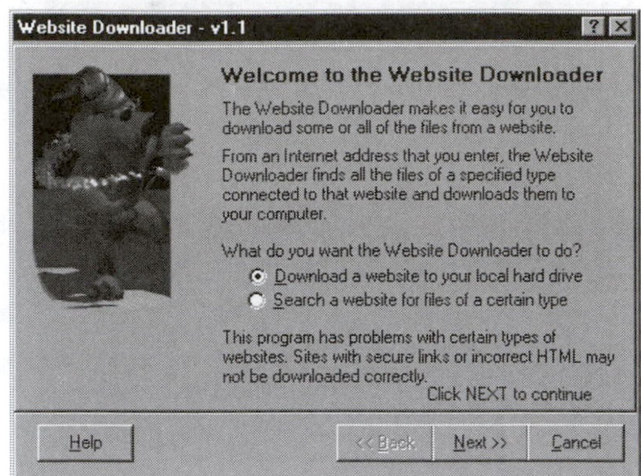

Figure 9. When you launch the **Website Downloader**, tell it to download a Web site by clicking the **Download a website to your local hard drive** radio button.

To download an existing Web site from a server with the Website Downloader

1. Select **Website Downloader** from the **SuperToolz** menu.
2. When the **Website Downloader** dialog box appears, as shown in Figure 9, select the **Download a website to your local hard drive** radio button, then click the **Next** button.
3. When the **Website to download** dialog box appears, as shown in Figure 10, enter the Web site's URL in the **Please enter your address below** text field.
   - **A.** Enter the name of the main page (usually **index.html**) in the **Please enter the name of the first page** text field.
   - **B.** Specify a folder on your computer for storing the Web site by entering a directory path (or by clicking the folder icon to browse for a folder) in the **Where do you want to save the downloaded files?** text field.
   - **C.** Click the **Next** button.

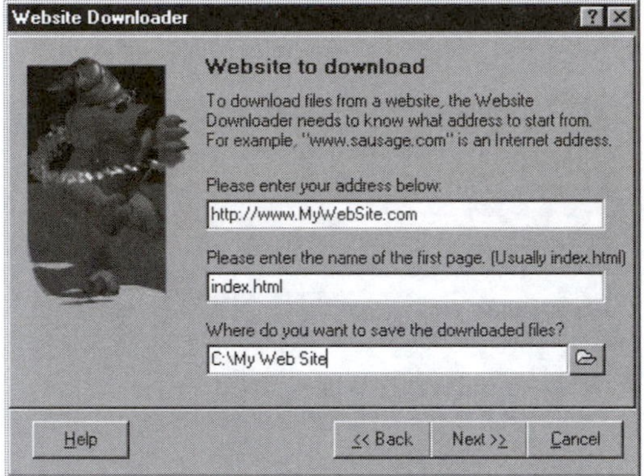

Figure 10. The **Website to download** dialog box prompts you for downloading information.

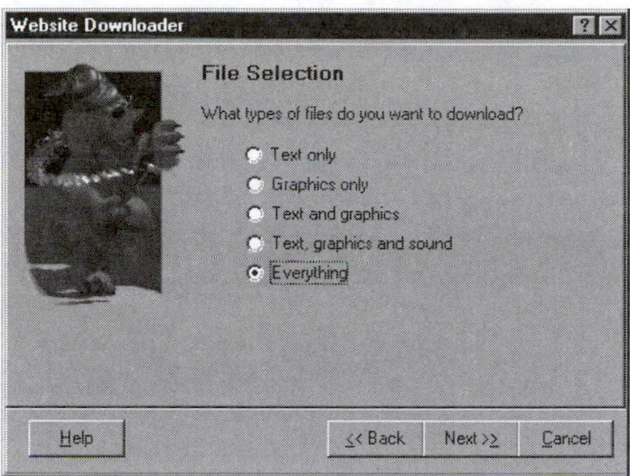

Figure 11. The **File Selection** dialog box asks which types of files you'd like to download.

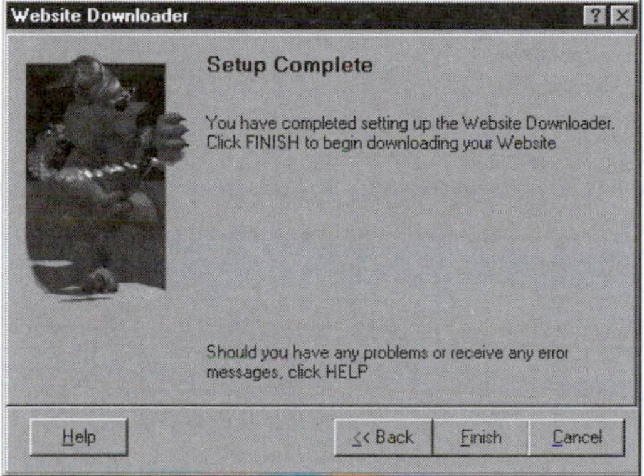

Figure 12. The **Setup Complete** dialog box tells you that you're ready to download now.

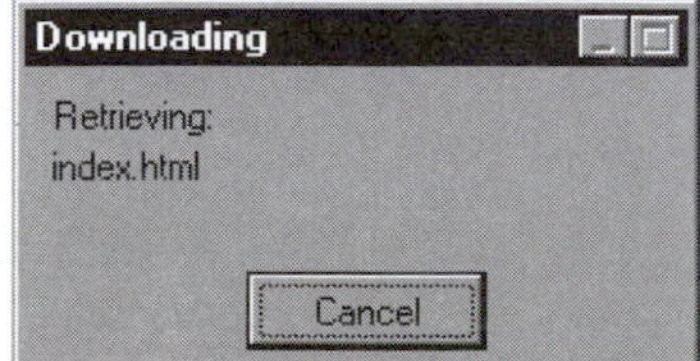

Figure 13. The **Downloading** dialog box tells you which files the **WebSite Downloader** is retrieving.

4. When the **File Selection** dialog box appears, as shown in Figure 11, choose which types of files you want to download by clicking a radio button (I recommend that you choose the **Everything** radio button), then click the **Next** button.

5. When the **Setup Complete** dialog box appears, as shown in Figure 12, click the **Finish** button to begin downloading the Web site, click **Cancel** to cancel the download, or click **Back** to return to previous dialog boxes to change information.

6. When the **Downloading** dialog box appears, it tells you which files the **Website Downloader** is currently downloading. You can cancel at any time by clicking the **Cancel** button.

✔ Tip

- Go online before launching the **Website Downloader**.

Importing Files Into Your WebSite

Now, let's talk about the **WebSites** Manager again. In order for the **WebSites** Manager to work properly, you need to import all of your files into the HotDog Pro WebSite you created earlier in this chapter. If you already have a full-blown Web site, you can import all of your files into it at once. Or you can add documents one by one as you create them.

To import files into your WebSite

1. Select the **Resource Manager** from the **View** menu, then select **WebSites** from the cascading list to display the **WebSites** Manager.
2. When the **WebSites** Manager appears in the right resources window pane, click your Web site with your right mouse button (all HotDog Pro WebSites appear as items on the list).
3. When the pop-up menu appears, select **Properties**.
4. When the **WebSite Properties** dialog box appears, select **Files** from the list.
5. When the **WebSite Properties—Files** dialog box appears, as shown in Figure 14, click the **Add** button.
6. When the **Add Documents to Project** dialog box appears, as shown in Figure 15, select the HTML file (or files) you wish to add, and click the **Open** button.
7. When you return to the **WebSite Properties—Files** dialog box, the selected files appear on the list. Click **OK** to add the files, or click **Cancel** to restore the previous list without the additions. You can also click the **Add** button to import more files, or select files and click the **Remove** button to delete them from the list.

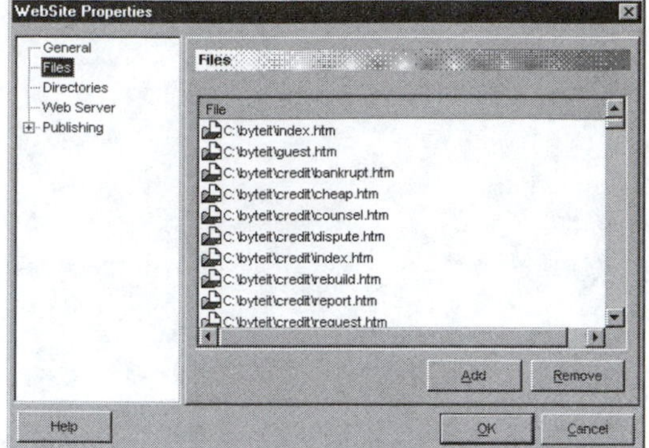

Figure 14. To add files, display the **WebSite Properties—Files** dialog box and click the **Add** button.

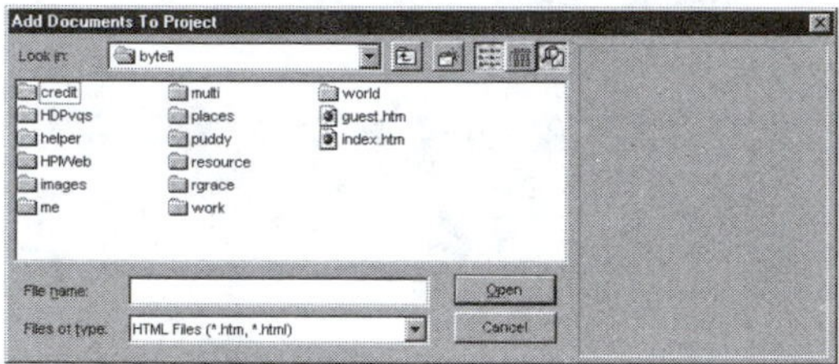

Figure 15. When the **Add Documents to Project** dialog box appears, you can select files to add.

Creating a Web Page

Whew! Now that you've downloaded, installed, and set up HotDog Pro, let's start making Web pages. What? You've never created a Web page in your life? You're used to graphical editors like Microsoft FrontPage or Adobe PageMill? No problem. HotDog Pro makes entering and formatting text as easy as working with a word processing program. This chapter covers the basics of creating, opening, and saving Web pages, setting up your document properties, and formatting text.

Creating, Opening, and Saving Web Pages

There are several ways to work with Web pages. You can either create new ones, or open existing ones and edit them. Even if you created a Web site in a different HTML application, you can still edit your pages with HotDog Pro.

To create a new Web page

1. Select **New** from the **File** menu.
2. When the **New** dialog box appears, as shown in Figure 1, select a template and click **OK**.

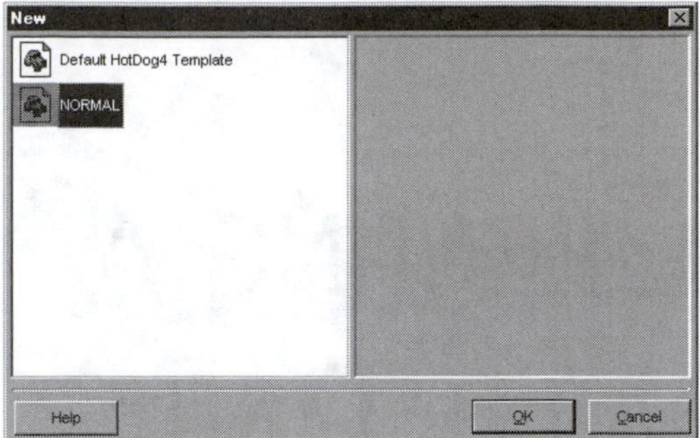

Figure 1. When you select **New** from the **File** menu, the **New** dialog box displays with a list of templates. Select a template and click **OK**.

To open an existing Web page

1. Select the **Open** icon from the standard toolbar, or select **Open** from the **File** menu, or use the **CTRL+O** key combination.
2. When the **Open File** dialog box appears, as shown in Figure 2, browse for your file.
3. Select a file and click the **Open** button.

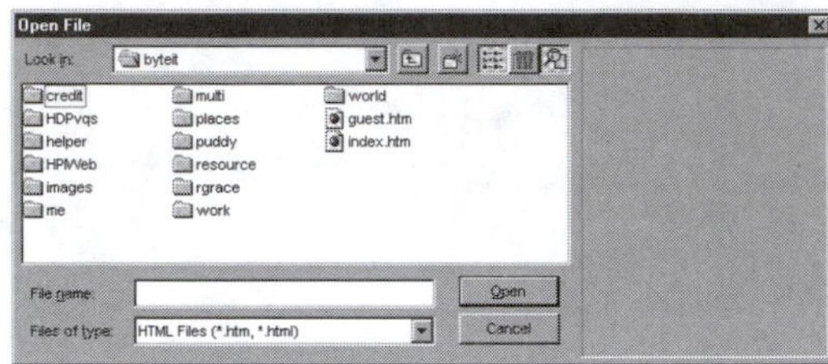

Figure 2. The **Open File** dialog box lets you browse for a file.

To save and name a Web page

1. Click the **Save** icon on the Standard toolbar, or select **Save** from the **File** menu, or use the **CTRL+S** key combination.
2. When the **Save As** dialog box appears, as shown in Figure 3, browse for the folder you want to save your document into.
3. Enter the name of your document in the **File name:** text field (don't enter the .HTM or .HTML file name extension—HotDog Pro does that automatically).
4. Make sure the **HTML Files** list item is selected from the **Save as type** pull-down list.
5. Click the **Save** button.

✔ Tips

- HotDog Pro comes with a couple of default templates that set up a basic HTML document for you.
- You can also build your own templates, as explained in the "Creating a Template" section of this chapter.
- If you click the **New** button on the Standard toolbar, a new document immediately appears in the application window with the default template settings. The **New** dialog box does not appear.
- Default body text information includes text, link, and background colors. The "To pick colors for your Web page" section in this chapter tells you how. You can use either a solid color or a GIF or JPEG image for your page's background (for more about GIFs and JPEGs, see Chapter 5).

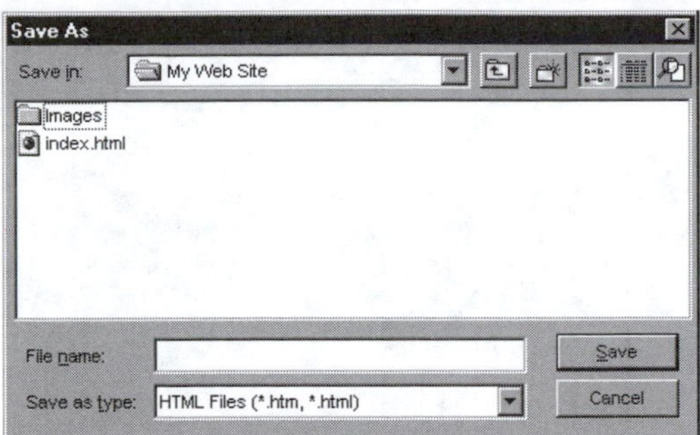

Figure 3. When the **Save As** dialog box appears, you can save and name your Web page.

HotDog Pro Default Template Code	
DEFINITIONS	**HTML CODE**
Document type	<HTML>
Header information	<HEAD>
Document Title (Displays in browser title bar)	<TITLE> type_Document _Title_here
Title closing tag	</TITLE>
Meta tag information and attributes	<META NAME="generator" CONTENT="Sausage Software HotDog Professional">
Header information closing tag	</HEAD>
Default body text	<BODY>
Default body text closing tag	</BODY>
Document type closing tag	</HTML>

Table 1. Basic HTML properties tags with definitions. All HTML documents should contain these elements (thought the Meta tag information is optional).

✔ Tips

- Meta tag information can include a brief summary of your page's topics, what application you created the page with, and the name of the author or company.
- Meta tag information gets picked up by search engines so your intended audience can find your site more easily.

Setting Up Document Properties

Document properties are default settings and header information for your Web pages. When you create a new Web page with the **HotDog Pro Default** template, a document with the HTML codes shown in Table 1 appears in the application window. But don't worry—you don't need to memorize or know much about these codes. HotDog Pro's easy-to-follow **Document Properties** dialog boxes prompt you for the information. HotDog Pro then generates the HTML codes and text for you.

Document Properties

- **Document type:** The **<HTML>... </HTML>** document opening and closing tags contain the text and identify the document as a Web page.
- **Header information:** The **<HEAD>... </HEAD>** tags enclose the header information—such as the page's title and meta tag information.
- **Page title header information:** The **<TITLE>...</TITLE>** opening and closing tags contain the page title. The title appears on the browser application window's title bar.
- **Meta tag header information (optional):** The **<Meta>** tag header data provides additional information about your pages.
- **Default body text:** The **<BODY>... </BODY>** opening and closing tags contain settings for the Web page's default body text settings. This includes the page's text and background colors.

To pick colors for your Web page

1. Click the **Background Details** icon on the Formatting toolbar, or select **Document Properties** from the **Format** menu.
2. When the **Document Properties** dialog box appears, make sure the **Appearance** tab is selected (as shown in Figure 4).
3. Choose a background image by entering the directory path to a GIF or JPEG image file in the **Choose a background image** text field. You can also click the folder icon to browse for your image file.
4. Or pick a solid color for your background by clicking the **Background Colour** selection box and selecting a color when the **Color** palette dialog box appears (click **OK** after selecting your color).
5. Click the **Document Text** selection box to display the **Color** palette dialog box, select a color for the body text in your Web page, then click **OK** to return to the **Document Properties** dialog box.
6. Click the **Standard Link** selection box to pick a color for your links.
7. Click the **Active Link** selection box to pick the color you want links to become *while* the user is clicking on them.
8. Click the **Visited Link** selection box to pick the color you want links to turn after the user visits them.
9. When you're finished picking links, click **OK**.

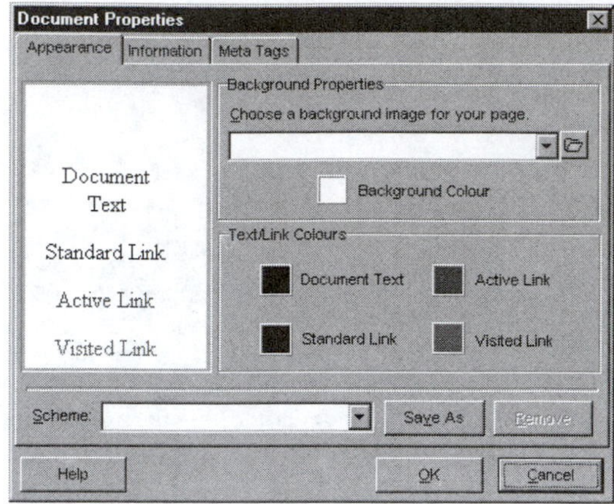

Figure 4. The **Document Properties—Appearance** dialog box makes it easy to pick color schemes.

✔ Tips

- If you create a new document by selecting **New** from the File menu, the **New** dialog box appears with a list of available templates, as shown in Figure 1.
- If you create a new document by clicking the **New** button on the Standard toolbar, HotDog Pro automatically generates your new document with the **Normal** template.
- Don't worry if you can't remember what each toolbar button does. Tooltips appear to remind you.
- When you pick colors, the new color appears in the appropriate selection box.
- You can preview your color scheme in the preview box to the left of the **Document Properties — Appearance** dialog box.
- If you look at your <BODY> tag source code after creating a color scheme, you'll see combinations of numbers preceded by a # sign. These are called *hexadecimal codes.* They represent colors.

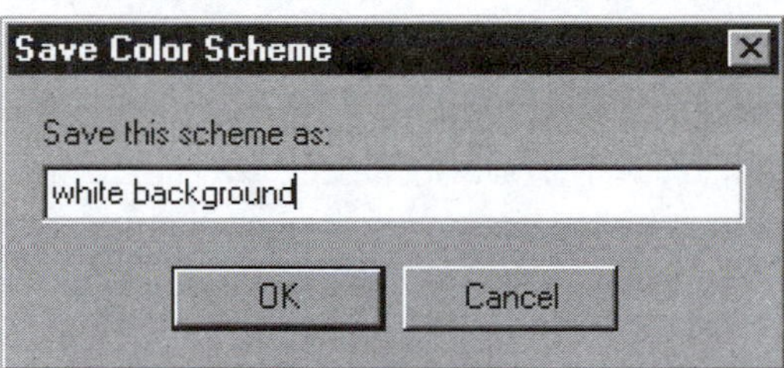

Figure 5. When the **Save Color Scheme** dialog box appears, you can save the color scheme you've just created for your Web page.

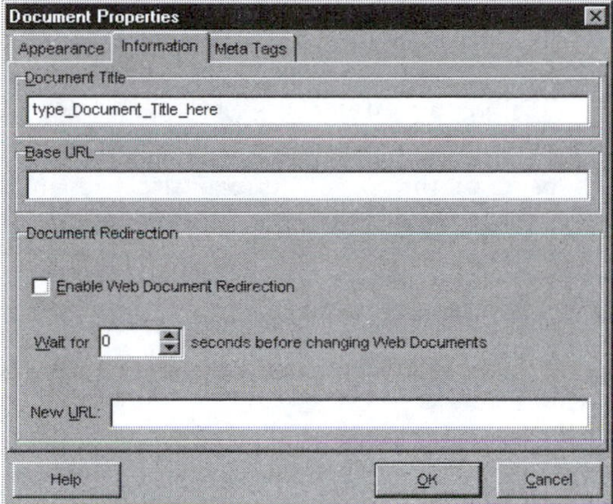

Figure 6. You can title your page in the **Document Properties—Information** dialog box.

✔ Tips

- For lists of hexadecimals and the colors they represent, go to Netscape's Background and Foreground Color Control Page at *home.netscape.com/assist/net_sites/bg/*.
- You can save color schemes, then apply them to Web pages by selecting them from the **Scheme** pull-down list.
- We'll be using the Format toolbar a lot in this chapter. To display the Format toolbar, select **Toolbars** from the **View** menu, then select **Format** when the cascading list displays.
- The **</BODY>** and **</HTML>** closing tags go at the bottom of your document.

To save a color scheme

1. After creating a color scheme that you like, click the **Save As** button.
2. When the **Save Color Scheme** dialog box appears, as shown in Figure 5, enter a name for your color scheme in the **Save this scheme as** text field.
3. Click **OK** to return to the **Document Properties—Appearance** dialog box.

To apply saved color schemes to a document

1. Click the **Background Details** icon on the Formatting toolbar, or select **Document Properties** from the **Format** menu.
2. When the **Document Properties** dialog box appears, make sure the **Appearance** tab is selected (as shown in Figure 4).
3. Select a saved color scheme from the **Scheme** pull-down list.
4. Click **OK**.

To title your Web page

When you enter a title for your Web page, the text appears in the browser's title bar when visitors view your page.

1. Click the **Background Details** icon on the Formatting toolbar, or select **Document Properties** from the **Format** menu.
2. When the **Document Properties** dialog box appears, select the **Information** tab.
3. When the **Document Properties—Information** dialog box appears, as shown in Figure 6, enter the title of your page in the **Document Title** text field.
4. Click **OK**.

To enter a base URL for your Web page

1. Click the **Background Details** icon on the Formatting toolbar, or select **Document Properties** from the **Format** menu.
2. When the **Document Properties** dialog box appears, select the **Information** tab.
3. When the **Document Properties—Information** dialog box appears, as shown in Figure 6, enter the full URL and document of the current page, such as: **http://www.ISP.com/my-web-site/index.html**.
4. Click **OK**.

To redirect the user's browser to a different Web page

1. Click the **Background Details** icon on the Formatting toolbar, or select **Document Properties** from the **Format** menu.
2. When the **Document Properties** dialog box appears, select the **Information** tab.
3. When the **Document Properties—Information** dialog box appears, as shown in Figure 6, enter the title of your page in the **Document Title** text field.
4. Select the **Enable Web Document Redirection** check box.
5. Select a number of seconds from the **Wait for __ seconds before changing Web Documents** number list by clicking the up or down arrows.
6. Specify the new document that you want to load automatically in the user's browser.
7. Click **OK**.

✔ Tips

- A base URL is an absolute Web site address for your HTML document. All path names for links, images, and page elements work relative to the base URL—even if the document gets moved to different location. This comes in handy for people who update and move pages frequently.
- You have to test pages with base URLs on the server. When you try to preview a page with a base URL locally, the images don't display and the links don't work.
- Redirecting a user's browser works like a mini-animation. When a user visits the page, another page automatically loads in their browser after a few seconds. Try it—it's neat!
- Don't make visitors wait more than a couple of seconds for the second Web page to load.
- Entering meta tag information isn't necessary, but it does give you more control over what search engines pick up from your pages and include in their databases. Search engines send out "robots" to automatically gather and catalog information from Web pages.

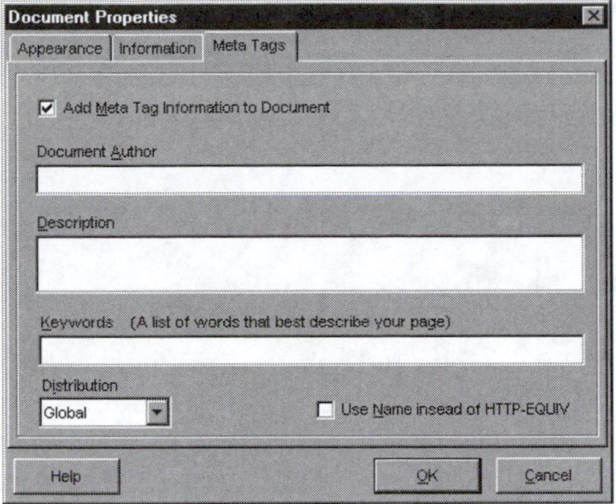

Figure 7. The **Document Properties—Meta Tags** dialog box lets you specify information that helps search engines catalog your site more accurately so visitors can find your page.

To include meta tag information in your document

1. Click the **Background Details** icon on the Formatting toolbar, or select **Document Properties** from the **Format** menu.
2. When the **Document Properties** dialog box appears, select the **Meta Tags** tab.
3. When the **Document Properties—Meta Tags** dialog box appears, as shown in Figure 7, select the **Add Meta Tag Information to Document** checkbox.
4. Enter your name or your organization's name in the **Document Author** text field.
5. Enter a quick description of your Web page in the **Description** text field.
6. Enter a few key words (separated by commas) that best summarize your Web page in the **Keywords** text field.
7. From the **Distribution** pull-down list, choose either **Global** (for distribution to the public via the Internet) or **Local** (for distribution across an organization via a private network).
8. Click **OK**.

Entering, Editing, Copying, and Pasting Text

You can enter, edit, and format text in an HTML document the same way as you do with a word processing document. To enter text, place your cursor where you want to insert the text and start typing. To edit text, select the text with your cursor and start typing the new text. You can even copy text from a file created in a different application and then paste it into your HTML document

To enter text

1. Place your cursor where you want to insert the text.
2. Start typing.

To edit text

1. Select the text you want to replace by placing your cursor, holding down your mouse button, and dragging it over the text.
2. Type the new text.

To copy text into an HTML document

1. Open the document you want to copy text from with the application that you created the document in.
2. Select the text you want to copy.
3. Use the **CTRL+C** key combination to copy the text onto your system's clipboard.
4. Return to the HotDog Pro application window and open the HTML document you want to paste the text into.
5. Use the **CTRL+V** key combination to paste the text into your HTML document.

✔ Tips

- You can copy and paste text from documents created in word processing and desktop publishing applications with a text editor — such as Microsoft Word, Corel WordPerfect, PageMaker, and Quark Xpress.
- The pasted text does not retain its formatting attributes (such as font styles, paragraphs, and bulleted lists). You need to reformat the text in HTML as explained in the following sections of this chapter.
- Consider breaking up long documents into separate HTML documents connected by links (Chapter 6 tells you how to make links).
- Less is more! Too much text formatting can make your page look confusing.

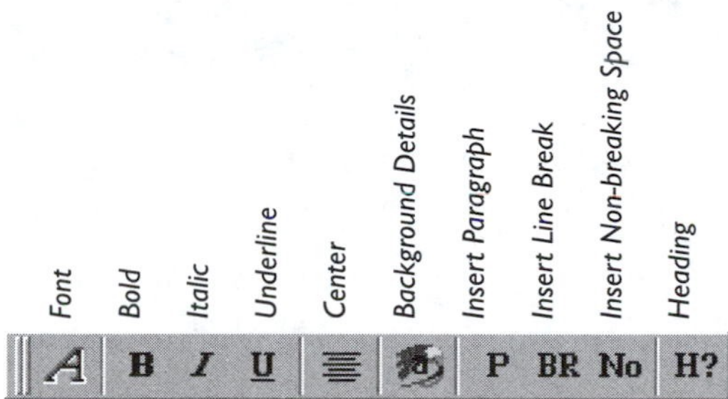

Figure 8. The **Format** toolbar makes it easy for you to perform common text formatting tasks.

Basic Text Formatting

HotDog Pro makes basic text formatting as simple as selecting text (or placing your cursor) and clicking a button on the Format toolbar. To display the Format toolbar (if you haven't yet), as shown in Figure 8, choose **Toolbars** from the **View** menu, then select **Format** from the cascading list. When the toolbar appears, anchor it as explained in Chapter 2. In addition, you can create lists (discussed later in this chapter) and insert other page elements (discussed in later chapters throughout the book) with the Insert toolbar.

Format toolbar options

- **Font:** Displays a list of fonts available on your system that you can select from.
- **Bold:** Formats selected text with the **<B>...</B>** bold opening and closing tags.
- **Italic:** Formats selected text with the **<I>...</I>** italic opening and closing tags.
- **Underline:** Formats selected text with the **<U>...</U>** underline opening and closing tags.
- **Center:** Aligns selected text to the center with the **<CENTER>...</CENTER>** center opening and closing tags.
- **Background Details:** Displays the **Document Properties** window so you can create color schemes and add document information as explained in the previous sections.
- **Insert Paragraph:** Inserts a **<P>** paragraph tag at your cursor's insertion point. A paragraph tag creates a line break separates the previous and following text with a double space. Paragraph **<P>** tags do not require **</P>** closing tags unless you plan to use cascading style sheets.

- **Insert Line Break:** Inserts a **
** line break tag at your cursor's insertion point. A line break tag creates a line break, but does not separate the previous and following text with an extra space. Line break **
** tags do not require closing tags.
- **Insert Nonbreaking Space:** Web browsers do not recognize extra spaces beyond one space per text element when you enter them in your text. To insert extra spaces, click the **Nonbreaking Text** toolbar button to enter the ** ** extended character string at the cursor's insertion point. For more about extended characters, see the section on the **HTML Tags** Manager later in this chapter.
- **Heading:** Click to display a list of headings (levels 1-6, with level 1 as the largest). Choose a heading level to apply it to the selected text. Figure 9 shows a Web page displayed in Internet Explorer with a level 1 heading applied.

To format text with the Formatting toolbar

1. Select the text you wish to format (or place your cursor at the insertion point to insert a paragraph, line break, or nonbreaking space).
2. Click the appropriate toolbar button on the **Format** toolbar.

HotDog Pro inserts the HTML tags for you. Wasn't that simple?

To apply fonts to text

1. Select the text you want to apply a font to.
2. Click the **Format** toolbar's **Font** button.
3. When the **Font** dialog box appears, as shown in Figure 10, choose a font from the **Font** list.

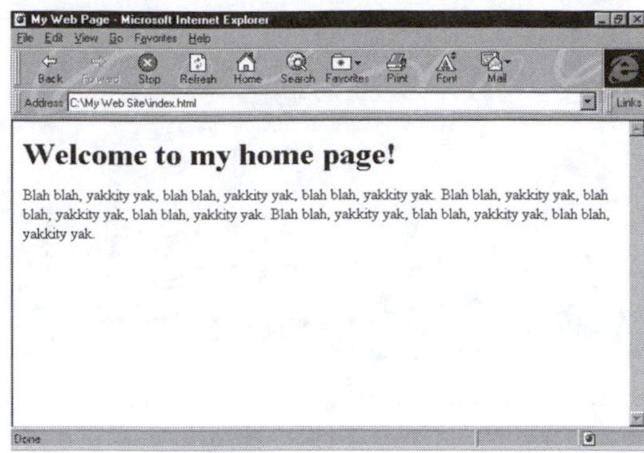

Figure 9. If you can select text and apply a heading tag, you can create a basic Web page.

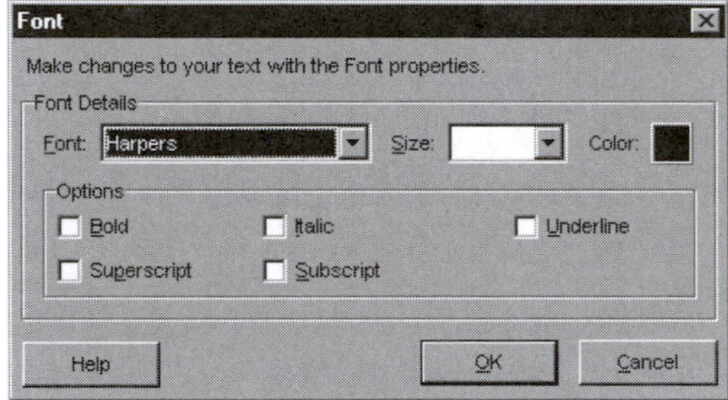

Figure 10. You can apply font attributes to selected text to give your pages a unique look by selecting options from the **Font** dialog box.

✔ Tips

- Remember—text formatting only displays in a Web browser or HotDog Pro's **Rover** resource, not in the HotDog Pro application window's document pane.
- Inserted page elements, such as tables and images, only display in a Web browser. The HotDog Pro application window's document pane only displays text and HTML tags.

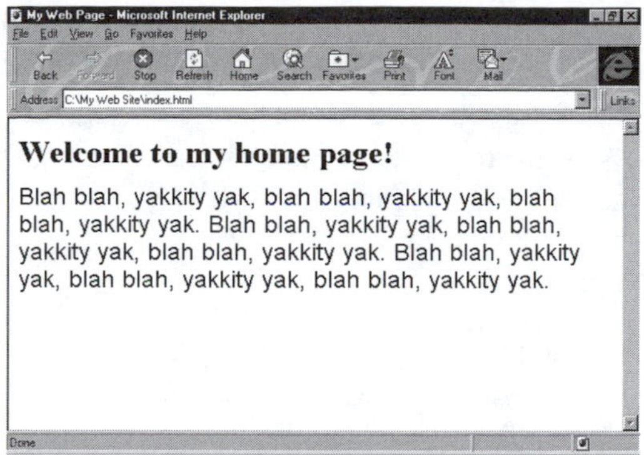

Figure 11. To see how your text looks with font attributes applied (I use the Arial font for the paragraph text), **you** need to preview them with your Web browser or with HotDog Pro's **Rover** resource.

✔ Tips

- If you decide to use fonts on your Web pages, stick with fonts that most people have on their systems—like Arial, Helvetica, Times Roman, Palatino, Courier, and Avant Garde. If visitors do not have the font you specify on their system, your pages will not display as you intend.
- This chapter mainly discusses **Format** toolbar options. But you'll also use the **Insert** toolbar to create bulleted lists and to insert a horizontal line. I explain other **Insert** toolbar options in later chapters.
- I don't recommend using the **Underline** formatting attribute. Since links generally appear with underlines, your visitors might mistake your underlined text for a link. They then get frustrated when the "link" doesn't work.

4. Choose a font size from the **Size** list.
5. You can also pick a font color (which overrides the default body text) by clicking the **Color** box to display the **Color** palette dialog box.
6. You can also choose to format text as bold, italic, superscript, subscript, or underlined by clicking the appropriate check boxes.
7. Click **OK** when you're finished selecting font attributes.
8. Preview your text with your browser or HotDog Pro's **Rover**. Figure 11 shows a Web page with the Arial font applied to the paragraph text displayed in Internet Explorer.

Making Lists

Bulleted, numbered, and nested lists are great for organizing information, and making important points stand out on your Web page. Browsers display these types of lists as indented text, and HotDog Pro automatically indents the text and inserts the bullets or numbers for you. To create lists, you first need to display the **Insert** toolbar. If you haven't done this already, select **Toolbars** from the **View** menu, then choose **Insert** from the cascading list.

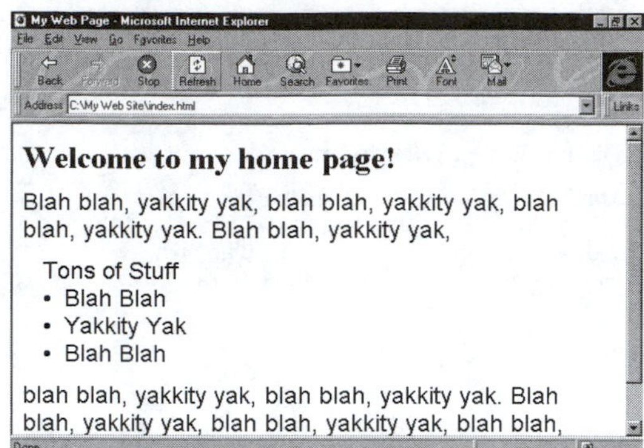

Figure 12. Bulleted lists are ideal for calling attention to specific topics discussed in your Web page.

Types of lists

- **Bulleted Lists:** Bulleted lists, as shown in the Web page in Figure 12, are indented lists of items preceded by a bullet. HotDog Pro even offers a few bullet styles to choose from.
- **Numbered Lists:** Numbered lists, as shown in the Web page in Figure 13, are indented lists of items preceded by a number. HotDog Pro automatically numbers the list items for you and offers commonly used numbering styles to choose from.
- **Nested Lists:** Nested lists, as shown in the Web page in Figure 14, are indented lists of items *within* a bulleted or numbered list. A nested bulleted or numbered list is inserted below an item in an existing list. HotDog Pro automatically indents the nested list farther towards the right.

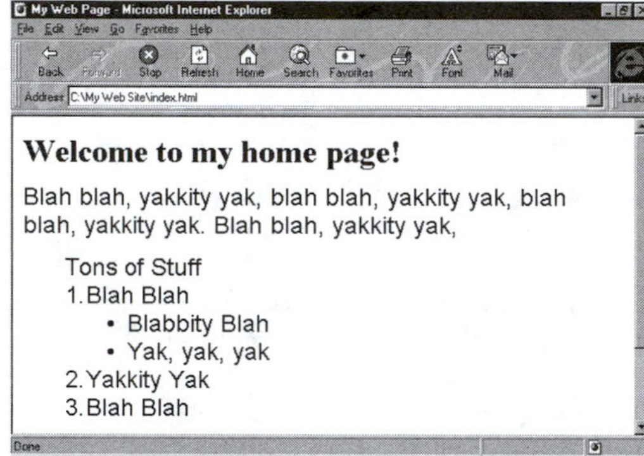

Figure 13. Numbered lists are ideal for explaining tasks (as I frequently do in this book), or listing items in order of importance.

To create a bulleted list

1. Place your cursor where you plan to insert your list.
2. Click the **Insert** toolbar's **List** button.
3. When the **Create List** dialog box displays, as shown in Figure 15, click the **Bulleted** radio button from the **List Type** options.

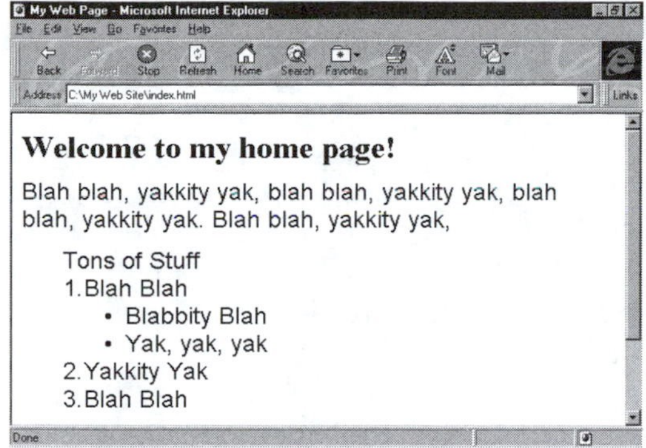

Figure 14. Nested lists help you visually organize more complex lists — such as a table of contents.

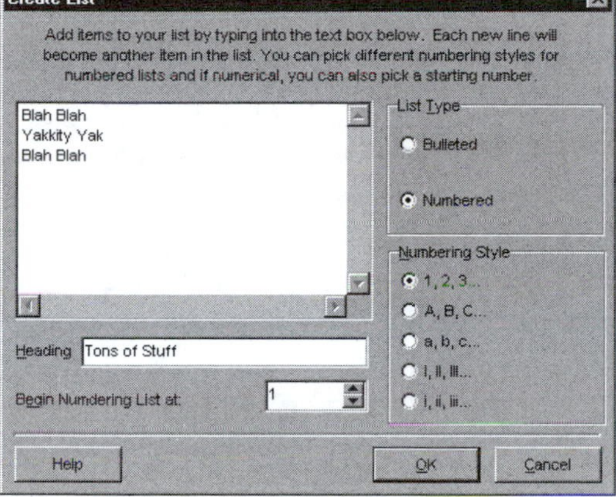

Figure 15. The **Create List** dialog box guides you through creating a bulleted or numbered list.

4. When the **Bullet Style** options list appears, select a bullet style by clicking a radio button.
5. Enter the items you wish to include in your list, and separate each item by pressing the **Enter** key on your keyboard.
6. You can also enter a heading for your list in the **Heading** text field.
7. Click **OK**.

To create a numbered list

1. Place your cursor where you plan to insert your list.
2. Click the **Insert** toolbar's **List** button.
3. When the **Create List** dialog box displays, as shown in Figure 15, click the **Numbered** radio button from the **List Type** options.
4. When the **Numbering Style** options list appears, select a number style by clicking a radio button.
5. Enter the items you wish to include in your list, and separate each item by pressing the **Enter** key on your keyboard.
6. You can also enter a heading for your list in the **Heading** text field.
7. Select the number that you wish to begin your list with from the scrolling **Begin Numbering List at** list.
8. Click **OK**.

To create a nested list

1. Insert the cursor beneath the list item you wish to create a nested list under.
2. Follow the previous instructions for creating a bulleted or numbered list.

Using Extended Characters

Web browsers don't recognize many commonly used extended characters—like letters with accents or symbols. Instead, extended characters (also often referred to as "special characters") are represented by odd-looking combinations of alphabetical characters—such as **©** for the © copyright symbol. Web browsers can interpret these combinations and display them as the correct special characters. But how can anyone possibly remember all these combinations? Never fear—HotDog Pro's **Extended Characters** resource, as shown in the right resource window pane of Figure 16, contains a list of commonly used characters. You can easily select, drag, and drop list items into your HTML document.

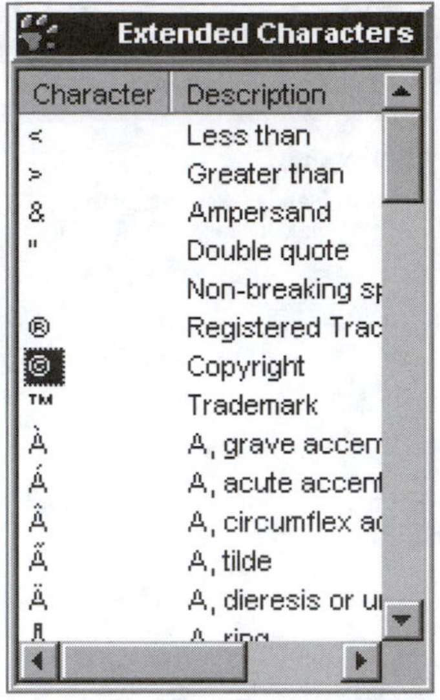

Figure 16. You can drag and drop special characters into your HTML document from the **Extended Character** resource list.

To add extended characters

1. Display the **Extended Characters** resource by choosing **Resource Manager** from the **View** menu, then selecting **Extended Characters** from the cascading list.
2. Place your cursor in the part of your HTML document where you want to insert a special character.
3. Scroll down the **Extended Characters** list to find the desired character.
4. Select a list item and double-click on it. Or you can drag and drop it into your document.
5. To display your Web page with special characters inserted (like the one shown in Figure 17), launch your Web browser or HotDog Pro's **Rover** resource.

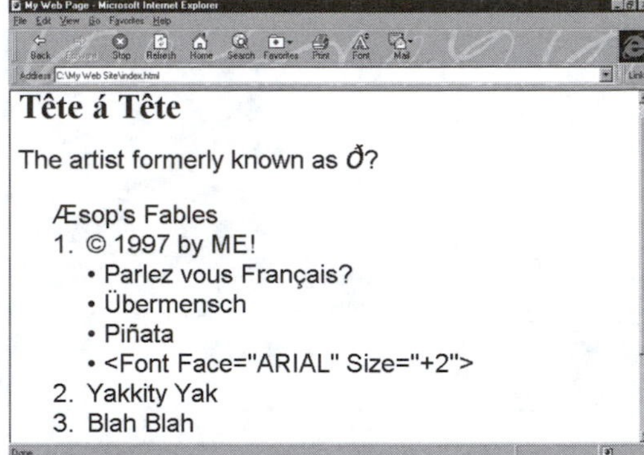

Figure 17. This page shows examples of commonly used extended characters.

✔ Tips

- Uppercase and lowercase letters with accents each have separate list items. Make sure you select the correct one.
- All extended character codes begin with **&** and end with **;**. This enables browsers to tell them apart from the rest of your text.
- The **Properties** dialog box's **Description** box gives you a definition of what the selected tag does.

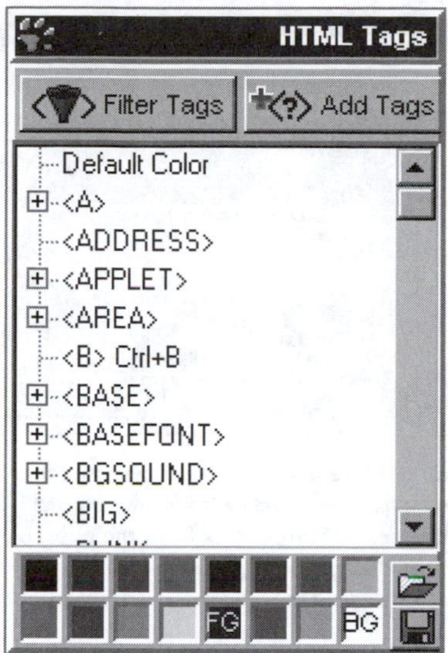

Figure 18. The **HTML Tags** Manager helps you insert a variety of HTML tags.

✔ Tips

- The **Defined in** box tells you which browsers support the tag. A list of permissible tag attributes displays in the list box on the left (if any attributes for that tag exist).
- Tag attributes are additional characteristics that can be entered within an HTML tag.

Working with the HTML Tags Manager

If HotDog Pro had toolbar buttons for every single HTML tag, there wouldn't be any room left on your computer screen. However, HotDog Pro does have the **HTML Tags** Manager. The **HTML Tags** Manager is a list of common HTML tags that displays in the right resource window pane. You can select list items and drag and drop them into your document when you need them. If you forget what a particular item of HTML code does, you can view the tag properties to jog your memory. HotDog Pro also gives you flexibility. If you use HTML codes that aren't supported by the **HTML Tags** Manager, you can add them to the list.

To insert tags with the HTML Tags Manager

1. Display the **HTML Tags** Manager by selecting **Resource Manager** from the **View** menu, then choosing **HTML Tags** from the cascading list.
2. When the **HTML Tags** Manager appears in the right resource window pane, as shown in Figure 18, insert your cursor where you want to place your tags in your HTML document.
3. Scroll through the list of tags until you find the one you're looking for.
4. Double-click on the list item you want to insert, or drag it from the list and drop it into your HTML document.
5. When the list item appears in your HTML document, insert your text or page element in between the opening and closing HTML tags.

To view HTML tag properties

1. Click an item from the **HTML Tags** Manager list with your right mouse button.
2. When the pop-up menu appears, select **Properties**.
3. When the **Properties** dialog box appears, as shown in Figure 19, you can view information about the selected HTML tag.
4. Click **OK** when you're finished viewing the tag's properties.

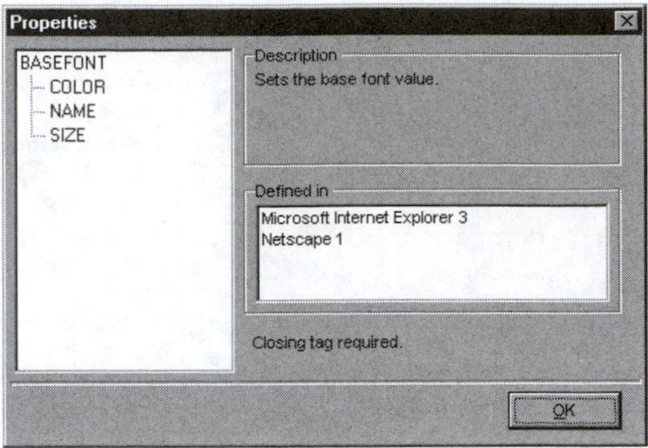

Figure 19. If you don't remember what a tag listed in the **HTML Tags** Manager does, click it with your right mouse button, then select **Properties** from the pop-up list. The **Properties** dialog box displays information about the tag and its attributes.

To add custom HTML codes to the tags manager

1. Click the **HTML Tags** Manager's **Add Tags** button.
2. When the **Add New Tag** dialog box appears, as shown in Figure 20, enter the name of the new tag in the **Element Name** text field.
3. Create a tag attribute by entering the attribute name in the **Name** text field, selecting the type of attribute from the **Type** list, and clicking the **Add** button.
4. When the attribute appears on the **Attributes** list, you can add more tag attributes.
5. Click **OK**.

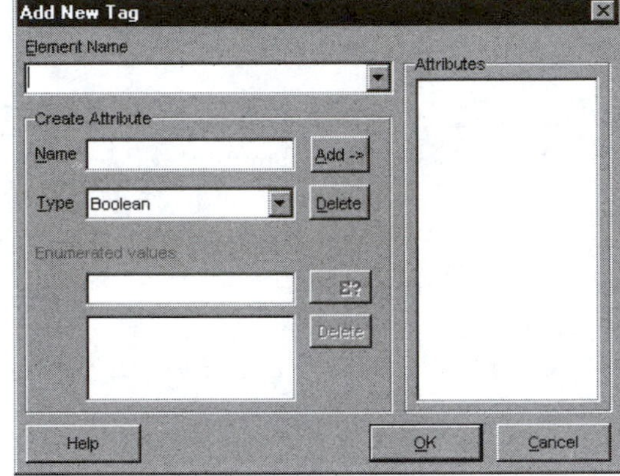

Figure 20. The **Add New Tag** dialog box lets you add new tags to the **HTML Tags Manager** list.

✔ Tips

- There are different types of tag attributes—**Boolean**, **Enumerate**, **String**, etc. These determine how attributes are specified. Once again, you may need an HTML whiz friend to help you with this.
- The **Add New Tag** dialog box can come in handy when you need to add material to your page that launch plug-ins or call up CGI scripts from your server.

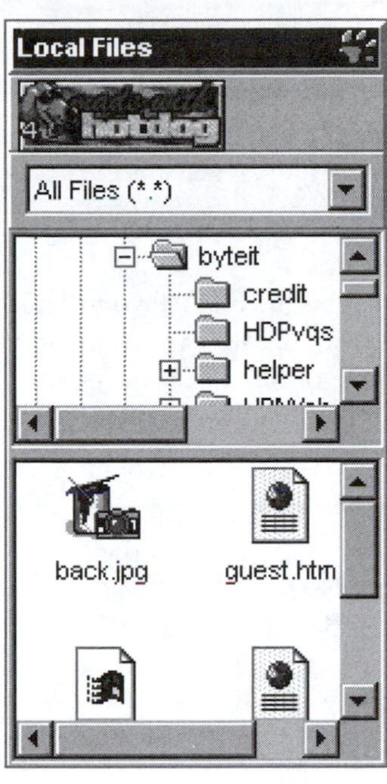

Figure 21. The **Local Files** Manager makes it easy for you to locate and display files on your computer.

Using the Local Files Manager

The **Local Files** Manager helps you work with files more easily. It displays a list of all the folders available on your computer, so you can browse for and open files without leaving the HotDog Pro application window. The **Files Manager** also lets you create links and add images by dragging and dropping list items into your HTML document, or by double clicking on them.

To view local files

1. Display the **Local Files** Manager by selecting **Resource Manager** from the **View** menu, then selecting **Local Files** when the cascading menu appears.
2. When the **Local Files** Manager appears in the left resource pane, as shown in Figure 21, select a file type from the pull-down list of file types. You can choose HTML Files, Graphics, or All Files (I recommend selecting **All Files** so you can see everything).
3. Browse through the folders on your computer by scrolling through the **Directories** list, and double-clicking the folder that contains the files you want to work with.
4. When you open a folder, your HTML and/or graphics files (depending on which item you selected from the **File Types** list) appear in the **Files** list.

To open a local HTML file

1. Display the **Local Files** Manager and browse for the folder where the file you want to open is located.
2. When the HTML document you want to open displays in the **Files** list, double click on it.

✔ Tips

- The **Add New Tag** dialog box is not for beginners. You need to know how HTML works in order to use it (or you can get a little help from a friend who does).
- The procedure described for opening files from the **Local Files** Manager only works if you have no documents open (otherwise, it creates a link). If you have an HTML document displayed in the document window, open files by clicking the Standard toolbar's **Open** button, selecting **Open** from the **File** menu, or using the **CTRL+O** key combination.

3. When the HTML document opens in the application window's document pane, you can begin working on it.

To rename a local file

1. Display the **Local Files** Manager and browse for the folder where the file you want to rename is located.
2. When the HTML document you want to rename displays in the **Files** list, click the file icon once. Wait a couple of seconds then click directly on the file name below the file icon (do not double-click).
3. When a selection box appears around the file name, you can type a name for the file.

To create a link to a local file

1. Display the **Local Files** Manager and browse for the folder where the file you want to link to is located.
2. Place your cursor at the place where you want to insert the link in your HTML document.
3. Select the file you want to create a link to from the **Files** list and double click on it.

To insert an image

1. Display the **Local Files** Manager and browse for the folder where the image file you want to insert is located.
2. Place your cursor at the place where you want to insert the link in your HTML document.
3. Select the file you want to create a link to from the **Files** list and double click on it.

✔ Tips

- You can make a link to any type of file (such as a QuickTime or AVI movie or other multimedia file). When a user clicks the link, the appropriate application launches.
- If you link to a multimedia file, you should include some text on your page that tells people what type of file it is. Some of your visitors may not have the appropriate application or plug-in.
- You can also insert links and images by dragging and dropping them into your document. Simply select a file, hold down your left mouse button, drag it to the insertion point of your document, and then release the mouse button.
- Templates *must* be saved to the default templates directory with the **.TPL** file name extension or they don't work. Unless you specify a different directory in your Preferences, as explained in Chapter 2, templates are located in: C:\PROGRAM FILES\HOTDOG4\Templates.
- If your template does not appear in the **New** dialog box list, don't panic. Browse for your template in the **Local Files** Manager. Make sure it is located in your default template directory and that it has the .TPL file name extension. If the document is located in the wrong directory, open the document and select **Save As** to save it to the correct directory. If the document has the wrong file name extension, rename it.

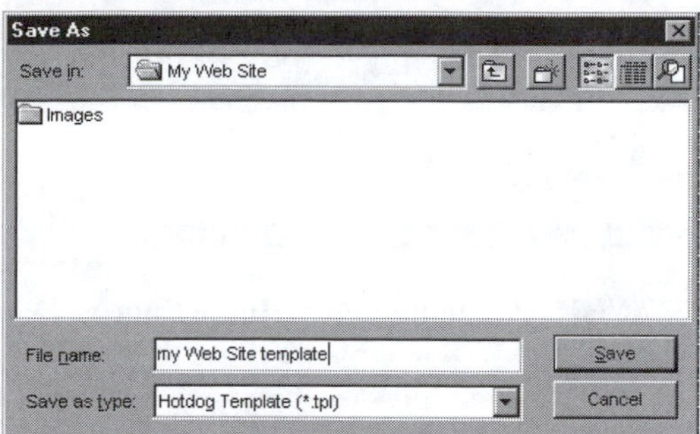

Figure 22. When the **Save As** dialog box appears, you can save and name your Web page template.

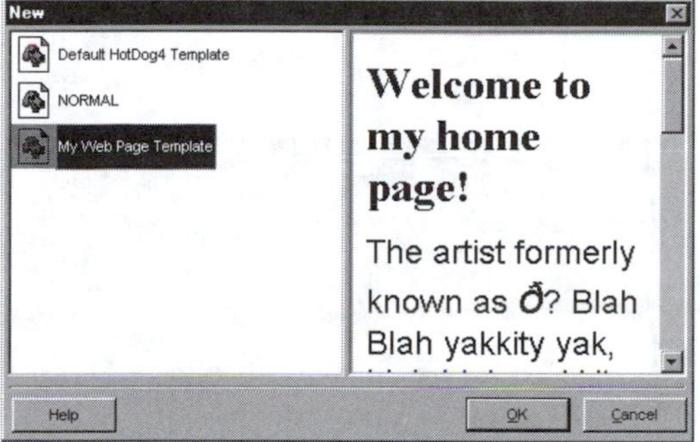

Figure 23. The **New** dialog box displays a list of available templates that you can choose from.

✔ Tips

- HotDog Pro comes with two basic templates with the basic codes required for HTML documents.
- The **New** dialog box displays a preview of the selected template so you can make sure that you're opening the right one.

Creating a Template

Most Web sites contain pages with common elements, such as color schemes, navigation buttons, and contact information. Entering these elements over and over again every time you add a new page to your Web site can get awfully tedious. That's why HotDog Pro lets you create templates. Once you create a page that contains the basic layout and elements that you want to include throughout your Web site, you can save it as a template that you can apply to other documents.

To save the current page as a template

1. Click the **Save** icon on the standard toolbar, or select **Save** from the **File** menu, or use the **CTRL+S** key combination.
2. When the **Save As** dialog box appears, as shown in Figure 22, browse for the default **Template** directory from the **Save In** list.
3. Enter the name of your template document, followed by the **.TPL** file name extension in the **File name** text field.
4. Make sure the **HotDog Template** list item is selected from the **Save as type** pull-down list.
5. Click **OK**.

To apply a template to a new HTML document

1. Select **New** from the **File** menu, or use the **CTRL+N** key combination.
2. When the **New** dialog box appears, as shown in Figure 23, select a template from the list and click **OK**.

When the HTML document appears in the application window's document window pane, you can begin working on your page.

Adding Horizontal Lines

You can use horizontal lines (also called "horizontal rules" or "page dividers") to divide your page into different sections. For example, the horizontal line on Rich Grace's home page (shown in Figure 24) divides the title image and navigation buttons from the rest of the document.

Figure 24. The horizontal line divides Rich Grace's home page at *www.byteit.com/rgrace/*.

To add a horizontal line

1. Insert the cursor at the place in your document where you want to add the horizontal line.
2. Click the **Insert Line** toolbar button.
3. When the **Horizontal Rule** dialog box appears, as shown in Figure 25, choose an option for how thick you want the line to be by selecting a number from the **Thickness** scrolling list.
4. You can choose a width for your line by selecting a number from the **Width** list.
5. You can also choose to specify the line width as a percentage (%) of the page width, or as a number of pixels. Simply select an option from the list to the right of the **Width** list.
6. Select the **Include Line Shading** text box to give your line a three-dimensional effect.
7. Choose whether you want to align your horizontal line to the **Center**, flush **Left**, or flush **Right** by selecting an option from the **Alignment** pull-down list.
8. Click the **OK** button.

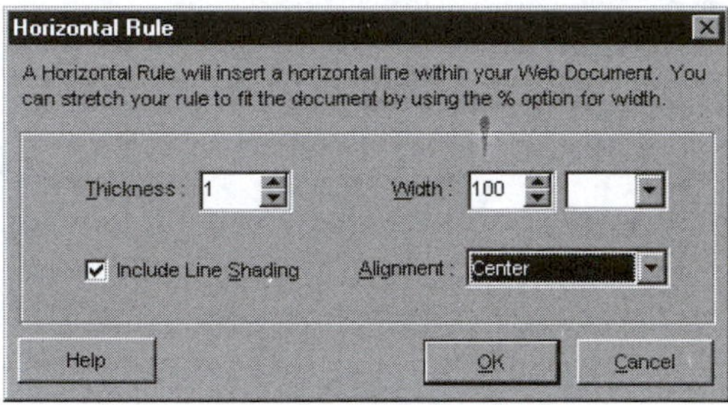

Figure 25. The **Horizontal Rule** dialog box helps you format your horizontal rule.

✔ Tips

- *Pixels* are the unit of measurement used on the Web. The size of a pixel varies depending on the size and resolution of the user's computer screen. Pixels are tiny. Open your word processor and display the ruler. An inch on that ruler equals roughly 100 pixels.
- To make a horizontal rule span the entire width of your Web page, select **100%** from the **Horizontal Rule** dialog box's **Width** options.

5

ADDING IMAGES

Images make the Web cool and fun. Even if you aren't a professional designer, you can use a few well-placed images to jazz up your page and make your site more navigable. HotDog Pro makes it easy for you to insert images and position them on your page so they look good with your page layout. In addition, the handy dandy **Button Editor** SuperTool helps you make simple changes to your images. It also converts BMP and PCX images to the GIF and JPEG formats used on the Web.

Images on the Web

Image files often take up huge amounts of disk space. Most of us wind up finding this out the hard way. When the Internet craze first started gathering steam, developers realized that large image files that take forever to download wouldn't do. And so the GIF and JPEG image file formats were born. GIF and JPEG files work well on the Web because they are tiny, yet the images still look good. Would you believe that the Web page shown in Figure 1—images and all—weighs in at a slender 104 KB? Besides, you *have* to use them, since most graphical Web browsers can *only* display GIF and JPEG files.

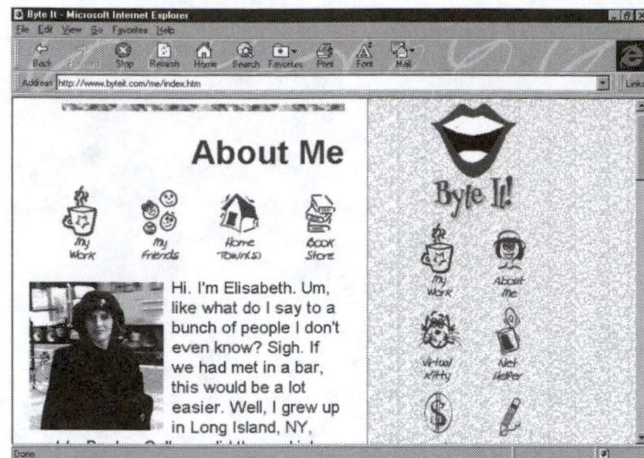

Figure 1. GIF and JPEG image files are small—this Web page (*www.byteit.com/me/index.htm*) has lots of images and still only takes up 104 KB in disk space—which takes 32 seconds to download with a 28.8 modem. That's even a bit piggy for a Web page.

Inserting Images

Before we begin, I should tell you that the images displayed on people's Web pages aren't *really* part of the HTML source document. Images are stored with the Web site as separate files. You then enter codes in your HTML document that tell the browser where and how to display the images. But thanks to HotDog Pro, you don't have to think about code and other technical things like that. The **Image Wizard** helps beginners place images quickly and easily. Meanwhile, if you're an advanced user, you'll find that the **Insert Image** dialog box provides options for the latest image attributes so you can tweak your page layout to your heart's content.

When you insert an image, HotDog Pro inserts the appropriate HTML codes in your document. While you don't *need* to know the codes, you should at least know what it looks like. You may need to find it later. The code appears similar to the following example:

```
<IMG SRC="images/my_image.gif" HEIGHT="213"
WIDTH="192" ALIGN="Left" BORDER="0"
VSPACE="5" HSPACE="5" ALT="Picture of cat">
```

The **<IMG SRC="images/my_image.gif">** tag tells the browser to display an image and

✔ Tips

- The GIF format works best for simple illustrations—such as cartoons, logos, icons, and line art.
- The JPEG format works best for scanned photographs and illustrations with lots of detail, shading, and subtle color gradients.

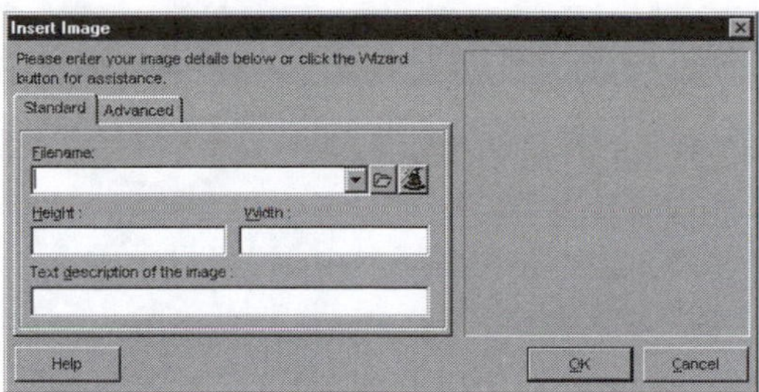

Figure 2. When the **Insert Image** dialog box appears, you can click the wizard hat icon to launch the **Image Wizard**. Or, advanced users can simply select options straight from the **Insert Image** dialog box.

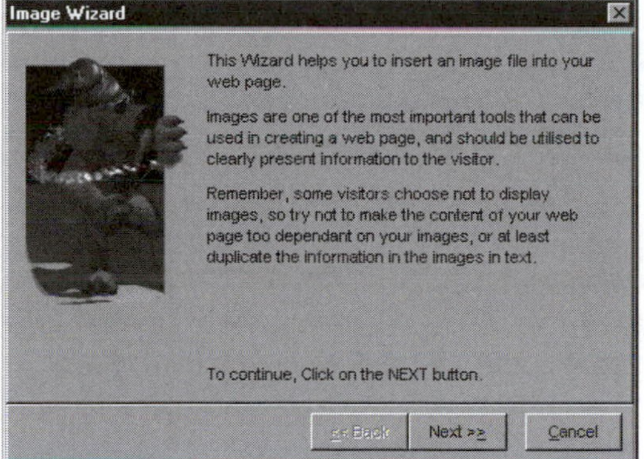

Figure 3. When the **Image Wizard** dialog box appears, read the instructions and click the **Next** button.

Figure 4. When the second **Image Wizard** dialog box appears, tell it where your image is located. If you want your image to function as a link, you can also specify a directory path or URL.

specifies the image's directory path so the browser can locate it. The rest of the items in the sample line of code are image source tag *attributes*. Attributes enable you to specify details for how a browser should handle page elements.

To insert an image with the Image Wizard

1. Place your cursor at the insertion point of your document, then click the **Image** toolbar button on the **Insert** toolbar, or select **Image** from the **Insert** menu.
2. When the **Insert Image** dialog box appears, as shown in Figure 2, click the **Wizard** button (with the wizard hat icon).
3. When the **Image Wizard** dialog box appears, as shown in Figure 3, read the instructions and click the **Next** button.
4. When the second **Image Wizard** dialog box appears, as shown in Figure 4, enter the directory path to the image in the top text field. Or you can click the folder icon to display the **Open** dialog box and browse for the file.
5. If you want your image to also function as a link, enter the directory path to the image in the bottom text field. Or you can click the folder icon to display the **Open** dialog box and browse for the file.
6. Click the **Finish** button to place your image. Or click **Cancel** to return to the HotDog Pro application window without placing the image.

To insert an image with the Insert Image dialog box

1. Place your cursor at the insertion point of your document, then click the **Image** toolbar button on the **Insert** toolbar, or select **Image...** from the **Insert** menu.
2. When the **Insert Image** dialog box appears, as shown in Figure 5, enter the directory path to your image in the **Filename** dialog box. Or you can click the folder icon to display the **Open** dialog box shown in Figure 6 to browse for the file.
3. When the image preview appears on the right, you can specify new height and width measurements (in pixels) for your image in the **Height** and **Width** text fields. However, HotDog Pro enters the correct measurements automatically.
4. Enter a brief description of your image in the **Text description of the image** text field.
5. Click the **Advanced** tab to enter more options.
6. When the **Insert Image**—Advanced dialog box appears, you can choose an alignment option from the **Alignment** pull-down list.
7. If you plan to link your image, you can specify a border width from the **Border Width** scrolling list. Or leave the measurement at **0** if you prefer not to display a border around your graphical link.
8. You can create a buffer around your image (so text doesn't butt up against it) by selecting a number of pixels from the **Horizontal Distance** and **Vertical Distance** scrolling lists.
9. Click **OK**.

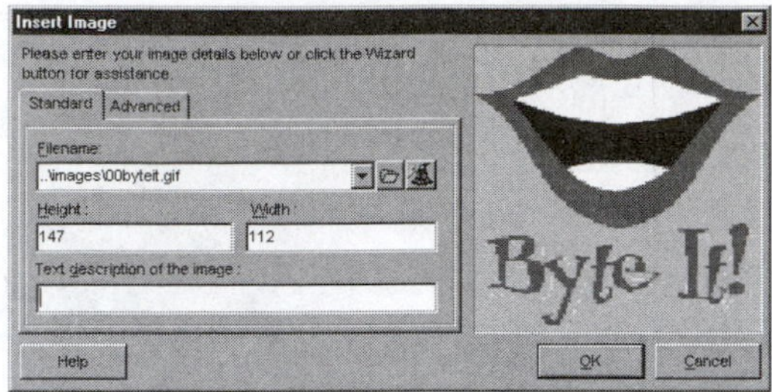

Figure 5. The **Insert Image** dialog box provides options for inserting your image.

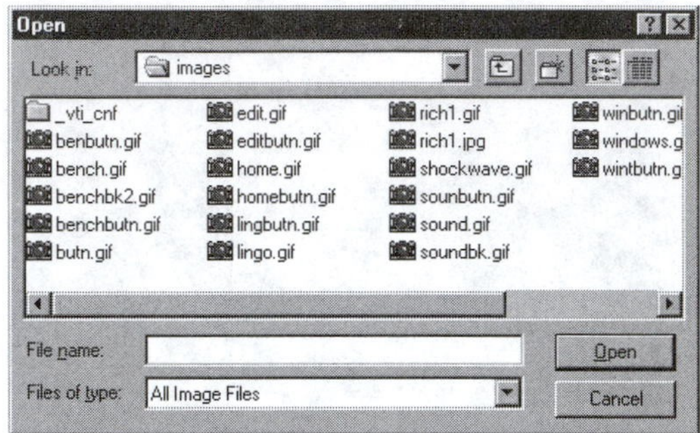

Figure 6. Click the folder icon to display the **Open** dialog box so you can browse for your image.

✔ Tips

- You must use the .GIF or .JPEG file name extension when naming your GIF and JPEG files, or else they won't display on your Web pages.
- If you choose to resize an image, make sure you do it proportionally so the image doesn't distort. This is simple when working with an image that is a perfect square (enter any numbers you want, but make sure that the **Height** and **Width** pixel measurements match each other).
- Another easy way to resize an image is to enter percentages (such as 50%) in the **Height** and **Width** text fields, rather than trying to calculate the proportionate number of pixels for each measurement.

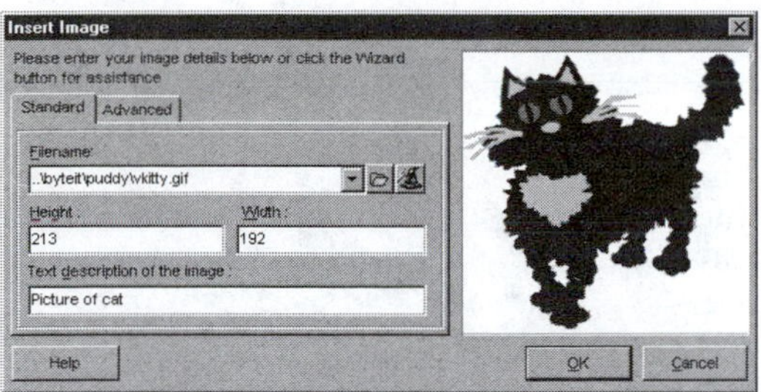

Figure 7. When you enter the directory path (or browse) for your image, a preview displays so you can make sure that you've selected the correct image.

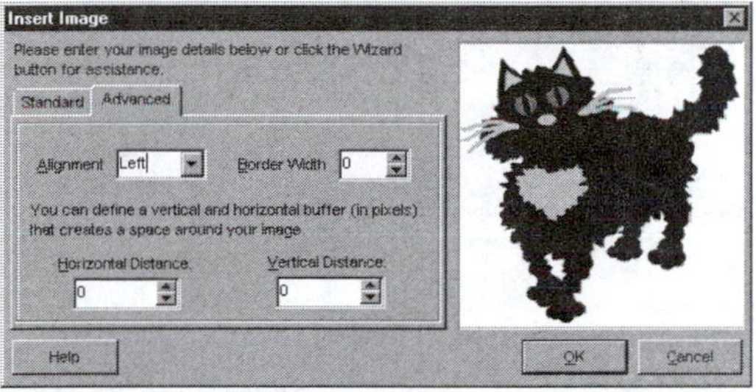

Figure 8. The **Insert Image—Advanced** dialog box offers additional options.

✔ Tips

- If you don't choose an **Alignment** option, the image automatically aligns to the left side of your page and the text wraps around it.
- Aligning text with images is tricky. You may have to experiment.
- How many pixels do you need to create an adequate buffer between an image and the surrounding text? Try selecting the number **5** from the **Horizontal Distance** and **Vertical Distance** scrolling lists.

To edit an image's attributes

1. Locate the document's HTML code for the image you want to change the attributes for.
2. Select the line of image source code you want to edit by dragging your cursor over it while holding down your mouse button—it will look similar to the following example:

```
<IMG SRC="images/my_image.gif"
HEIGHT="213" WIDTH="192" ALIGN="Left"
BORDER="0" VSPACE="5" HSPACE="5"
ALT="Picture of cat">
```

3. Click the **Image** button from the **Insert** toolbar.
4. When the **Insert Image** dialog box appears, as shown in Figure 7, you can view the settings for the image tag attributes and make changes.
5. You can click the **Advanced** tab for additional options, as shown in Figure 8.
6. When you're finished making changes, click **OK**.

Converting and Editing Images with the Button Editor

The Web requires GIF and JPEG images. However, you may have Bitmap (BMP) and Paint (PCX) formatted images that you would like to use in your Web pages. With HotDog Pro's **Button Editor** SuperTool, this isn't a problem. The **Button Editor** can convert these files to GIFs and JPEGs in a snap. In addition, this versatile tool also helps you crop and resize images—or add a beveled border and text. Pretty nifty, huh?

To launch the Button Editor

1. Select **Button Editor** from the **SuperToolz** menu.
2. When the **Button Editor** appears, as shown in Figure 9, you can begin working with images.

To open an image in the Button Editor

1. Launch the **Button Editor**.
2. When the **Button Editor** application window appears, as shown in Figure 9, click the **Open** toolbar button, select **Open** from the **File** menu, or use the **CTRL+O** key combination.
3. When the **Open** dialog box appears, as shown in Figure 10, browse for the image you want to convert, select the image, then click the **Open** button.

To save an image in the Button Editor

1. Click the **Save** button. Or you can select **Save** from the **File** menu, or use the **CTRL+S** key combination.

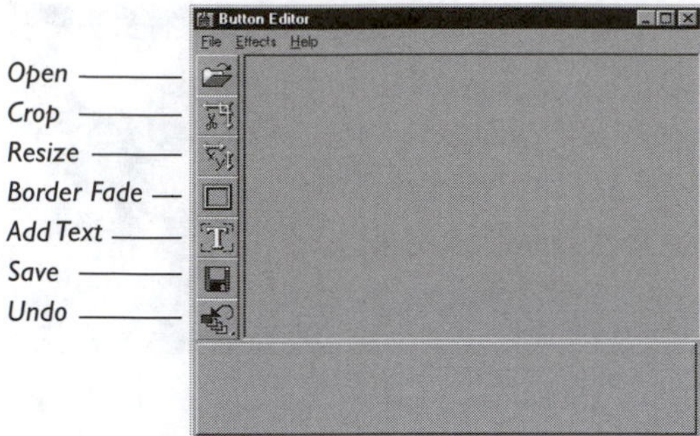

Figure 9. The **Button Editor** makes it easy for you to convert and make simple changes to your images.

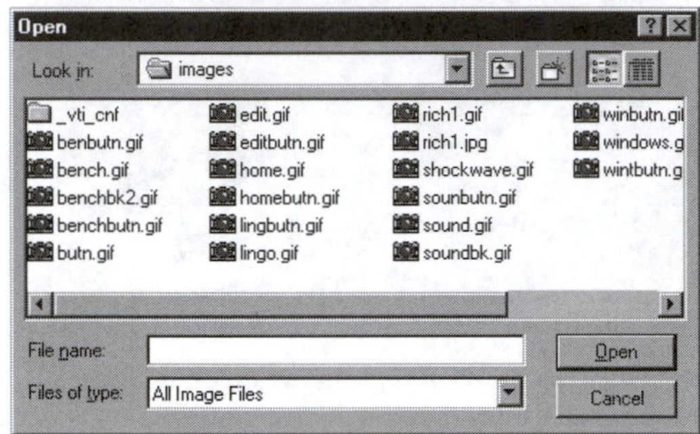

Figure 10. When the **Open** dialog box appears, you can browse for an image.

✔ Tips

- Trust the Button Editor. It knows whether your converted image would work best as a GIF or a JPEG and converts your file automatically. You can tell which file format the **Button Editor** has chosen by looking at the **File of type** list. Either the **GIF** or **JPEG** radio button automatically selects.
- When the **File Format** list's **JPEG** radio button is selected, a slider appears so you can determine the image's *compression level*: **Full** compression reduces your image's file size, but also diminishes the quality of your image; **None** results in the highest quality image. I recommend leaving the slider set at **None** to maintain the details in your image.

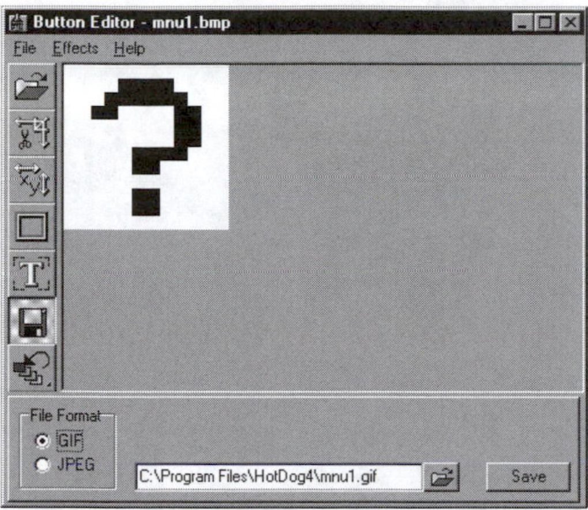

Figure 11. If the **Button Editor** converts your image to a **GIF** file, click the **Save** button.

Figure 12. If the **Button Editor** converts your image to a **JPEG** file, you can select a compression level by moving the **Compression** slider, then save your image by clicking the **Save** button.

✔ Tip

- When you convert images, the Button Editor renames your file with the correct file name extension.

To convert an image to a GIF or JPEG from a BMP or PCX file

1. Launch the **Button Editor**.
2. When the **Button Editor** application window appears, as shown in Figure 9, click the **Open** toolbar button, select **Open** from the **File** menu, or use the **CTRL+O** key combination.
3. When the **Open** dialog box appears, as shown in Figure 10, browse for the image you want to convert, select the image, then click the **Open** button.
4. When the image displays in the **Button Editor**, click the **Save** button. Or you can select **Save** from the **File** menu or use the **CTRL+S** key combination.
5. When the **File Format** options display at the bottom of the **Button Editor** application window, as shown in Figures 11 and 12, enter a directory path for your image. Or, you can browse for a directory by clicking the folder icon.
6. Click the **Save** button.

You can crop an image to get rid of unwanted background areas.

To crop an image

1. Launch the **Button Editor** and open an image.
2. When the image displays, click the **Crop** toolbar button.
3. When the cross hair cursor appears, drag it diagonally to draw a square selection box around the part of the image you want to crop to—as I did with the image shown in Figure 13.
4. When you're finished, click **Crop**, then click the **Save** button to save the image, or click the **Undo** button to cancel your changes.

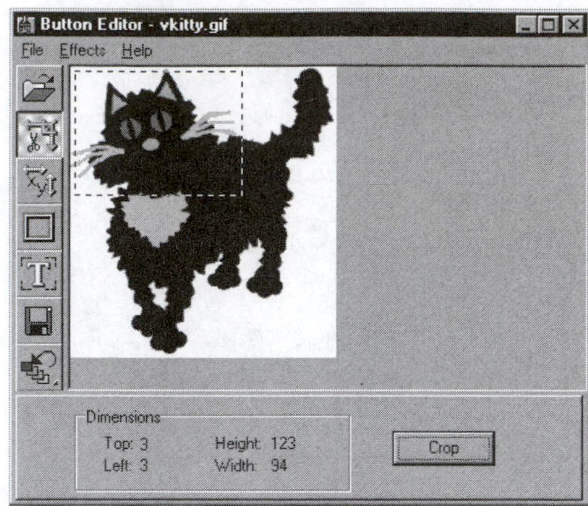

Figure 13. To crop an image, select the **Crop** tool, draw a selection box around the area you want to crop, then click the **Crop** button.

To resize an image

1. Launch the **Button Editor** and open an image.
2. When the image displays, click the **Resize** toolbar button.
3. When the **Resize** options appear at the bottom of the **Button Editor** application window, as shown in Figure 14, make sure the **Proportional** checkbox is selected. This ensures that the **Button Editor** proportions your resized image correctly.
4. Enter a new pixel measurement in the **Height** or **Width** text field. The other measurement changes automatically if you have the **Proportional** checkbox selected.
5. Click the **Resize** button to display the newly resized image.
6. Click the **Save** button to save the image or click the **Undo** button to undo your changes.

Figure 14. To resize an image, enter new pixel measurements for the image, then click the **Resize** button.

✔ Tips

- You can adjust the size of the cropping area. Pass your cursor over one of the selection box's sides or corners. When the double-arrow appears, hold down your left mouse button and drag the selected side or corner inwards or outwards.
- Images may distort slightly when you resize them.

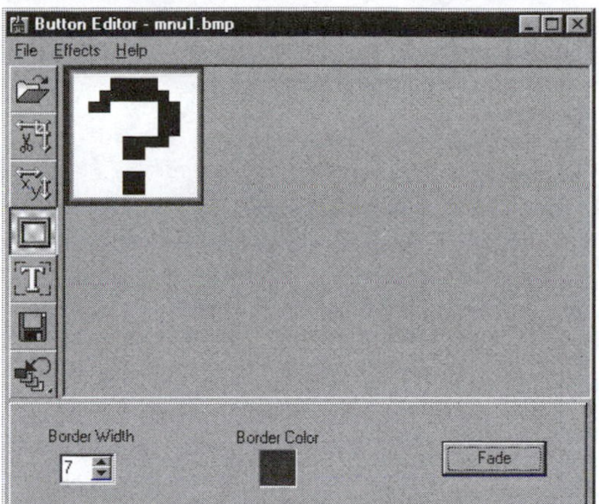

Figure 15. Click the **Border Fade** toolbar button to display options for applying a shaded border to your image.

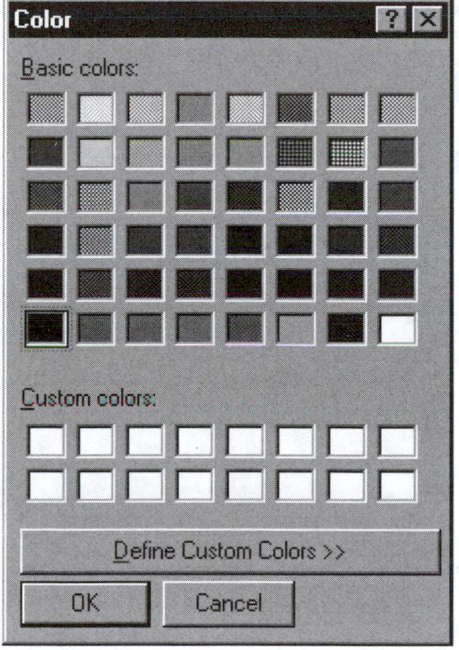

Figure 16. Pick a color for your border with the **Color** palette dialog box, then click **OK** to return to the **Button Editor** application window.

You can apply a border fade to turn rectangular and square images into beveled buttons.

To apply a Border Fade

1. Launch the **Button Editor** and open an image.
2. When the image displays, click the **Border Fade** toolbar button.
3. When the **Border Fade** options appear at the bottom of the application window, as shown in Figure 15, choose a width (in pixels) for your border from the **Border Width** scrolling list.
4. Choose a color for your border by clicking the **Border Color** selection box.
5. When the **Color** palette dialog box appears, as shown in Figure 16, click on a color, then click the **OK** button to return to the **Button Editor** application window.
6. Click the **Fade** button and then click the **Save** button save your changes, or click **Undo** to cancel your changes.

✔ Tips

- When you resize or crop an image that you have already inserted into your HTML document, remember to change the height and width attributes to reflect your changes. You can either edit or reinsert the image, as explained earlier in this chapter ("Inserting Images"). Otherwise your image will not display correctly.
- The **Border Fade** and **Text** tools are great for creating navigational buttons for your Web site (you can use Windows 95's Paint program to make a rectangle or square).
- The **Border Fade** tool works best with simple two-color images.

To add text to an image

1. Launch the **Button Editor** and open an image.
2. When the image displays, click the **Add Text** toolbar button.
3. When the text options appear at the bottom of the application window, as shown in Figure 17, select a font from the **Font** list.
4. Select a font size from the **Size** list. You can also choose to bold, italicize, or underline your text by clicking the appropriate buttons.
5. Click the **Colour** selection box to display the **Color** palette dialog box so you can pick a color for your text.
6. Enter the text you want to include in the **Text** text field.
7. Click the **Make Caption** button to format your text as a caption, like the one shown in Figure 18. Or click one of the **Alignment** buttons to center your text at the middle, top, or bottom of the image.
8. Click the **Save** button to save your changes, or click **Undo** to cancel your changes.

✔ Tips

- You can use any font you want, because the text becomes part of your image. It will display correctly in people's browsers no matter what fonts they have installed on their systems.
- The **Undo** button comes in handy—when you click it, a list of the things you've done appears so you can choose which actions to undo.

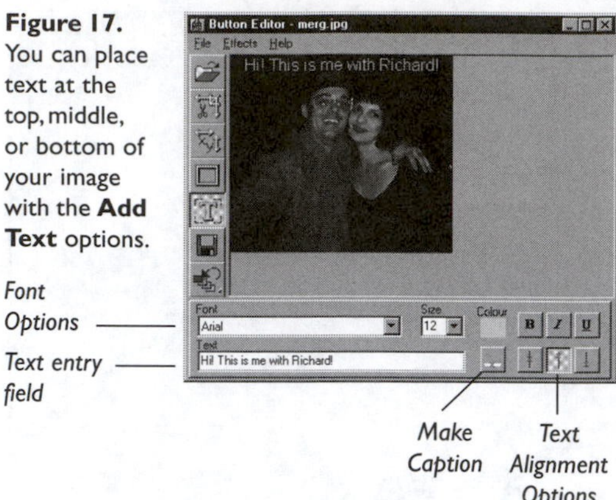

Figure 17. You can place text at the top, middle, or bottom of your image with the **Add Text** options.

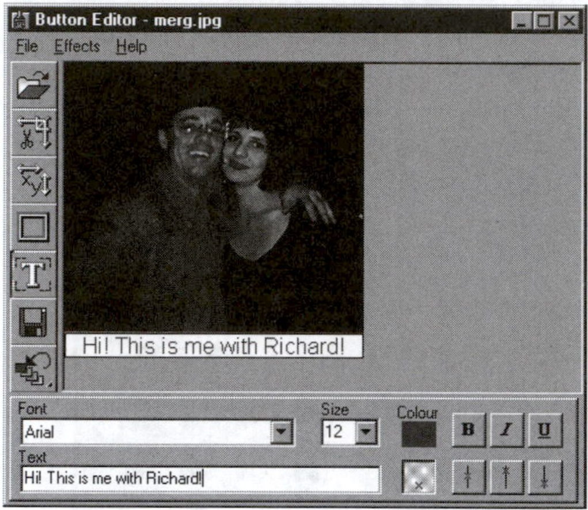

Figure 18. You can also add a caption to your image by clicking the **Make Caption** button.

6

MAKING LINKS

What's the key to the Web? Links, of course! Links make the Web exciting and interactive. Click a link and something happens—a new page displays, a Java applet or multimedia file launches, a virtual reality world appears, or any other number of things. And best of all, making links isn't hard at all. HotDog Pro's **Insert Link Wizard** takes you through the steps. Or you can enter your information in the **Insert Link** dialog box.

Magazines and other print publications refer people to information by listing a reference (such as "turn to page 6," "read such-and-such article," or "call 1-800-try-2buy"). Web publications refer people to information with links. Links give you a convenient way to refer people to resources without making your visitors turn pages, make phone calls, send away for a brochure, or visit the library.

If you run your own business, you can make links to your online portfolio, downloadable information packets, or multimedia demonstrations of your products or services. For example, you can click the images on Margaret Weigel's home page (shown in Figure 1) to download her Macromedia Director animations and view them.

Making Links

The easiest way to make a link is by following the **Insert Link Wizard**'s instructions. Making links used to require entering lots of tedious URLs and directory paths—and remembering the protocols for different types of links. Now HotDog Pro's **Insert Link Wizard** does everything for you. All you need to know is the location of the places and files you want to link to, and what type of link you want to create. If you have more experience with Web pages and get annoyed by following numerous dialog boxes, you can also insert links straight from the **Insert Link** dialog box. When HotDog Pro inserts the link source code into your HTML document, it looks similar to the following example:

<A HREF="http://www.cool_site.com/cool/index.htm">Really awesome, cool Web site</A>

Types of links

- **Web site link:** Select this option to link to a page or file on another Web site.
- **File link:** Select this option to link to a page or file on your own Web site.
- **FTP link:** Select this option to link to an FTP site (this stands for File Transfer Protocol—an older type of site that displays downloadable files but not text or images).
- **Email link:** Select this option to link to an email address. When users click the link, the email program launches. The specified email address appears in the email program's **To** text field, so users can compose and send a message instantly.
- **News group link:** Select this option to link to a news group. When users click the link, their news reader application launches and the news postings from the specified news group begin downloading.

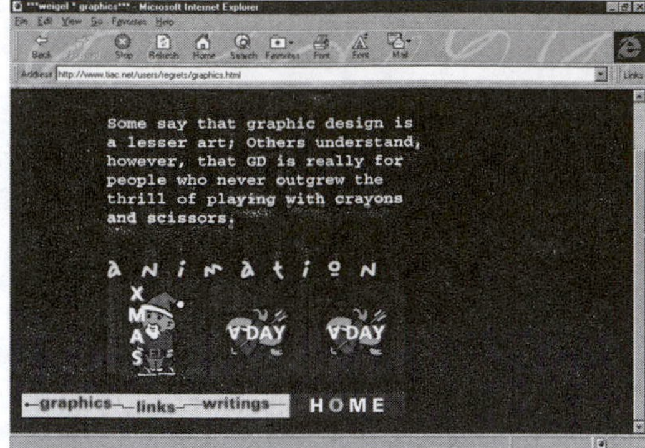

Figure 1. Margaret Weigel's home page at **www.tiac.net/users/regrets/** works as an interactive portfolio. You can click on links to see demonstrations and examples of her work.

✔ Tips

- Graphical links look really cool. To make an image into a link, select the source code for the image you want to link from your HTML document (instead of regular text), then follow this chapter's instructions. For more about locating source code for your images, see Chapter 5.
- Most people can view Web pages and send email. Web browsers like Internet Explorer and Netscape Navigator can also display the contents of FTP and Gopher sites. However, some people may not have a news reader or Telnet application. Warn visitors when linking them to other types of sites.
- Some people don't have fancy browsers and plug-ins. Warn visitors if you link to Java or ActiveX activated pages—or files that require plug-ins. People get annoyed when a Web site wastes their time or (yikes!) crashes their browser.
- If you have page content that requires plug-ins—like multimedia or portable document files—make a link to the place where they can get the plug-in.

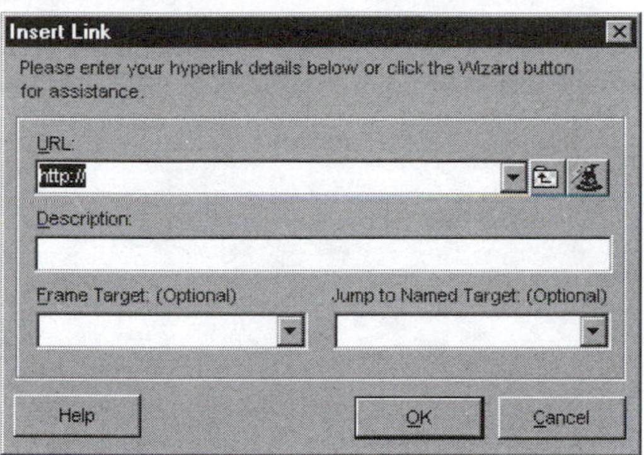

Figure 2. To launch the **Insert Link Wizard**, click the **Link** button on the **Insert** toolbar to display the **Insert Link** dialog box, then click the **Wizard** button.

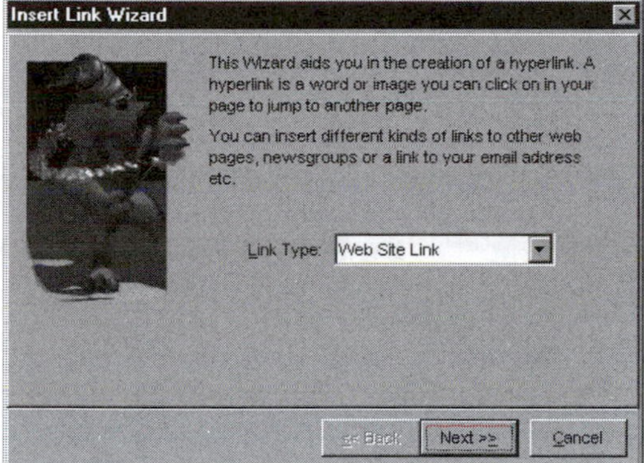

Figure 3. When the first **Insert Link Wizard** dialog box appears, choose the type of link you want to create, then click the **Next** button.

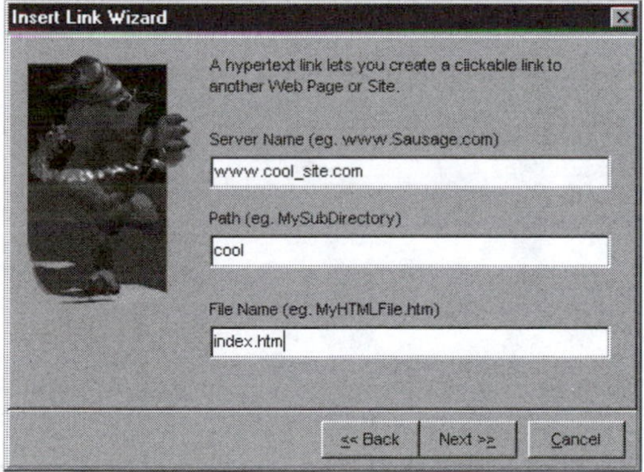

Figure 4. When the second **Insert Link Wizard** dialog box appears, enter the server name, directory path, and file name, then click the **Next** button.

- **Telnet link:** Select this option to link to a Telnet site. When users click the link, their Telnet program (Windows systems come with HyperTerminal) launches and data from the specified Telnet site displays.
- **Gopher link:** Select this option to link to a Gopher site (this is an older type of site that displays text but not images).

To make a link with the Insert Link Wizard

1. Insert your cursor where you want to make a link, or highlight the text or image source code you want to link.
2. Click the **Link** button on the **Insert** toolbar, or select **Hyperlink** from the **Insert** menu.
3. When the **Insert Link** dialog box appears, as shown in Figure 2, click the **Wizard** button (the icon looks like a wizard hat).
4. When the first **Insert Link Wizard** dialog box appears, as shown in Figure 3, select the type of link you want to create from the **Link Type** list (as explained in the "Making Links" section), then click the **Next** button.
5. When the second **Insert Link Wizard** dialog box appears, as shown in Figure 4, enter the name of the server in the **Server Name** text field—such as: **www.website.com**.
6. Enter the name of the sub-directory or chain of sub-directories (if any)—separated by back slashes in the **Path** text field, as in: **users/username**.
7. Enter the name of the file in the **File Name** text field (as in, **index.html** for a Web page or **file.exe** for a downloadable application), then click the **Next** button.

8. When the third **Insert Link Wizard** dialog box appears, as shown in Figure 5, enter the text that you want linked in the **Description** text field. If you have already selected text or source code for an image, the text appears in the **Description** text field automatically.

9. If you have frames on your Web site, select a target from the **Target Frame** list (this determines which frame a linked Web page displays in—for more about frames, see Chapter 8).

10. Click the **Finish** button, or click the **Advanced** button for more options. You can also click the **Back** button to move backwards and make changes. Or you can cancel your link by clicking the **Cancel** button.

    A. If you click the **Advanced** button, the fourth **Insert Link Wizard** dialog box appears, as shown in Figure 6. You can enter a server port number in the **Port Number** dialog box. This is rarely ever necessary. Servers provide access to different types of services (such as access to Web pages) through ports. Web servers usually use port 80.

    B. You can also enter the name of a page target or select one from the **Target** pull-down list (for more about targets, see the "Creating Link Targets and Internal Links" section later in this chapter). When you're done, click the **Finish** button.

11. When you return to the **Insert Link** dialog box, click **OK**.

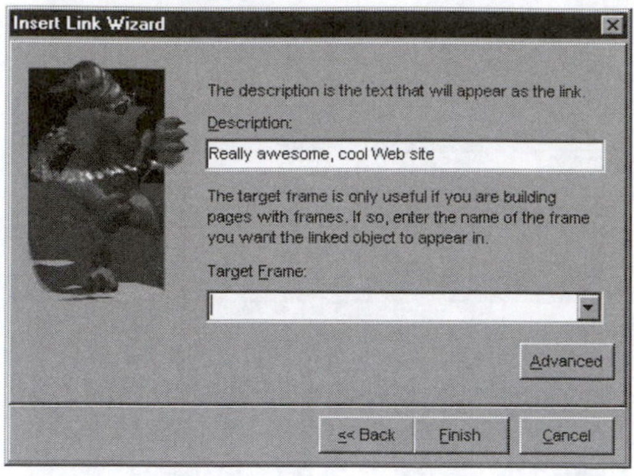

Figure 5. When the third **Insert Link Wizard** dialog box appears, enter the text you wish to enclose in your link (selected text automatically appears). You can also select a target frame if your site has frames. Click the **Finish** button, or click the **Advanced** button for additional options.

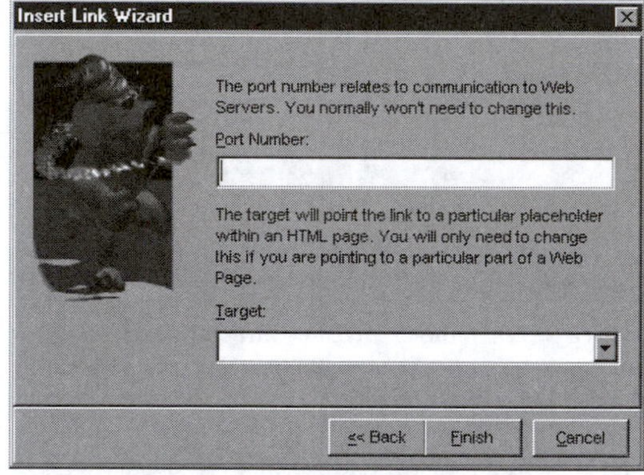

Figure 6. The fourth **Insert Link Wizard** dialog box offers advanced options. You can specify a port number and a link target. When you're done, click the **Finish** button.

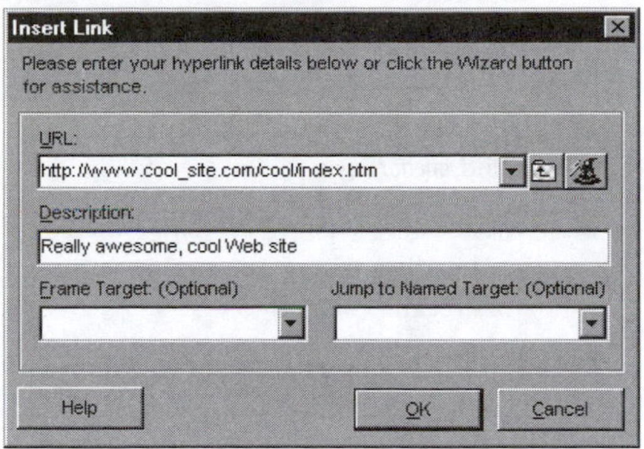

Figure 7. If you're confident about HTML and specifying URLs, you can create links straight from the **Insert Link** dialog box.

✔ Tips

- The **Insert Link Wizard** dialog box appearances may vary, depending on which item you select from the **Link Type** list.
- When you link to an email address, the second dialog box prompts you only for your email address.

To create a link with the Insert Link dialog box

1. Insert your cursor where you want to make a link, or highlight the text or image source code you want to link.
2. Click the **Link** button on the **Insert** toolbar, or select **Hyperlink** from the **Insert** menu.
3. When the **Insert Link** dialog box appears, as shown in Figure 7, enter the full URL or directory path to your link. If you link to a file within your Web site, you can click the folder button to browse for a file.
4. Enter the text you want to link in the **Description** text field (if you selected text or image source code from your HTML document, HotDog Pro enters it automatically).
5. If your Web site has frames, select a Frame target from the **Frame Target** list. You can also enter the frame target's name manually as you would enter text in a text field (for more on frames, see Chapter 8).
6. If you want to link to a link target, you can select it from the **Jump to Named Target** list or enter it manually as you would enter text in a text field.
7. Click **OK**.

To edit a link

1. Select the source code for your link—link source code looks similar to the following example:

```
<A HREF="http://www.cool_site.com/cool/
index.htm">Really awesome, cool Web
site</A>
```

2. Click the **Link** button from the **Insert** toolbar.
3. When the **Insert Link** dialog box appears, you can either edit your link properties from the **Insert Link** dialog box or launch the **Insert Link Wizard** dialog box for additional options.

✔ Tips

- Tags that have to do with links are called *anchor* tags.
- Just about any page element—such as a heading, paragraph, image, or table—can be targeted.
- When you click the **Jump to Named Target** list scroll button, a list of all the named targets in your document displays. The **Jump to Named Target** list also functions as a text field so you can enter targets located on other Web pages or Web sites.
- If you import all of the pages from your site into the **WebSites** Manager (as explained in Chapter 3), the **Jump to Named Target** list displays a list of the available target names on your site.

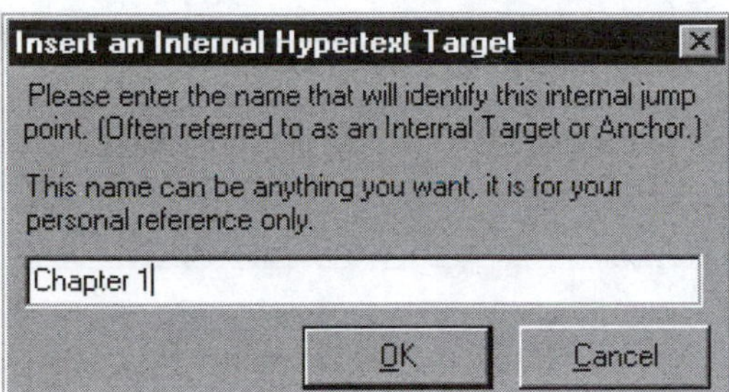

Figure 8. When the **Insert an Internal Hypertext Target** dialog box appears, enter a name for your link target.

Creating Link Targets and Internal Links

By now, you might have started wondering what a "link target" is (don't confuse link targets with *frame* targets—which I discuss in Chapter 8). Link targets enable you to create links to different parts of the same Web page. Once you create a link target, you can then make a link to the target. This works well for long documents with a table of contents. Users can click table of contents items and jump to the corresponding section of the document. When you create a link target, the HTML code looks similar to the following:

```
<A NAME="name_of_your_target">My Link Target
</A>
```

The link *to* the target is coded as follows:

```
<A HREF="#chapter 1">Go to My Link
Target!</A>
```

To create a link target

1. Place your cursor where you want to create a target (for example, next to the text you're targeting).
2. Click the **Target** button on the **Insert** toolbar.
3. When the **Insert an Internal Hypertext Target** dialog box appears, as shown in Figure 8, enter a name for your target in the text field.
4. Click **OK**.

To link to a target in the same document

1. Insert your cursor where you want to make a link, or highlight the text or image source code you want to link.
2. Click the **Link** button on the **Insert** toolbar, or select **Hyperlink** from the **Insert** menu.
3. When the **Insert Link** dialog box appears, as shown in Figure 9, enter the text you want to link in the **Description** text field. When you select text or image source code from your HTML document, HotDog Pro enters it automatically.
4. Select a target name from the **Jump to Named Target** list.
5. Leave the **URL** text field blank.
6. Click **OK**.

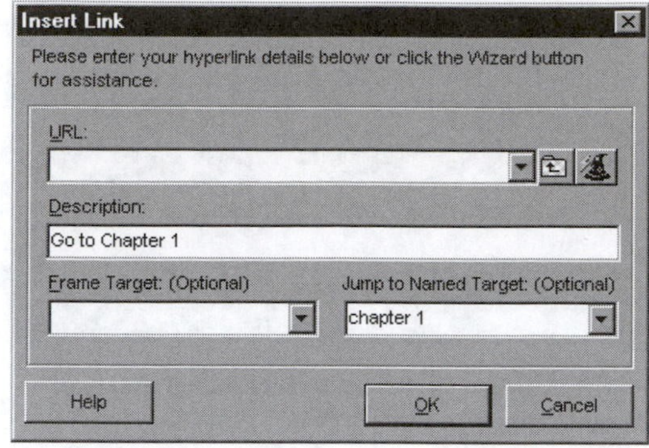

Figure 9. To link to a target, launch the **Insert Link** dialog box, and select a target name in the **Jump to Named Target** text field.

To link to a target in a different document

1. Follow the instructions for creating a regular link (either with the **Insert Link Wizard** or straight from the **Insert Link** dialog box).
2. From the **Insert Link** dialog box (the **Insert Link Wizard** returns you to this dialog box), enter the name of your target in the **Jump to Named Target** text field.Linking to Netscape Bookmarks and Internet Favorites.
3. Click **OK**.

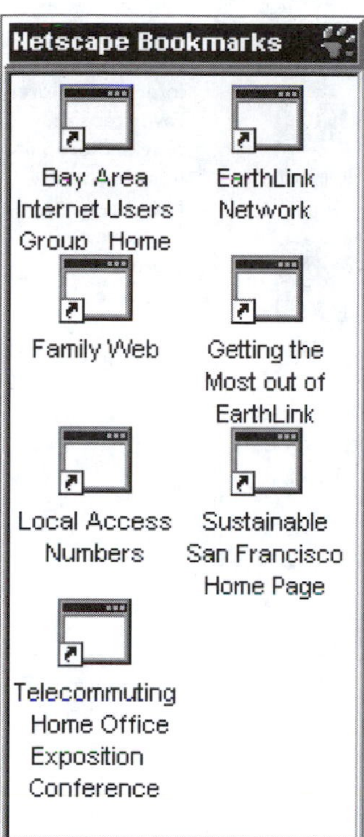

Figure 10. To link to a Netscape Bookmark site, drag and drop an item from the **Netscape Bookmarks** resource.

Linking to Your Bookmarks and Favorites

Since your Netscape Bookmarks and Internet Explorer Favorites contain links to your favorite places to visit, you may want to include them in your Web pages. HotDog Pro imports Bookmarks and Favorites from your Web browsers. It displays them in your **Netscape Bookmarks** and **Internet Favorites** resources, so you can link to them effortlessly.

To link to a Netscape Navigator Bookmarks site

1. Select **Resource Manager** from the **View** menu, then select **Netscape Bookmarks** from the cascading list.
2. When the **Netscape Bookmarks** resource displays in the left resource pane, as shown in Figure 10, place your cursor where you want to insert the Bookmark link.
3. Select a bookmark and double-click it. Or you can drag and drop a Bookmarks list item into the insertion point of your document. HotDog Pro automatically creates the link.

To link to an Internet Favorites site

1. Select **Resource Manager** from the **View** menu, then select **Internet Favorites** from the cascading list.
2. When the **Internet Explorer Favorites** resource displays in the left resource pane, as shown in Figure 11, place your cursor where you want to insert the Favorites link.
3. Select a Favorite and double-click it. Or you can drag and drop a Favorites list item into the insertion point of your document. HotDog Pro automatically creates the link.

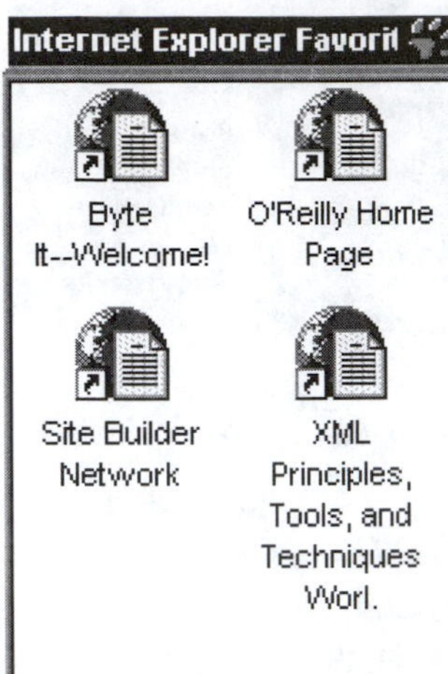

Figure 11. To link to a Internet Explorer Favorites site, drag and drop an item from the **Internet Explorer Favorites** resource.

7 CREATING TABLES

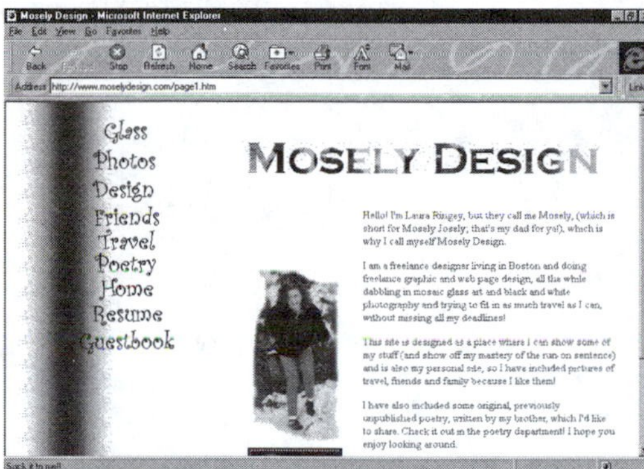

Figure 1. Mosely Design's home page (at **www.moselydesign.com**) uses tables to create this complex but seamless layout.

If you're a graphic designer (or even if you aren't), you've probably noticed something. Laying out Web pages isn't as simple as laying out documents with a desktop publishing or word processing application. But thanks to tables, you can still control placement of your text and images. You can even create some pretty sophisticated page layouts, like the Mosely Design site shown in Figure 1. Tables have been around for a while, but few applications give you HotDog Pro's ease and versatility.

Creating and Formatting Tables

HotDog Pro gives you many ways to create and work with tables. If you're an experienced HTML coder, **Quick Table** helps you quickly set up a basic table, which you can format by entering the appropriate codes yourself. If you don't know much HTML, never fear. HotDog Pro's **Table Wizard** and the **Visual Table Editor** SuperTool save the day. The **Table Wizard** guides you through the process of generating commonly used table lay outs, and the **Visual Table Editor** makes it easy for you to customize your table and insert elements.

Tables aren't difficult to understand once you get the hang of them. Think of them as a primitive spreadsheet. Tables are composed of rows, columns, and cells. Cells contain table data (text and other page elements), and are formed where the rows and columns intersect. For example, a simple two-column, two-row table would look similar to the one shown in Table 1. If you use **Quick Table** to generate a two-column, two-row table, HotDog Pro inserts the code shown in Table 2.

Cell 1	Cell 2
Cell 3	Cell 4

Table 1. This is what a simple two-column, two-row table looks like.

Two-Row, Two-Column Table

HTML CODE	DEFINITION
<TABLE>	Begins table
<TR>	Begins first table row
<TD></TD>	Encloses data for cell 1 (insert object between opening and closing tags)
<TD></TD>	Encloses data for cell 2 (insert object between opening and closing tags)
</TR>	Ends first table row
<TR>	Begins second table row
<TD></TD>	Encloses data for cell 3 (insert object between opening and closing tags)
<TD></TD>	Encloses data for cell 4 (insert object between opening and closing tags)
</TR>	Ends second table row
</TABLE>	Ends table

Table 2. HTML code for a two-column, two-row table.

Table Elements

- **<TABLE>...</TABLE>:** Encloses the table.
- **<TR>...</TR>:** Encloses table rows.
- **<TD>...</TD>:** Encloses table cells.

To create a table with Quick Table

1. Click the **Quick Table** button from the **Insert** toolbar.
2. When the **QuickTable** pop-up table appears, as shown in Figure 2, select a number of rows and columns by holding down your left mouse button and dragging it across the squares.

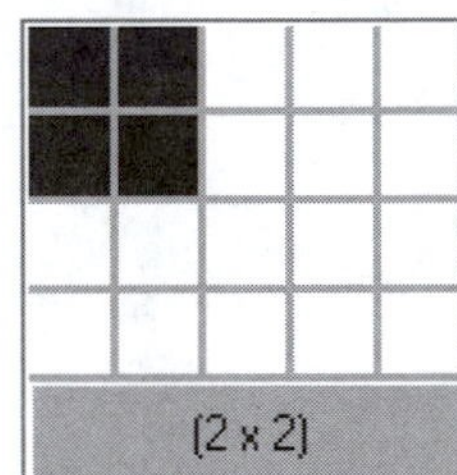

Figure 2. You can quickly insert a basic table by selecting cells from the **Quick Table** pop-up table.

✔ Tips

- Working with tables requires planning ahead. Make a rough sketch of your table if that makes things easier.
- To cancel inserting a table with **Quick Table**, press the **Esc** (Escape) key. To undo a table that you've just inserted, click the **Undo** button on the **Standard** toolbar.

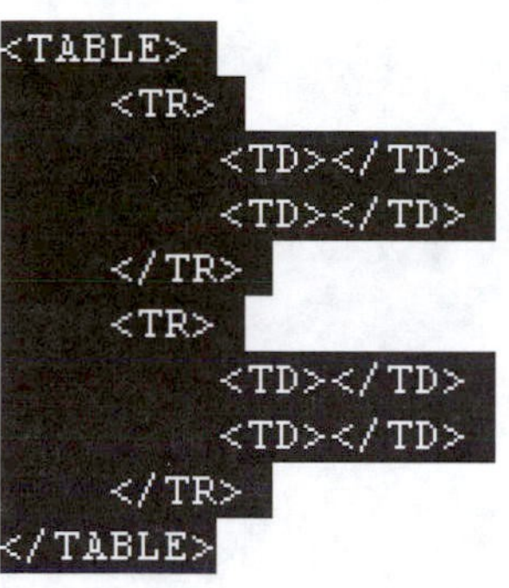

```
<TABLE>
    <TR>
        <TD></TD>
        <TD></TD>
    </TR>
    <TR>
        <TD></TD>
        <TD></TD>
    </TR>
</TABLE>
```

Figure 3. HotDog Pro automatically selects your new table code so you can display it in the **Visual Table Editor**.

3. When the number of rows and columns you wish to include in your table are highlighted, release the mouse button.
4. When the HTML code for your table appears in your document, as shown in Figure 3, you can begin working with it. HotDog Pro automatically selects the source code for you so you can launch the **Visual Table Editor** to compose your table and insert page elements. You can also deselect the table and work with it manually.

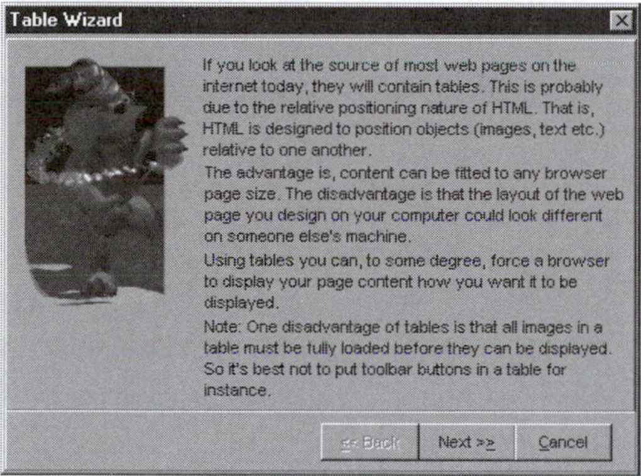

Figure 4. When the first **Table Wizard** dialog box appears, click the **Next** button.

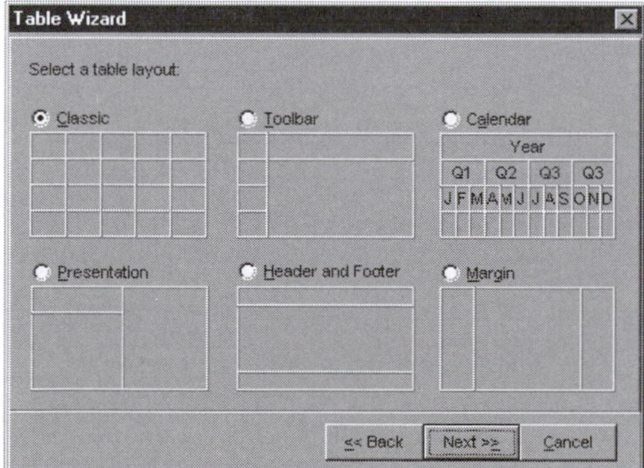

Figure 5. When the second **Table Wizard** dialog box appears, pick a table layout and click the **Next** button.

To create a table with the Table Wizard

1. Click the **Table** button on the **Insert** toolbar (not to be confused with the **Quick Table** button).
2. When the first **Table Wizard** dialog box appears, as shown in Figure 4, read the instructions and click the **Next** button.
3. When the second **Table Wizard** button appears, as shown in Figure 5, choose the table layout you want to create. Select a radio button from the **Select a table layout** options, then click the **Next** button.
4. When the third dialog box appears, as shown in Figure 6, pick a number of rows from the **Rows in table** list, and pick a number of columns from the **Columns** list. You can also constrain the table height and width by selecting a unit of measurement (pixels or percentages) and entering a number for the **Minimum width of table** and **Minimum height of table** settings.
5. Choose whether you want your table to align to the left, center, or right of your page from the **Alignment of table** list, and click the **Next** button.

6. When the fourth **Table Wizard** dialog box appears, as shown in Figure 7, choose a thickness for your border (in pixels) from the **Border Thickness** list.

7. You can also choose a color for your table cells (**Cell colour**), the table border's highlight color (**Border colour light**), and the border color's shadow (**Border colour dark**). Click the selection button for each item. When the **Color** palette dialog box displays, as shown in Figure 8, pick a color, then click the **OK** button to return to the fourth **Table Wizard** dialog box.

8. When you finish selecting colors, click the **Next** button to move forward, or click the **Restore** button to undo your color settings.

9. When the fifth **Table Wizard** dialog box appears, as shown in Figure 9, choose **Cell Spacing** and **Cell Padding** measurements from the lists and click the **Next** button.

10. When the sixth **Table Wizard** dialog box appears, as shown in Figure 10, choose an option for placing row and column numbers in your table cells. Or leave the selection boxes blank and click the **Finish** button (I explain this option more fully in the following tip list). HotDog Pro automatically selects the new table source code so you can view your table in the **Visual Table Editor**.

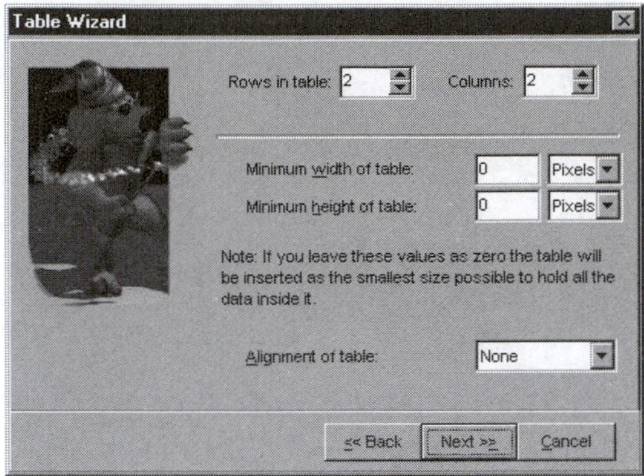

Figure 6. When the third **Table Wizard** dialog box appears, pick your number of columns and rows and your table alignment.

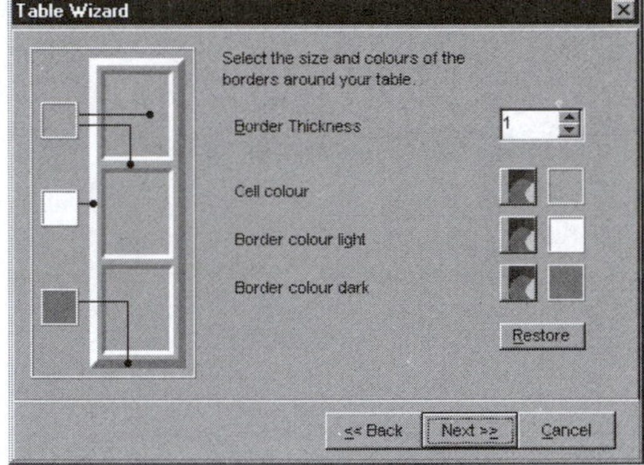

Figure 7. When the fourth **Table Wizard** dialog box appears, choose a number (in pixels) for the thickness of your table border. You can also pick colors for your table cells and the border highlight and shadow.

✔ Tips

- To enter text in a table cell from your HTML document, place your cursor in between the **<TD></TD>** table cell tags and start typing.
- To insert an image in a table cell from your HTML document, place your cursor in between the **<TD></TD>** table cell tags and click the **Image** button

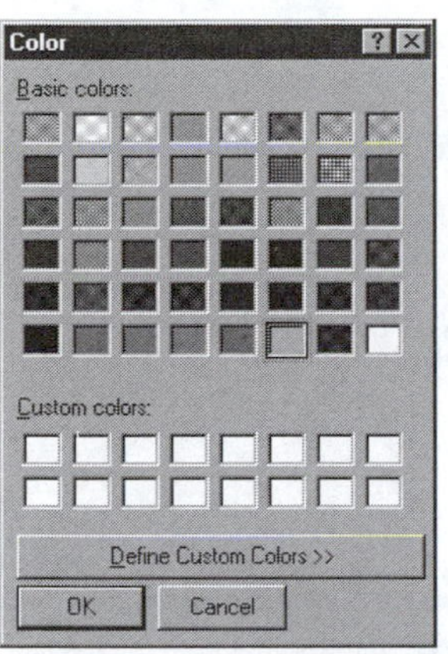

Figure 8.
You can pick border and table cell colors from the **Color** palette dialog box, then click **OK** to return to the fourth **Table Wizard** dialog box.

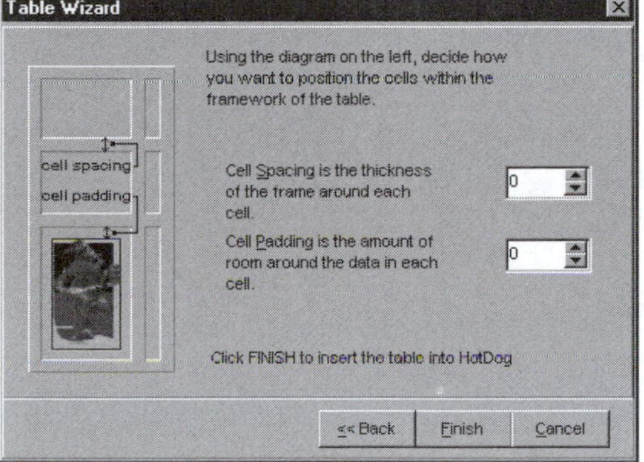

Figure 9. When the fifth **Table Wizard** dialog box appears, choose a pixel measurement for your cell spacing and cell padding attributes, then click the **Next** button.

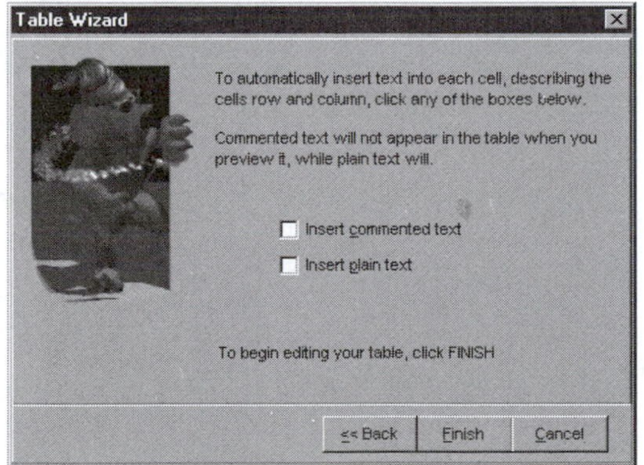

Figure 10. When the sixth **Table Wizard** dialog box appears, choose an option for placing row and column numbers in your table cells or leave the selection boxes blank and click the **Finish** button.

✔ Tips

- If you don't understand how the **Minimum width of table** and **Minimum height of table** settings work, you can ignore them for now. You can specify a minimum width or height for your table later with the **Visual Table Editor.** The "Editing Tables with the Visual Table Editor" section explains this further.
- The **Table Wizard**'s third dialog box may look slightly different than the one shown in Figure 6, depending on which table layout you choose. But don't worry. Each dialog box gives you detailed information and instructions.
- You don't *need* to pick colors for your table cells and borders. If you leave these options blank, the table cells and borders match the background color on your Web page.
- If you'd rather use the **Visual Table Editor** than fiddle with source code, leave the sixth **Table Wizard** dialog box options blank. Having the **Table Wizard** generate row and column numbers for your table cells is only useful if you plan on working directly with the source code.
- If you prefer working directly with your source code, select the sixth **Table Wizard**'s **Insert Commented Text** option. This inserts row and column numbers in your table cells to help you keep track of your table cells. Commented text does not appear when the document loads in a browser.

Editing Tables with the Visual Table Editor

The **Visual Table Editor**, as shown in Figure 11, gives you a graphical, intuitive way to compose and edit tables once you've created them. You can insert text, links, and images into table cells, make easy edits, and preview your changes. The **Visual Table Editor** even helps you create new tables and save tables as HTML documents for future use.

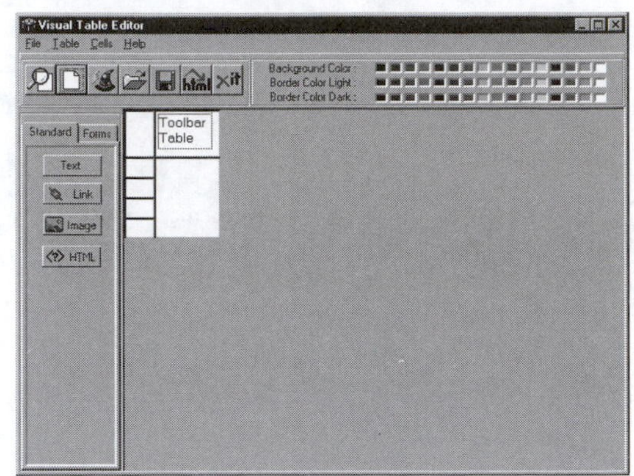

Figure 11. The Visual Table Editor makes working with tables easy.

To launch the Visual Table Editor

1. Select **Visual Table Editor** from the **SuperToolz** menu.
2. When the **Visual Table Editor** application window displays, as shown in Figure 11, you can create a table.

To edit a table with the Visual Table Editor

1. Select your table by placing your cursor above the **<TABLE>** opening tag, holding down your mouse key and dragging it below the **</TABLE>** closing tag. If you've just created a table with the **Table Wizard** or **Quick Table**, HotDog automatically selects your table source code for you.
2. Launch the **Visual Table Editor**.
3. When the **Visual Table Editor** application window displays with your table, you can begin working.

To start a new table with the Visual Table Editor

1. Launch the **Visual Table Editor**.
2. When the **Visual Table Editor** application window appears, click the **New** toolbar button to generate a simple two-row, two-column table.

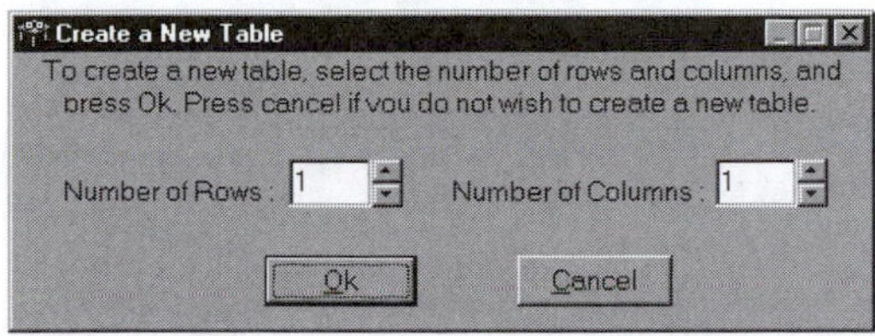

Figure 12. To create a new table, click the **New** button from the **Visual Table Editor**'s toolbar, then pick a number of rows and columns when the **Create a New Table** dialog box appears.

3. You can also select **New** from the **File** menu to display the **Create a New Table** dialog box, as shown in Figure 12.

4. When the **Create a New Table** dialog box appears (if you select **New** from the **File** menu), select an item from the **Number of Rows** list, and an item from the **Number of Columns** list.

5. Click the **OK** button.

Inserting, Editing, and Removing Objects

Before you can begin working with the **Visual Table Editor**, you first need to think the way it thinks. And the **Visual Table Editor** thinks of Web page elements—like text, links, images, and HTML source code—as *objects*. To place Web page elements, you select a type of object from the **Standard** list and drag it into a table cell. Depending on which type of object you select, the appropriate dialog box appears so you can enter text or browse for a file. When you need to make changes, you can do so by editing an object's properties.

To insert text into a table cell

1. Click the **Text** button and drag your cursor into a table cell.
2. When the **Insert Text** dialog box appears, as shown in Figure 13, enter the text you want to place in the table cell. You can also paste text that you've cut or copied onto the clipboard using the **CTRL+V** key combination.
3. You can also choose colors and styles for your text by selecting it and choosing options from the toolbar.
4. When you're finished, click **OK**.

To insert a link

1. Click the **Link** button and drag your cursor into a table cell.
2. When the **Insert Link** dialog box appears, as shown in Figure 14, enter a URL or document name in the **URL** text field.
3. Enter the text that you want the link to enclose in the **Description** text field.

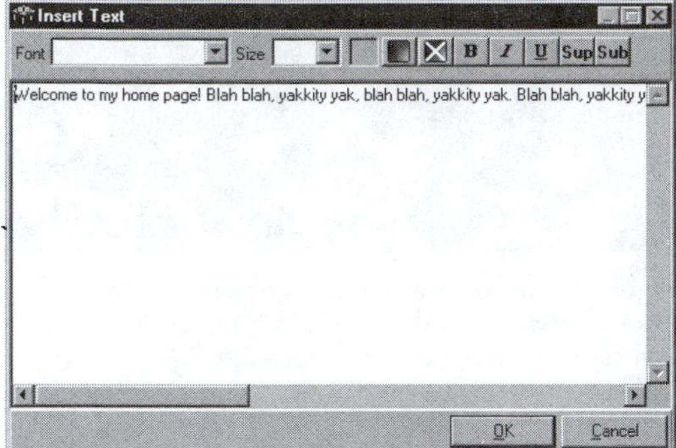

Figure 13. When the **Insert Text** dialog box appears, you can enter or paste the text you want to place in the table cell.

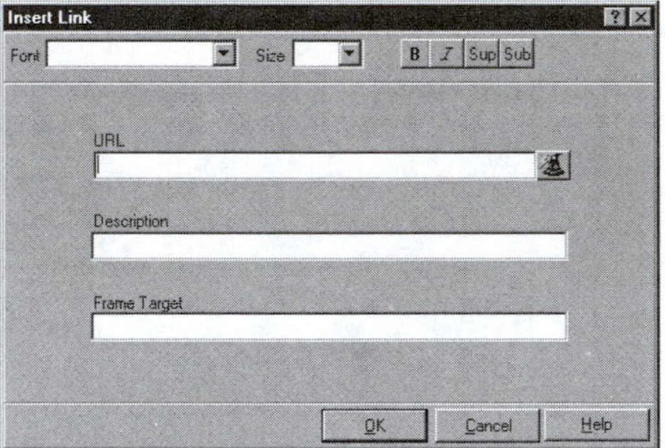

Figure 14. When the **Insert Link** dialog box appears, you can either enter your link information in the text fields or click the button with the wizard hat to launch the **Insert Link Wizard**.

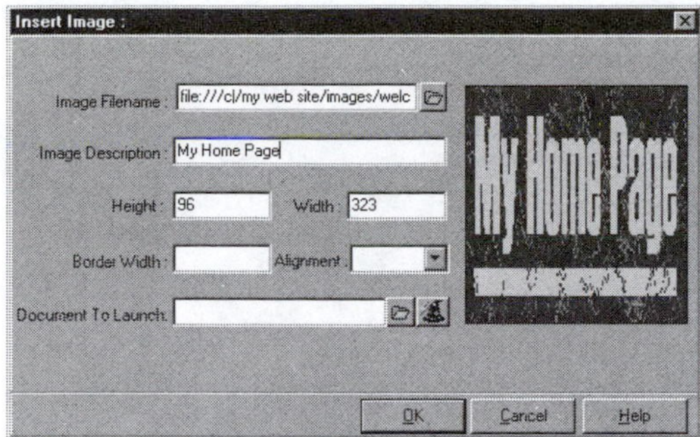

Figure 15. When the **Insert Image** dialog box appears, you can enter or paste the image you want to place in the table cell.

✔ Tips

- At the time of this writing, the **Visual Table Editor** (along with some of the other SuperToolz) doesn't handle relative path names correctly. When you browse for images and documents, the **Visual Table Editor** specifies the absolute path name, such as: **file:///c|/my web site/images/image.gif**, instead of: **images/image.gif**. Obviously, this means that the links and images in your table won't work correctly.
- You can use HotDog Pro's find and replace feature or the **Publisher—AutoReplace** preferences to get rid of the extra path information. Also, the people at Sausage Software constantly update HotDog and its components. Check the AutoDownloader for new versions of the **Table Editor** and other SuperToolz .

4. If your Web site uses frames, enter the name of a frame target in the **Frame Target**.
5. You can also choose colors and styles for your text by selecting it and choosing options from the toolbar.
6. When you're finished, click **OK**.

To insert an image

1. Click the **Image** button and drag your cursor into a table cell.
2. When the **Insert Image** dialog box appears, as shown in Figure 15, browse for your image file by clicking the **Image Filename** text field's folder icon.
3. Enter a quick description of your image.
4. If you want your image to function as a link, enter a URL for the document in the **Document to Launch** text field. You can also click the folder button to browse for a file, or click the wizard button to launch the **Insert Link Wizard**.
5. Images that function as links can also have a border. You can enter a number of pixels in the **Border Width** text field.
6. When you're finished, click **OK**.

To insert an HTML element

1. Cut the source code you want to insert in a table cell by selecting the code from your HTML document and using the **CTRL+X** key combination. You can also click the **Cut** button on the Standard toolbar or select **Cut** from the **Edit** menu.
2. Return to (or select your table, then launch) the **Visual Table Editor**.
3. Click the **HTML** button and drag your cursor into a table cell.
4. When the **Edit Unknown Tag** dialog box appears, as shown in Figure 16, paste your source code from the clipboard by using the **CTRL+V** key combination. You can also enter your code from scratch.
5. When you're finished, click **OK**.

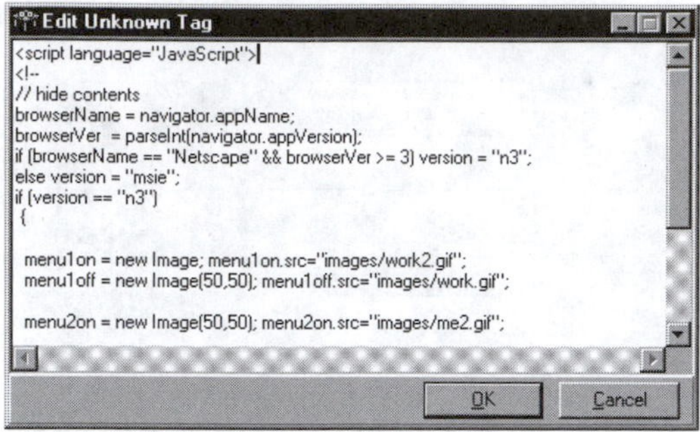

Figure 16. When the **Edit Unknown Tag** dialog box appears, you can enter or paste the HTML code you want to place in the table cell.

✔ Tips

- When you insert an HTML element (such as commented text, or an embedded multimedia object), the **Visual Table Editor** displays a place holder rather than an accurate rendering of what the object looks like.
- The **HTML** element button is useful for specifying a Java applet or embedded object. You can cut the source code from your HTML document and paste it into the **Edit Unknown Tag** dialog box's text window.

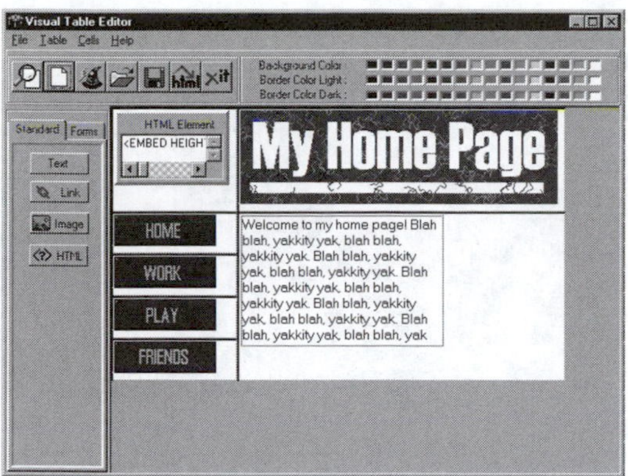

Figure 17. Once you've assembled your table, you can substitute images or edit your text, links, and HTML elements by selecting an object and editing its properties.

Editing Object Properties

Once you finish inserting objects into cells, your table starts to look good. For example, after inserting some text, a few images, and an HTML element, my empty-looking toolbar layout (which you saw in Figure 11) now appears as shown in Figure 17. Although the **Visual Table Editor** won't display your table *exactly* as it would appear in a browser, it comes pretty darned close. But what do you do if you want to substitute an image or make changes to your text, links, or HTML elements? That's no problem. You can simply select an object and edit its properties.

To edit object properties

1. Select an object by clicking on it with your *right* mouse button.
2. When the pop-up menu appears, select **Object**, then select **Properties** when the cascading menu appears.
3. When the **Insert Text**, **Insert Link**, **Insert Image**, or **Edit Unknown Tag** dialog box appears, you can make your changes.
4. When you're finished, click **OK**.

To remove an object

1. Select an object by clicking on it with your *right* mouse button.
2. When the pop-up menu appears, select **Object**, then select **Remove Object** when the cascading menu appears.

Editing Table Properties

When creating a table, it helps to plan ahead. But after looking over your table, you may find that you want to change some of the settings you entered when creating your table with the **Insert Table Wizard**. For example, you may want to widen the table border or change the background color. The **Visual Table Editor** makes editing your table properties simple.

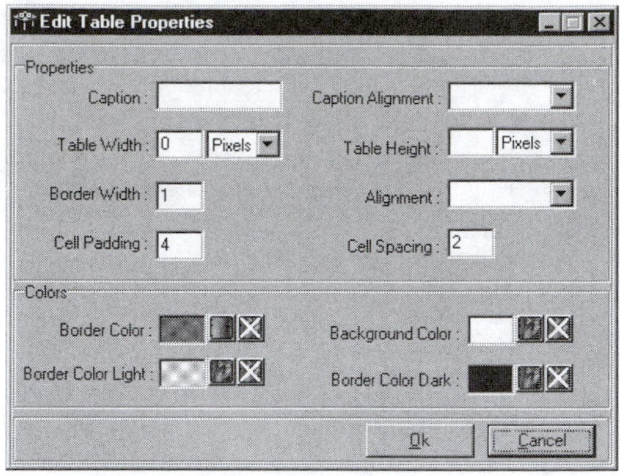

Figure 18. You can change the appearance of your tables by entering new settings in the **Edit Table Properties** dialog box.

To edit table properties

1. Click anywhere on the table with your right mouse button.
2. When the pop-up menu appears, select **Table**.
3. When the cascading menu appears, select **Properties**.
4. When the **Edit Table Properties** dialog box appears, as shown in Figure 18, change your settings, then click **OK**.

Table properties

- **Caption:** You can give your table a caption by entering text in the **Caption** text field.
- **Caption alignment:** You can choose whether your caption appears above or below the table by selecting an option from the **Caption Alignment** list.
- **Width:** You can constrain the width of your table by selecting a unit of measurement (**Pixels** or **Percentage** width in relation to the entire Web page) from the **Table Width** list, and then entering a number in the **Table Width** text field.
- **Height:** You can constrain the height of your table by selecting a unit of measurement (**Pixels** or **Percentage** height in relation to the entire Web page) from the **Table Height** list, and then entering a number in the **Table Height** text field.

✔ Tips

- If you don't choose an alignment option, the table automatically aligns to the left of your page.
- If the objects in your table cells look crowded, try padding your table cells in the **Edit Table Properties** dialog box. Enter a number of pixels in the **Cell Padding** text field (usually a number between **4** and **10** does the trick).
- To cancel colors that you've picked for your border or background colors in the **Edit Table Properties** dialog box, click the corresponding button with the **X** on it. When no color is selected, these settings conform to the Web page's default background color.
- You can constrain the table width in the **Edit Table Properties** dialog box by entering a value in the **Table Width** text field. This is helpful when you only want a table to fill part of the Web page.
- Constraining the table height can cause difficulties. If your text, images, and other table elements exceed the specified height, the table creates more space by expanding its width beyond the browser viewing area.

- **Border:** You can enter a number of pixels to determine the width of your border in the **Border Width** text field.
- **Alignment:** To determine whether the table aligns to the left, right, or center of your Web page, select an option from the **Alignment.**
- **Cell Padding**: You can enter a pixel value to determine the amount of space between table objects and the wall of the cell that encloses them.
- **Cell Spacing:** You can enter a pixel value to determine the width of the borders of the table cell walls.
- **Border:** Click the **Border Color** selection box to display the **Color Palette** dialog box so you can pick a different border color.
- **Border Light**: Click the **Border Color Light** selection box to display the **Color Palette** dialog box so you can pick a different color for the border's highlight.
- **Border Dark:** Click the **Border Color Dark** selection box to display the **Color Palette** dialog box so you can pick a different color for the border's shadow.
- **Background:** Click the **Background Color** selection box to display the **Color Palette** dialog box so you can pick a different color for the table's background.

Editing Table Cell Properties

You can also edit properties for individual table cells. Table cells can have their own background colors and alignment settings. First, I'll cover how to edit table cell properties with the **Edit Cell Properties** dialog box. Then I'll explain the **Edit Cell Properties** dialog box options in greater detail. In addition, you can split and merge cells to create more complex tables.

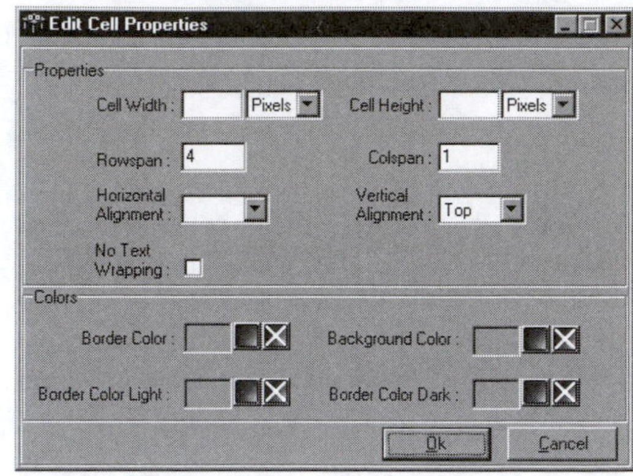

Figure 19. You can change the appearance of your table cells by entering new settings in the **Edit Cell Properties** dialog box.

To edit table cell properties

1. Click on a table cell with your right mouse button.
2. When the pop-up menu appears, select **Table Cell**.
3. When the cascading menu appears, select **Properties**.
4. When the **Edit Cell Properties** dialog box appears, as shown in Figure 19, change your settings, then click **OK**.

Table cell properties

- **Cell Width:** You can constrain the width of a table cell by selecting a unit of measurement (**Pixels** or **Percentage** width in relation to the entire table) from the **Cell Width** list, and then entering a number in the **Cell Width** text field.
- **Cell Height:** You can constrain the height of a table cell by selecting a unit of measurement (**Pixels** or **Percentage** height in relation to the entire table) from the **Cell Height** list, and then entering a number in the **Cell Height** text field.
- **Rowspan:** You can determine how many rows are spanned by a table cell by entering a number of rows in the **Rowspan** text field.

✔ Tips

- If you don't choose horizontal and vertical alignment options for table cells,table elements automatically align to the upper left of the cell.
- If the objects in your table cells look crowded, display the **Edit Table Properties** dialog box and enter a value in the **Cell Padding** text field.
- To cancel colors that you've picked for your border or background colors, click the corresponding button with the **X** on it. When no color is selected, these settings conform to the Table's default background color.
- The **Rowspan** and **Colspan** properties give you more options for arranging your table cells. For example, the right bottom table cell (which contains the text) of the table shown in Figures 20 and 21 spans four rows.
- When entering **Rowspan** settings, the number of rows specified can't exceed the total number of rows in the table.
- When entering **Colspan** settings, the number of columns specified can't exceed the total number of columns in the table.
- If you constrain the cell width for a table cell, all cells in the column also conform to the specified width.
- If you constrain the cell height for a table cell, all cells in the same row also conform to the specified height.
- Table cells can have individual background colors.

- **Colspan:** You can determine how many columns are spanned by a table cell by entering a number of columns in the **Colspan** text field.
- **Horizontal Alignment:** You can determine whether content aligns to the left, right, or center of the cell by selecting an option from the **Horizontal Alignment** list.
- **Vertical Alignment:** You can determine whether content aligns to the top, middle, or bottom of the table cell by selecting an option from the **Vertical Alignment** list.
- **No Text Wrapping:** If you select the **No Text Wrapping** checkbox, the table cell (and the width of the corresponding column) expand to fit the text.
- **Border:** Click the **Border Color** selection box to display the **Color Palette** dialog box so you can pick a different border color.
- **Border Light**: Click the **Border Color Light** selection box to display the **Color Palette** dialog box so you can pick a different color for the border's highlight.
- **Border Dark:** Click the **Border Color Dark** selection box to display the **Color Palette** dialog box so you can pick a different color for the border's shadow.
- **Background:** Click the **Background Color** selection box to display the **Color Palette** dialog box so you can pick a different color for the cell's background.

You can divide a cell, as shown in Table 3.

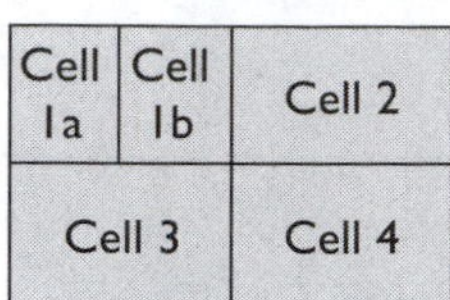

Table 3. You can split a cell into two parts.

To split a cell

1. Click on a table cell with your right mouse button.
2. When the pop-up menu appears, select **Table Cell**.
3. When the cascading menu appears, select **Split Cell**.

You can merge table cells, as shown in Table 4.

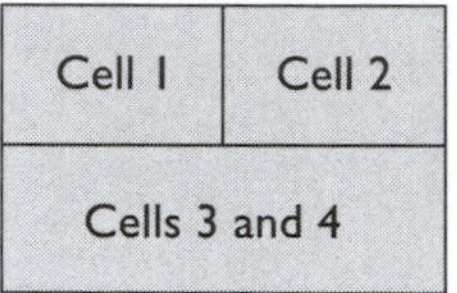

Table 4. You can merge adjacent table cells to design more interesting layouts.

To merge table cells

1. Select the cells you want to merge, then click with your right mouse button.
2. When the pop-up menu appears, select **Table Cell**.
3. When the cascading menu appears, select **Merge Cell**.

You can add a new cell, as shown in Table 5.

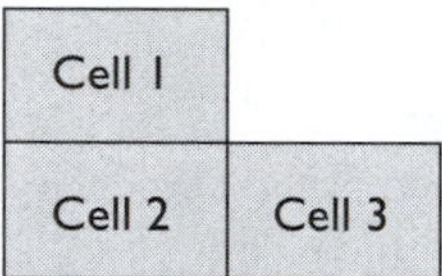

Table 5. You can add a new table cell (but remember to add a corresponding cell above or below it, so your table doesn't look funny).

To add a cell

1. Click on a table cell with your right mouse button.
2. When the pop-up menu appears, select **Table Cell**.
3. When the cascading menu appears, select **Add Cell**.

You can delete the adjacent table cell.

To delete a cell

1. Click on a table cell with your right mouse button.
2. When the pop-up menu appears, select **Table Cell**.
3. When the cascading menu appears, select **Delete Cell**.

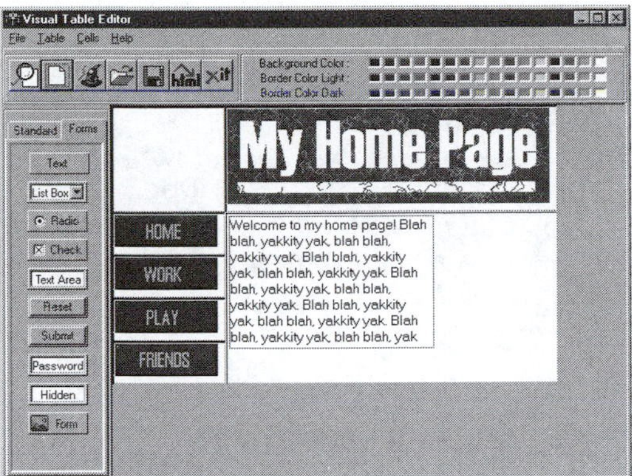

Figure 20. The **Visual Table Editor** provides a list of form elements so you can work with electronic forms.

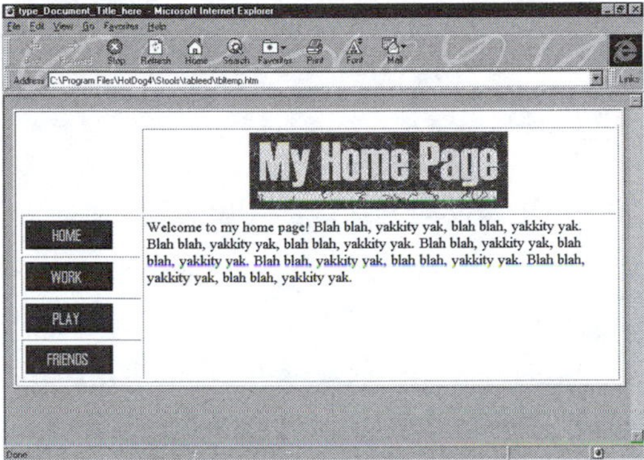

Figure 21. Click the **Preview Table in a Browser** button to view your table. The table displays by itself. To see it with the rest of your Web page, add the table to your HTML document and preview it from the HotDog Pro application window.

Arranging Forms in Tables

Tables also come in handy for arranging your electronic forms. The **Visual Table Editor** helps by providing a list of form elements. You can select and drag form elements into table cells. To display the list of forms elements, click the **Forms** tab. When the **Forms** list appears, as shown in Figure 20, you can select items and drag them into table cells. For more about setting up forms, see Chapter 14.

The Final Steps

Once you finish creating and editing your table, you can preview it in your favorite browser, and add the new table source code to your HTML document. If you like the table layout and plan to use it again, you can also save the table as a separate HTML document. You can open this document when you need to generate source code for the same (or similar) table.

To preview a table

1. Click the **Preview Table in a Browser** button, or select **Preview** from the **Table** menu.

2. When a browser launches, as shown in Figure 21, your table displays.

To place a table in the current HTML document

1. Click the **Compile Table to HTML** button, or select **Compile** from the **Table** menu to generate the HTML code in your HTML document.

2. When the **Information** dialog box tells you the table has been placed, you can exit the **Visual Table Editor** or make further changes.

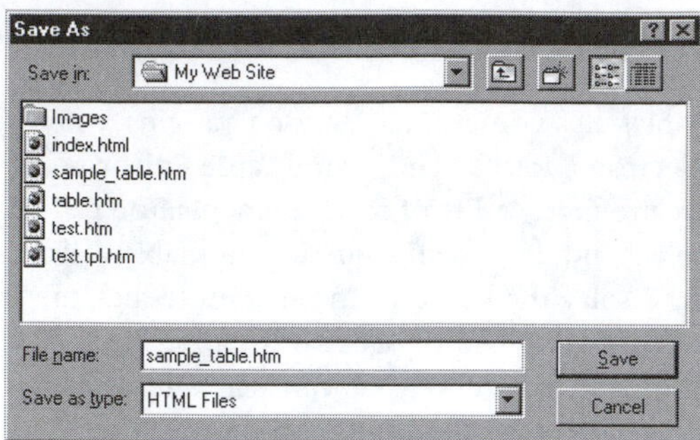

Figure 22. When the **Save As** dialog box appears, you can name and save your table.

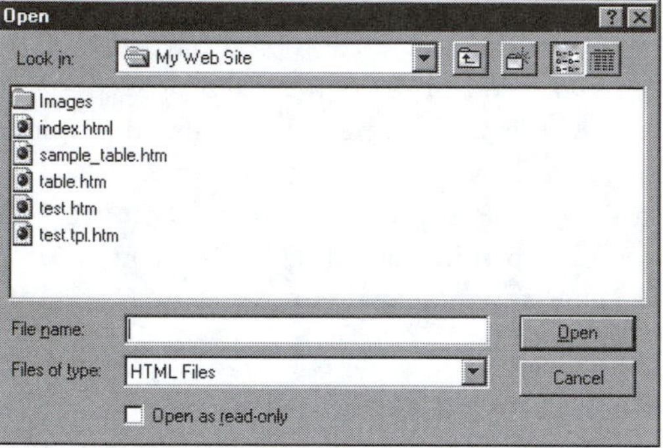

Figure 23. You can open a table document from the **Visual Table Editor** by browsing for your file with the **Open** dialog box.

To exit the Visual Table Editor

1. Click the **Exit** button, or select **Exit** from the **File** menu.
2. When you return to the HotDog Pro application window, you can preview your HTML document with the table by launching Rover or your favorite browser.

To save a table as a separate HTML document

1. Click the **Save** button, or select **Save** from the **File** menu.
2. When the **Save As** dialog box appears, as shown in Figure 22, browse for a folder and name your table.
3. Click the **Save** button.

To open an existing table document

1. Click the **Open** button, or select **Open** from the **File** menu.
2. When the **Open** dialog box appears, as shown in Figure 23, select a file and click the **Open** button.
3. When the table appears in the **Visual Table Editor**, you can click the **Compile Table to HTML** button to add the table to the current HTML document.

8

Building Frames

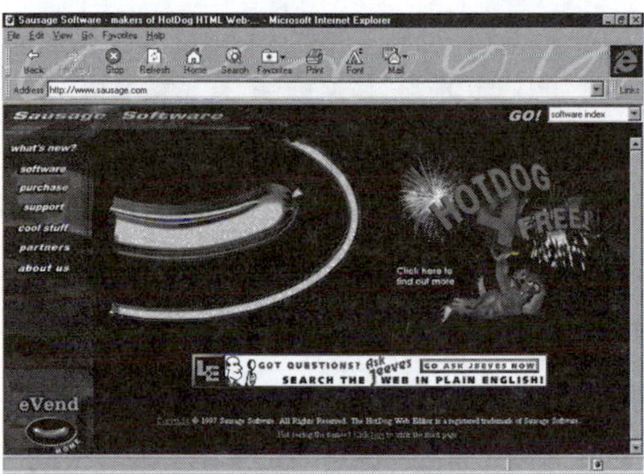

Figure 1. Sausage Software uses frames to keep its navigational links visible throughout their Web site.

You've probably seen Web pages with frames. Frames divide the browser viewing area into different parts, so you can display different Web pages simultaneously. Take Sausage Software's Web site (shown in Figure 1), for example. The left frame contains a document with a list of links and the right frame contains the welcoming page. When you click a link, the new page displays in the right frame, but the list of links remains unchanged. Frames are a useful tool for helping visitors navigate large, complex Web sites. Users can view different pages while keeping navigational links in view. Is creating a site with frames difficult? Not anymore. The **Frames Wizard** walks you through all the steps.

Building a Frame Set Document with the Frame Wizard

How do frames work? It's simple. An HTML frame set document tells the browser how to display the frame layout, and which Web page to load in each frame. If this sounds complicated, never fear. HotDog Pro's **Frame Wizard** guides you through the steps involved in building a frame set document. Frame set documents contain only the specifications for your frames—they do not include text, images, or other data that appears in the browser.

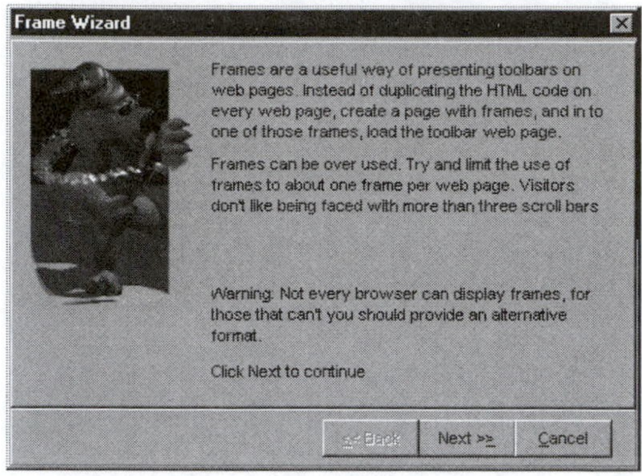

Figure 2. When the first **Frame Wizard** dialog box appears, read the instructions and click the **Next** button.

To create a frame set document with the Frame Wizard

1. Create or open a blank HTML document.
2. Click the **Frame Wizard** button on the **Insert** toolbar, or select **Frames** from the **Insert** menu.
3. When the first **Frame Wizard** dialog box appears, as shown in Figure 2, read the instructions and click the **Next** button.
4. When the second **Frame Wizard** dialog box appears, as shown in Figure 3, select either the **Rows** or **Columns** option from the **Arrange frames by** list. Then, select a number of rows or columns from the **Number** list.
5. Click the **Next** button.
6. When the third **Frame Wizard** dialog box appears, as shown in Figure 4, select a frame and enter settings for it by doing the following:

   A. Enter a name for the frame in the **Frame Name** text field.

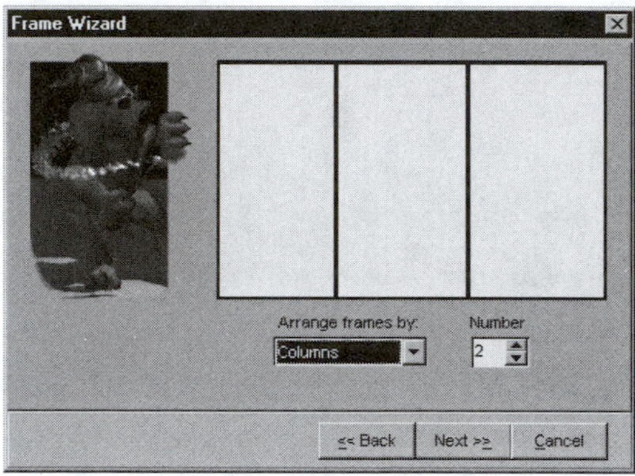

Figure 3. When the second **Frame Wizard** dialog box appears, choose options for how you want to arrange your frames.

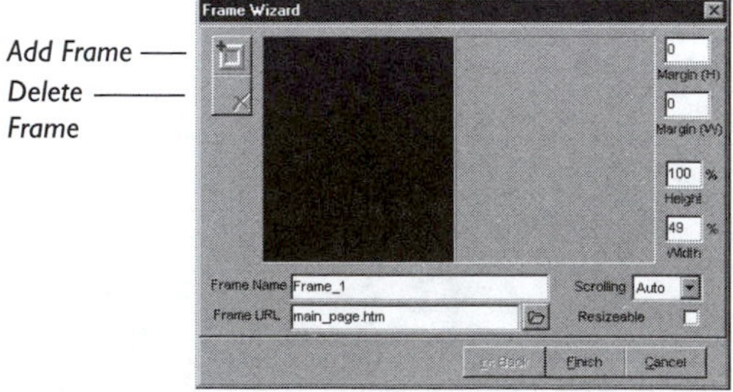

Figure 4. When the third **Frame Wizard** dialog box appears, select a frame and enter settings for it.

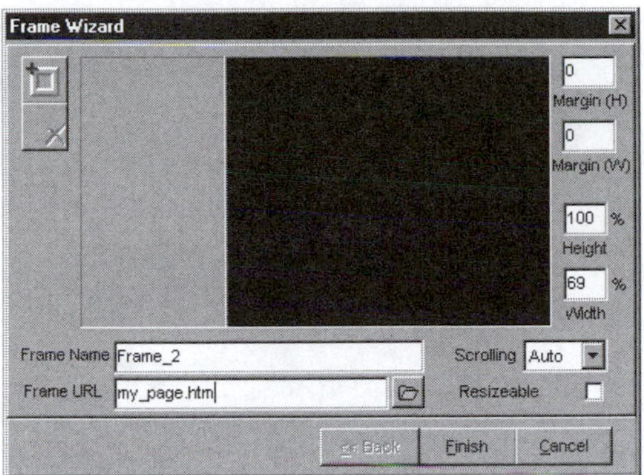

Figure 5. Select the next frame and enter settings for it as you did with the previous frame.

✔ Tips

- Keep things simple. Two frames is usually enough, and I don't recommend layouts with more than three frames.
- You can add a new frame by selecting a frame and clicking the **Add Frame** button in the third dialog box of the **Frame Wizard**. This helps you create more complex layouts.
- You can delete a frame by selecting a frame and clicking the **Delete Frame** button in the third dialog box of the **Frame Wizard**.
- To ensure that frames appear consistently throughout your Web site, you should set up your index file as the frame set document.

B. Enter the name of the HTML document you want displayed in the frame in the **Frame URL** text field (or click the folder icon to browse for a file).

C. You can set the height or width percentage of the frame by clicking your mouse on the border between the frames and dragging it. Or you can specify a height or width percentage in the **Height** or **Width** text fields.

D. You can also specify the height and width for margins (space between the frame's content and the frame's border) in the **Margin (H)** and **Margin (W)** fields.

E. To disable scrolling (so a scrollbar does not appear for the selected frame), select **No** from the **Scrolling** list.

F. To enable visitors to resize the frame, select the **Resizeable** checkbox.

7. Select the next frame (shown in Figure 5) and enter settings for it as you did for the previous frame.
8. Click the **Finish** button to insert the frame set source code into your HTML document. Or, you can click **Cancel** to cancel your frame set.

Working with Frames

Web sites with frames work a bit differently from regular Web sites. While you can still preview individual documents, they won't appear as visitors see them unless you view them through the frame set document. In addition, you need to specify frame targets for your links so pages display in the correct frame. A frame target determines which frame the linked document appears in. When you create links for documents that appear in a framed Web site, the **Link Wizard** and the **Insert Link** dialog boxes display an option for specifying a frame target. For more on links, see Chapter 6.

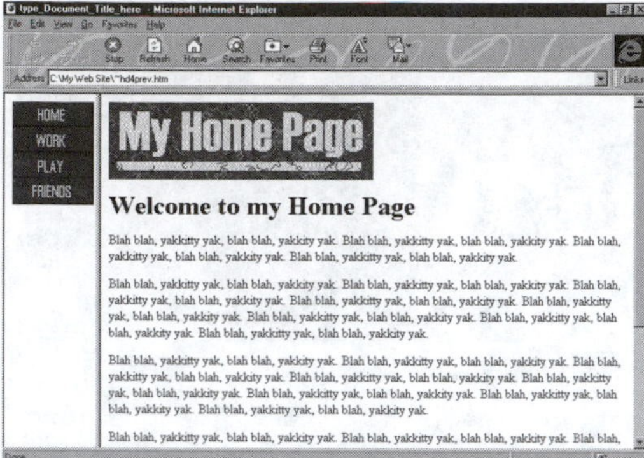

Figure 6. A frames layout organized by columns.

To preview your frames

1. From the HotDog Pro application window, open your frame set document.
2. Click the **Preview** button from the **Standard** toolbar, or select **Preview** from the **File** menu, or press the **F9** key.
3. When the browser launches, you can view your site with frames. Column layouts appear similar to the one shown in Figure 6. Row layouts appear similar to the one shown in Figure 7.

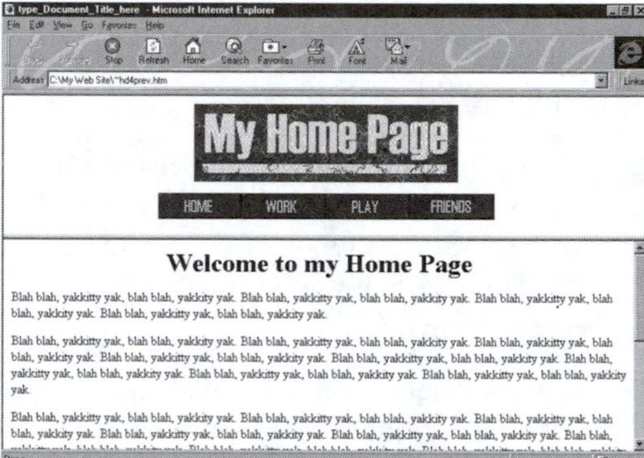

Figure 7. A frames layout organized by rows.

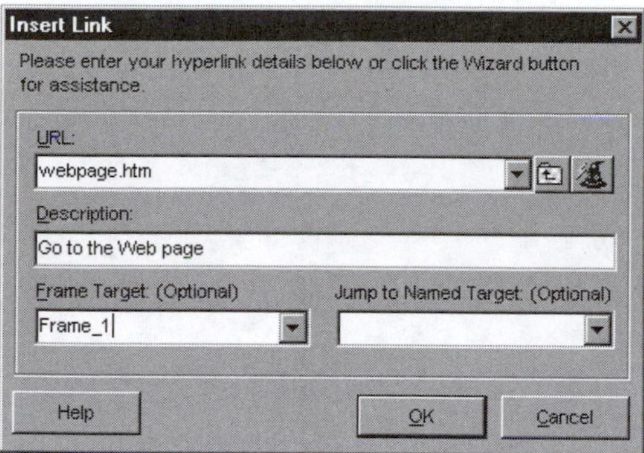

Figure 8. When creating a link, you also need to specify a target frame in the **Frame Target** text field to ensure that the linked page loads in the appropriate frame.

To create links for a Web site with frames

1. Open an HTML document in the HotDog Pro application window.
2. Select the text or image you want to link, or place your cursor where you want to make a link.
3. Click the **Link** button from the **Insert** toolbar.
4. When the **Insert Link** dialog box appears, as shown in Figure 8, enter your information in the **URL** and **Description** text fields as you normally would (for more about creating links, see Chapter 3).
5. Enter the name of the target frame in the **Frame Target** text field. When visitors click the link, the page loads in the specified frame.

✔ Tips

- When specifying **Height** and **Width** settings for individual frames in the third **Frame Wizard** dialog box (see Figures 4 and 5), the sum of all the frames must add up to 100%. If you resize borders by dragging them, the Frames Wizard automatically adjusts the other frames.
- The third **Frame Wizard** prompts you to name each of your frames when you size them (as shown in Figures 4 and 5). Naming your frames makes it easier for you to target links to them.
- You can target a link so the page loads in a new browser window by selecting **Blank** from the **Frame Target** list.
- If you don't specify a frame target for a link, the new page loads in the current frame.
- You can also preview individual documents in your Web site, but the frames won't appear unless you view your pages through the frame set document.
- Rover, HotDog Pro's built-in preview browser, cannot display frames.
- When you click the links in the frame set document preview, they may not work. When HotDog Pro launches your browser, it loads a temporary preview file instead of the real Web page. You can get around this by opening your frame set document as you would normally open a local file in your browser. With Internet Explorer, select **Open** from the **File** menu, click the **Browse** button when the **Open** dialog box appears, then browse for your frame set document.

Making Image Maps

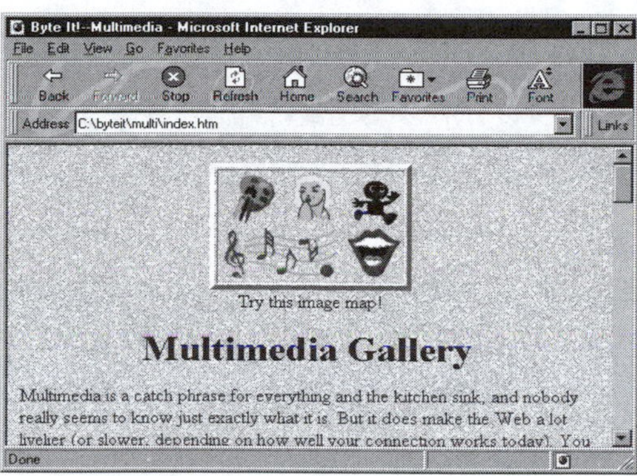

Figure 1. You can click different objects in this image map to visit different pages on the site (**www.byteit.com/multi/**).

Want to give visitors a visually appealing way to navigate your Web site? Make an image map like the one shown in Figure 1. HotDog Pro's **Image Mapper** SuperTool makes image maps simple and fun. With image maps, you use a single image and create linked *hot spots* so users can click on parts of the image to jump to different places. You don't have to be an artist to design an image map. You can use clip art that you either purchase or download from the Web, and arrange different pictures into a single image file. Or you can use a single image with clickable hot spots.

Creating a New Image Map

The **Image Mapper** makes it easy to make image maps. Load an image, create clickable hot spots by drawing shapes around parts of the image and specifying links, and add the code to your HTML document. When you draw a clickable hot spot, a dialog box appears so you can enter a URL for the link. When you finish creating the image map, you can insert the image map codes into the current HTML document. When you view your Web page in a browser, voila! You can click different parts of the image to navigate your site. You can also save the image map file as a separate document with the **.IM** file name extension so you can easily place it in other HTML documents.

To launch the Image Mapper

1. Place your cursor at the insertion point of your HTML document (the place where you want to insert the image map).
2. Select **Image Mapper** from the **SuperToolz** menu.

To load a new image

1. From the **Image Mapper** application, click the **New** button, select **New** from the **File** menu, or use the **CTRL+N** key combination.
2. When the **Open** dialog box appears, as shown in Figure 2, browse for your images folder.
3. Select an image and click the **Open** button.
4. When the **Add Default URL** dialog box appears, as shown in Figure 3, enter a default URL in the **URL** text field.
5. Click **OK**. When the image displays in the **Image Mapper** application window's work area, as shown in Figure 4, you can create hot spots for your image map.

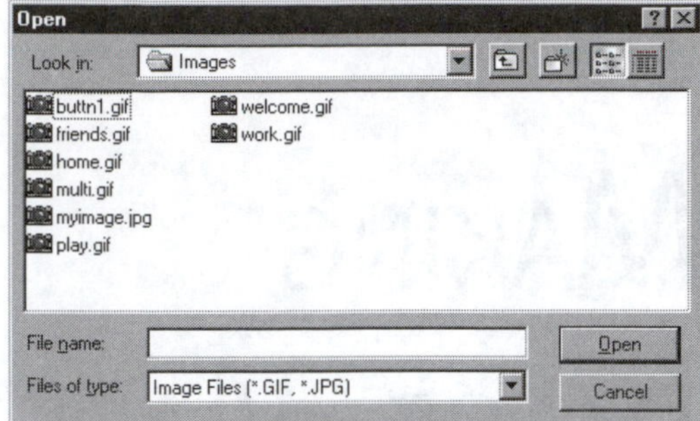

Figure 2. When the **Open** dialog box appears, select an image and click the **Open** button.

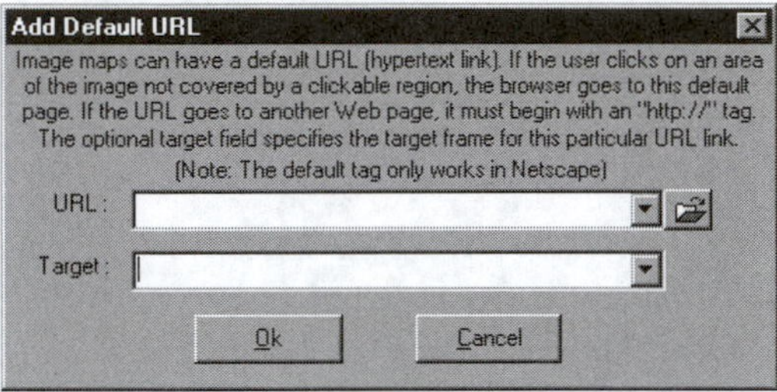

Figure 3. When the **Add Default URL** dialog box appears, enter a URL in the **URL** text box. You can also enter a frame target in the **Target** text field.

✔ Tips

- You can make image maps out of GIF or JPEG files.
- The *default URL* determines where visitors jump to if they click a part of the image map that is not defined by a clickable hot spot. The default URL attribute only works when viewed in the Netscape browser. You can also specify a frame target.
- You can create and arrange images with the built-in Windows Paint program (it creates PCX and BMP files), then convert them to GIF or JPEG files with the **Button Editor**. For more about converting and editing images, see Chapter 5.

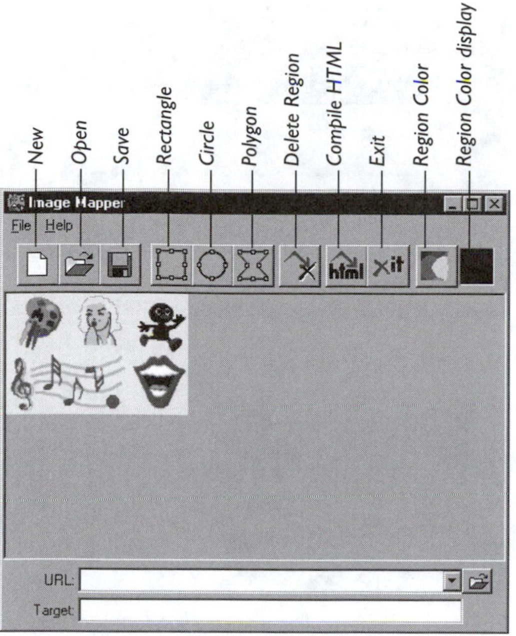

Figure 4. When the image appears in the **Image Mapper** application window's work area, you can begin creating hot spots for your image map.

Image Mapper toolbar buttons

- **New:** Opens a new image and displays it in the work area so you can create a new image map.
- **Open:** Opens an existing image map (.IM) document so you can place it in the current HTML document.
- **Save:** Saves the current image map as a separate document with the **.IM** file name extension.
- **Rectangle:** Defines a rectangular clickable hot spot.
- **Circle:** Defines a circular clickable hot spot.
- **Polygon:** Defines an irregular shape.
- **Delete Region:** Deletes the selected hot spot.
- **Compile HTML:** Adds the image map source code to the insertion point of the current HTML document.
- **Exit:** Exits the Image Mapper.
- **Region Color:** Changes the color of your clickable hot spots so you can see them better.
- **Region Color Display:** Displays the selected hot spot color.

To create a hot spot

1. Click the **Circle**, **Rectangle**, or **Polygon** toolbar button.

2. To define a circular or rectangular hotspot, click an area and drag the cursor diagonally. To define an irregular shape, draw the shape by clicking your left mouse button in different places (like a connect-the-dots game) and click the right mouse button when you finish.

3. When the **Add Hotspot URL** dialog box appears, as shown in Figure 5, enter a URL in the **URL** text field and the status bar text in the **Status Bar Text** text field. If your Web site uses frames, you can also specify a target in the **Target** text field.

4. Click **OK** and repeat the above steps to define other areas. When you finish defining hot spots, they display in your image, as shown in Figure 6.

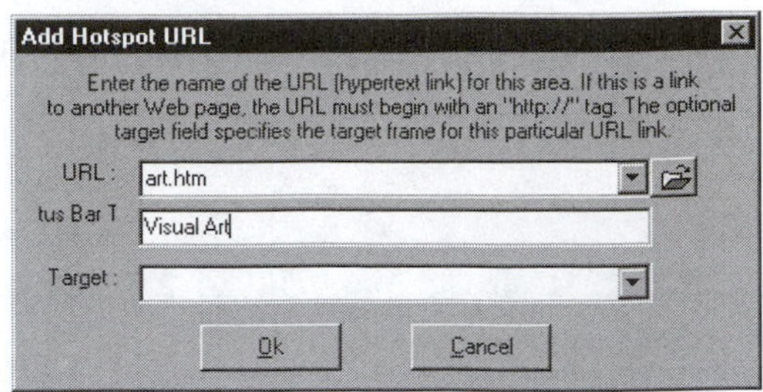

Figure 5. Enter a URL and status bar text for your clickable hot spot in the **Add Hotspot URL** dialog box.

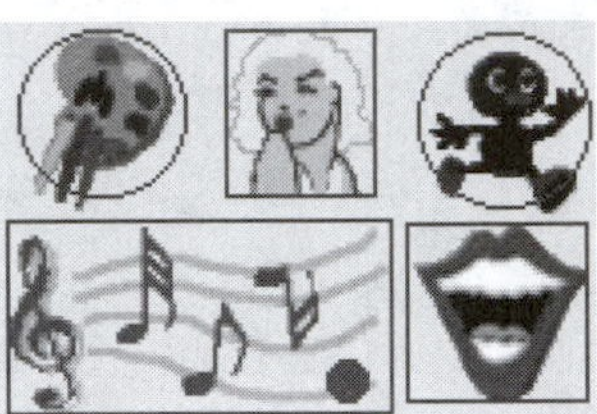

Figure 6. Image with hot spots defined (hot spots do not become part of the image file itself—they only appear when you display the image map in the **Image Mapper**).

✔ Tips

- Clickable hot spot *status bar text* appears in the browser's status bar when the user passes their cursor over a clickable hot spot.
- Dont worry if your hot spot isn't defined exactly the way you want. You can resize and reposition it later.
- You can change the color of your hot spots so you can see and work with them more easily.
- Hot spots do not appear in the image itself, or on the Web page when it displays in a browser.

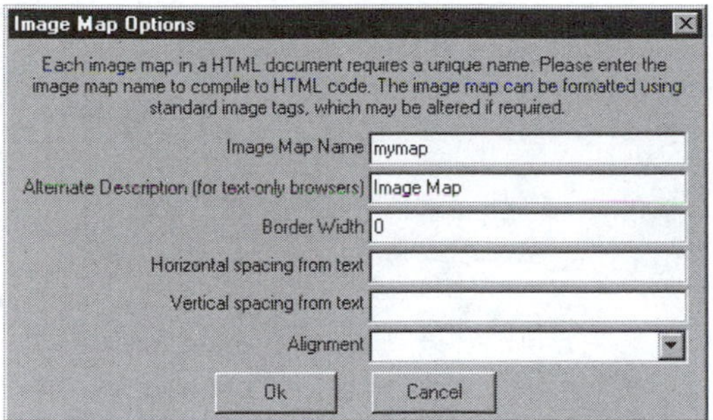

Figure 7. To place your image map code in the current HTML document, click the **Compile HTML** button and fill in the text field when the **Image Map Options** dialog box appears.

To place an image map in the current HTML document

1. Click the **Compile HTML** toolbar button (this tells the **Image Mapper** to generate the image map code and insert it in your HTML document).
2. When the **Image Map Options** dialog box appears, as shown in Figure 7, enter a name for your image map (such as **my image map**) in the **Image Map Name** text field.
3. Enter a description of the image map for people with text-only browsers in the **Alternate Description** text field.
4. Specify a width for the border around your image by entering a number of pixels in the **Border Width** text field (enter **0** if you do *not* want to display a border).
5. You can specify a buffer between your image and surrounding page elements by entering pixel measurements in the **Horizontal spacing from text** and **Vertical spacing from text** text fields.
6. Select an option from the **Alignment** list to determine how your image aligns in relation to surrounding text.
7. Click **OK** to place the image map source code in your HTML document.

Editing Hot Spots

Once you finish defining your hot spots, you can change the colors so you can see them better (hot spots don't appear when you view the image in a browser). You can also resize and reposition your hotspots.

To change hot spot colors for better visibility

1. Click the **Region Color** toolbar button.
2. When the **Color** dialog box appears, as shown in Figure 8, pick a color that contrasts with your image.
3. Click **OK**.

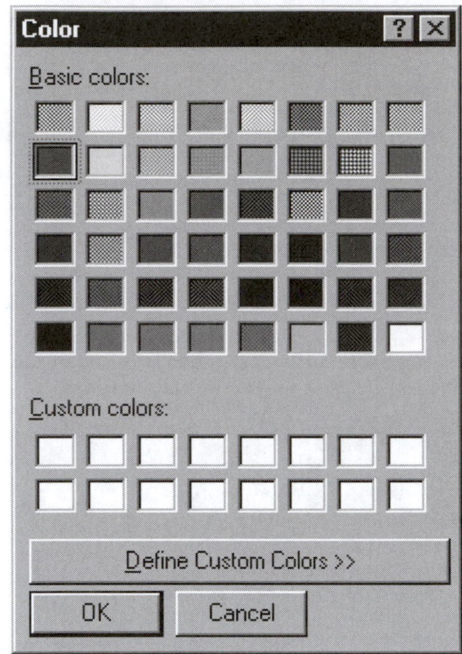

Figure 8. Pick a new color to display your hot spots from the **Color** dialog box.

To resize a hot spot

1. Select a hot spot by clicking on it.
2. When the hot spot turns into a selection box with dashed lines, as shown in Figure 9, click on a side or corner of the hot spot (if it's a circle, click anywhere on the outline of the circle).
3. When the two-sided arrow appears, drag inward to reduce the hot spot's size, or outward to enlarge the hot spot.

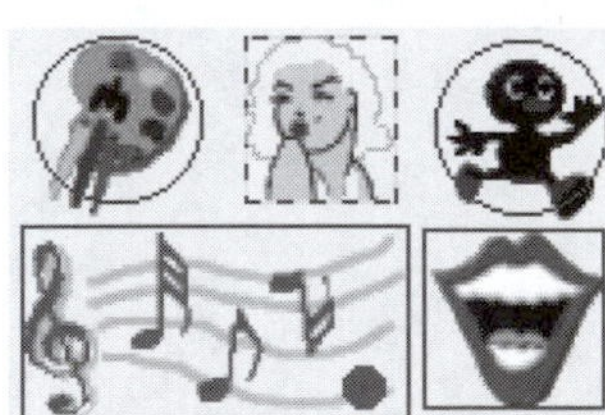

Figure 9. You can resize or move a hot spot by clicking on it to display the hot spot as an editable selection box.

To move a hot spot

1. Select a hot spot by clicking on it.
2. When the hot spot turns into a selection box with dashed lines, as shown in Figure 9, click inside the defined hot spot area.
3. When the four-way arrow appears, you can drag the hot spot to a new position.

To delete a hot spot

1. Select a hot spot by clicking on it.
2. Click the **Delete Region** toolbar button.

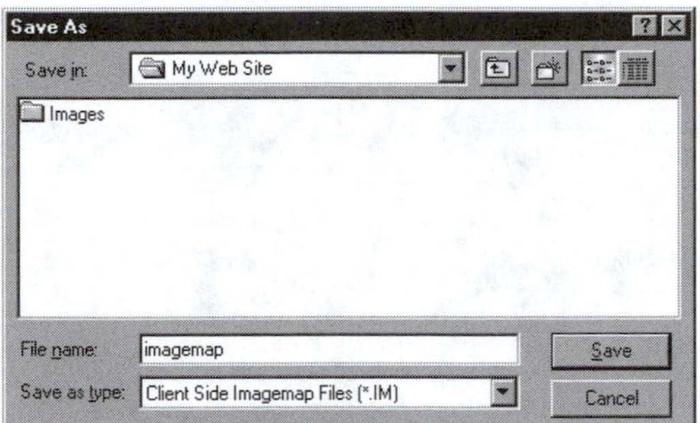

Figure 10. When the **Save As** dialog box appears, browse for a folder and name your image map file.

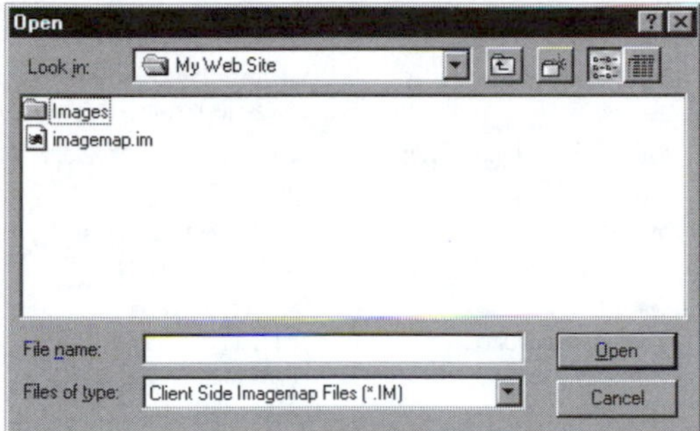

Figure 11. When the **Open** dialog box appears, browse for your image map (.IM) file.

✔ Tips

- An image map file is a text document that tells the browser to display an image, and specifies where the image's Hot Spot files are. Image map files have the .IM file name extension.
- To ensure that your internal links work when you use the image map in other documents, save the image map file to the folder you keep your HTML documents in.

Working with Image Map Files

In addition to placing an image map in a specific HTML document, you can save your image map as a separate image map document. This comes in handy when you want to use the same image map in different Web pages. You can open the image map document and place it in an HTML document whenever you need to.

To save an image map file

1. Click the **Save** toolbar button.
2. When the **Save As** dialog box appears, as shown in Figure 10, browse for a directory.
3. Name the file and click the **Save** button. HotDog Pro automatically saves your file with the **.IM** image map document file name extension.

To open an existing image map file

1. Launch the **Image Mapper**.
2. When the **Image Mapper** application window displays, click the **Open** toolbar button.
3. When the **Open** dialog box appears, as shown in Figure 11, browse for the image map (**.IM**) document.
4. Select the image map document and click the **Open** button.

Anatomy of an Image Map

If you're curious, take a look at your HTML document and the code generated for you by the **Image Mapper**. The **Image Mapper** does not change the appearance of the image itself. It displays the image so you can define clickable hot spots and specify URLs. The image map itself is a list of your clickable hot spots with specifications for the shape, coordinates (position relative to the image), and links, and consists of two components: the image source **<IMG SRC>** code, which tells the browser to display the image and make it behave as an image map, and the **<MAP>**...**</MAP>** code, which specifies the map information.

Compare the **Image Mapper** file displayed in Figure 12 with the image map source code shown in Table 1.

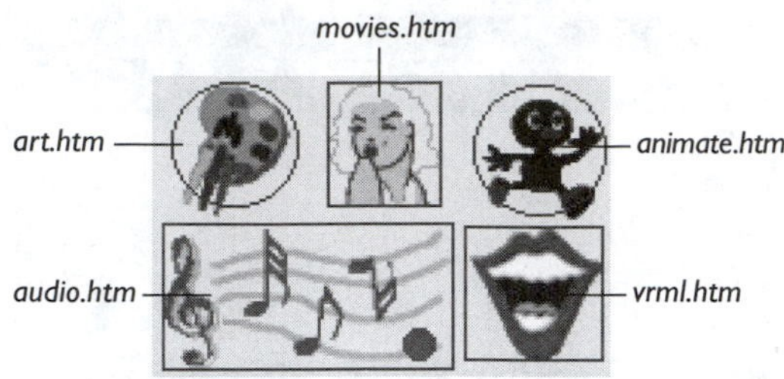

Figure 12. Image map with clickable hot spots that link to different documents. The code for this image is explained in Table 1.

Image Map Source Code

HTML code	What it means
<img src="multi.gif"	Points to the image file
alt="Multimedia Mega Sites"	Specifies alternative text to display in text-only browsers
width="151" height="100"	Specifies the image's width and height
border="0"	Tells the browser not to display a border
usemap= "index.htm#multimap">	Specifies an image map, points to the image map information, and closes the image source tag
<map name="multimap">	Specifies an image map and names the image map so the image file can point to it
<area shape="CIRCLE" coords="25,23,23" href="art.htm">	Defines a circle area for the art.htm link.
<area shape="RECTANGLE" coords="75,24,23" href="movies.htm">	Defines a rectangle area for the movies.htm link.
<area shape="CIRCLE" coords="128,26,23" href="animate.htm">	Defines a circle area for the animate.htm link
<area shape="RECTANGLE" coords="1,51,99,100" href="audio.htm">	Defines a rectangle area for the audio.htm link
<area shape="RECTANGLE" coords="127,73,23" href="vrml.htm">	Defines a rectangle area for the vrml.htm link.
</map>	Closing tag ends image map information

Table 1. HTML source code for the image map shown in Figure 12.

10

Making Java Animations

With HotDog Pro's **Java Animator** SuperTool, you can jazz up your page with simple Java animations. These animations are simple programs, called *Java applets*. However, you don't need to know any programming. All you have to do is create or collect a series of images, assemble the animation cells, and choose any special effects you want to add. When you finish, you can tell the **Java Animator** to generate Java programming code for you. You can even add a sound track and specify a background color or image for your Java animation applet.

The Java Animator

The Java Animator, as shown in Figure 1, makes it easy for you to place and arrange images for your animation, add a background, sound, and special effects. Java is the programming language of choice on the Web. It runs in people's browsers regardless of what kind of computer they use. With Java, you can do lots of neat stuff that used to require CGI programming and direct access to the server. While you would need to learn some programming to take advantage of the full range of Java's capabilities, the Java Animator lets even novices have a little fun.

Java animations consist of three basic components: the data files, the Java *class* file, and the HTML source code. When you place an animation applet in your HTML document, the Java Animator generates the HTML code needed to load the applet when you view the page in a browser.

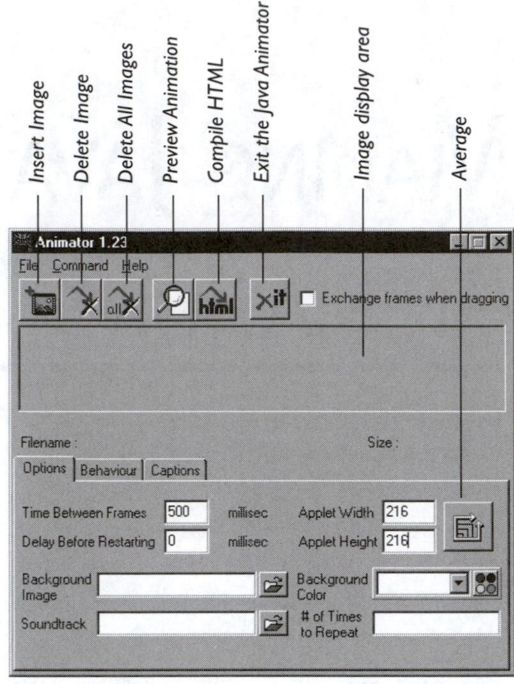

Figure 1. The **Java Animator** SuperTool makes it easy to create animated Java applets.

Java animation components

- **Data files:** The image and audio files used in your animations are not actually part of the applet generated by the **Java Animator**. They are stored as separate files that load into the applet when the applet runs in a Web browser.
- **Class files:** When you finish creating your animation, the **Java Animator** generates a little program for you. The Java applet (program) itself is called a *class file*. The **Java Animator** saves it with the **.CLASS** file name extension.
- **HTML source code:** When the **Java Animator** generates a class file, it also inserts HTML source code into the current Web page. The source code tells the browser to load the applet so the animation starts running.

✔ Tips

- If you use more than five or six images, your Java animation may take too long to load in the browser.
- Each image in an animation can also be called a *frame* or a *cel*.
- For best results, your images should all have the same width and height dimensions. Or you can click the **Average** button next to the **Height** and **Width** options to automatically specify height and width parameters that allow for images of different sizes.
- When you select an image displayed in the **Java Animator**, the file name, path information, and image size displays below the image display area (see Figure 3).

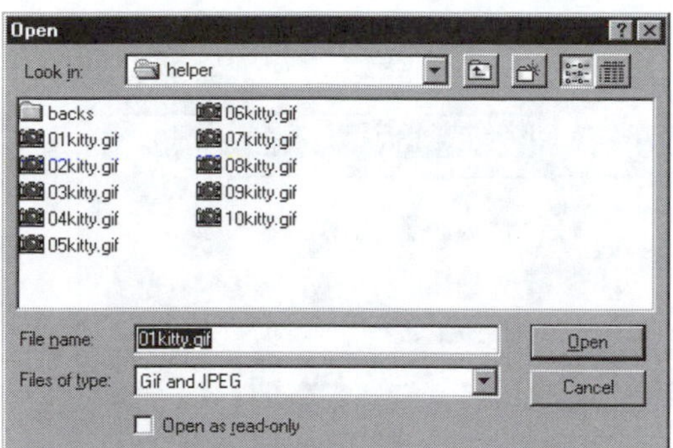

Figure 2. To insert images, click the **Open Image** button to display the **Open** dialog box and browse for an image.

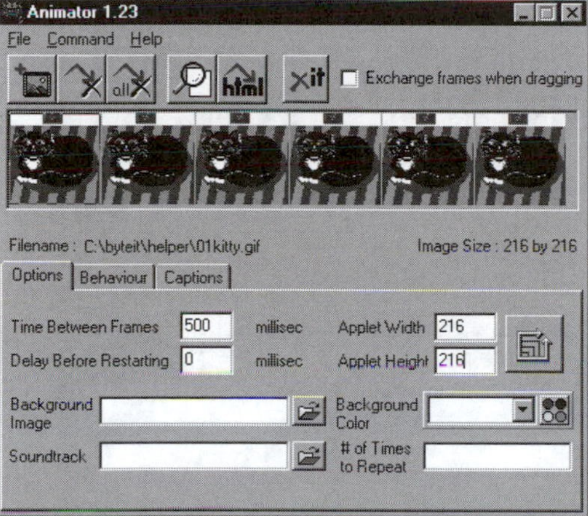

Figure 3. When you place your images, they appear in the **Java Animator** application window's work area.

✔ Tip

- You need to specify a background image or color for your applet.

To launch the Java Animator

1. Place your cursor at the insertion point of your HTML document (where you want the animation to appear).
2. Select **Java Animator** from the **SuperToolz** menu.
3. When the **Java Animator** application window displays, you can begin inserting your images.

To place images

1. From the **Java Animator**, click the **Insert Image** toolbar button.
2. When the **Open Image** dialog appears, as shown in Figure 2, browse for and select an image.
3. Click the **Open** button.
4. Repeat the above steps to insert more images. Images appear in the **Java Animator** application window's work area, as shown in Figure 3.

To remove an image

1. Select an image.
2. Click the **Delete Image** toolbar button.

To delete all images

1. Click the **Delete All Images** toolbar button.

To rearrange images

1. Select an image.
2. Drag it to another position in the animation. The image on the left displays first. The image on the right displays last.
3. You can move other images to different positions to rearrange the order in which images appear.

To choose animation Options

1. From the **Java Animator**, click the **Options** tab to display the selections shown in Figure 3.
2. Enter the amount of time you want to elapse between frames (in milliseconds) in the **Time Between Frames** text field.
3. Enter the amount of time you want to delay the animation before it loops again (in milliseconds) in the **Delay Before Restarting** text field.
4. Specify a size for your applet (in pixels) in the **Applet Width** and **Applet Height** text fields. This determines the amount of space the browser allows for the animation applet to display when the user views your page.
5. You can pick a background image by entering the directory path and name of an image in the **Background Image** text field. Or you can click the folder icon to browse for the image.
6. You can pick a background color for your applet by clicking the **Background Color** button. When the **Color Picker** palette displays as shown in Figure 4, pick a color and click **OK** to return to the **Java Animator** application window.
7. You can specify an audio file to use as a soundtrack by entering the name of the file in the **Soundtrack** text field. Or you can click the folder icon to display the **Open** dialog box and browse for the image.
8. Specify how many times you want your animation to repeat by entering a number in the **# of Times to Repeat** text field.

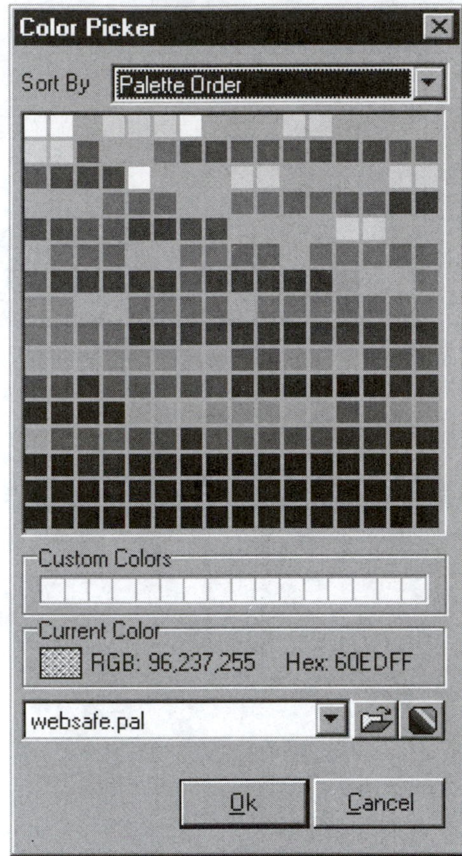

Figure 4. You can specify a background color for your applet by selecting a color from the **Color Picker**.

✔ Tips

- A *millisecond* is one thousandth of a second.
- You can only use .AU formatted audio files in Java applets.
- To find some cool .AU files that you can use, visit SunSite's Multimedia archive at sunsite.unc.edu/pub/multimedia/sun-sounds/.
- When you specify a soundtrack, the sound plays over and over again (so try to pick something that isn't too annoying!) while the animation runs.

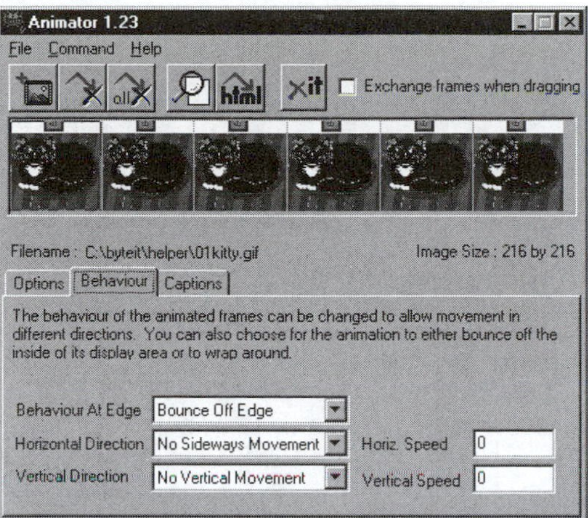

Figure 5. You can enter settings for how your images move and behave throughout the animation.

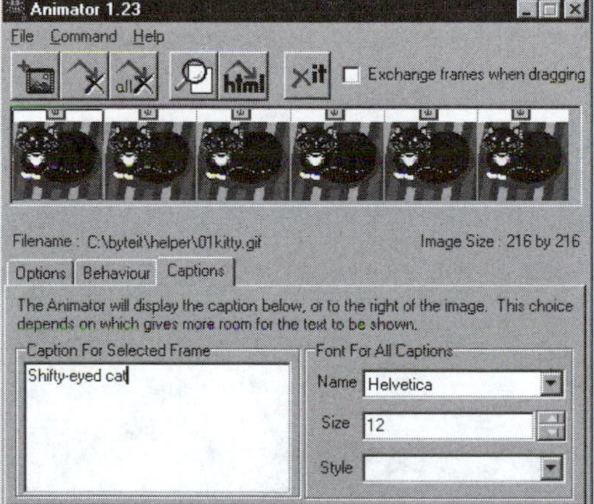

Figure 6. You can enter captions for your frames. The caption appears below the image when the animation runs in the browser.

To choose Behavior settings

1. Click the **Behavior** tab to display the options shown in Figure 5.
2. Select an option from the **Behavior At Edge** list. Here you can determine the movement of your frames.
3. You can select an option from the **Horizontal Direction** list to determine how your images move from side to side (or whether you want them to move).
4. You can select an option from the **Vertical Direction** list to determine how your images move up and down (or whether you want them to move up and down).
5. You can also enter numbers (in milliseconds) for the horizontal and vertical movement speeds in the **Horiz Speed** and **Vertical Speed** text fields.

To enter text captions

1. Click the **Captions** tab to display options for adding captions for each image, as shown in Figure 6.
2. Select the image you want to create a caption for.
3. Enter the text you want to include in the **Caption For Selected Frame** text field.
4. Pick a font from the **Name** list (with Java applets, you can only select basic fonts).
5. Pick a font size from the **Size** list.
6. Pick a text style (bold, italic, or underlined) from the **Style** list.
7. Repeat steps 2-6 for each image.

To preview your animation

1. Click the **Preview Animation** button.
2. If you have more than one browser specified in your HotDog Pro **Browser** Preferences, select an item from the pop-up list, as shown in Figure 7.
3. When the animation appears (with the applet source code below it), like the one shown in Figure 8, you can choose whether to generate the applet, or make changes.

To place your animation in your HTML document

1. Click the **Compile HTML** toolbar button.
2. When the **Compile Java Animation** dialog box appears, as shown in Figure 9, tell the **Java Animator** where your images are stored by selecting a radio button from the **In Which Remote Directory Will Your Animation Images Be Stored** list.
3. Specify a folder for the Java animation .CLASS file and name it by entering a directory in the **Copy Class Files To** text field and clicking the **Create** button. Or you can click the folder button to display the **Browse for Folder** dialog box shown in Figure 10, and locate your folder.
4. When you return to the **Compile Java Animation** dialog box, click the **Compile HTML** button. This creates the .CLASS applet files, and generates the HTML applet code and places it in your document.
5. When you return to the **Java Animator**, you can click the **Exit** button to return to the HotDog Pro application window.

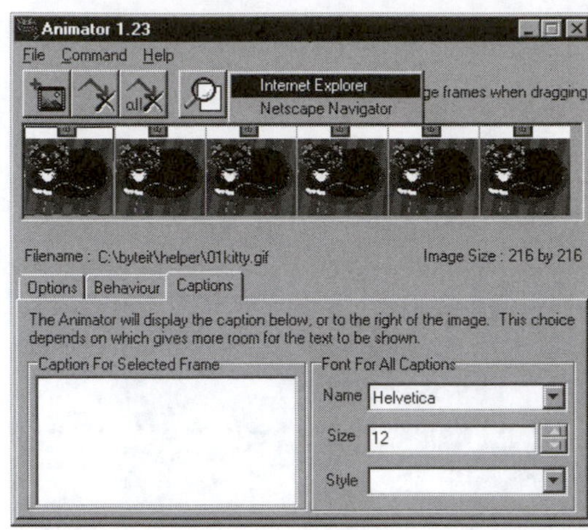

Figure 7. To preview your animation in a browser, click the **Preview** button. If you have more than one browser specified, a pop-up menu appears.

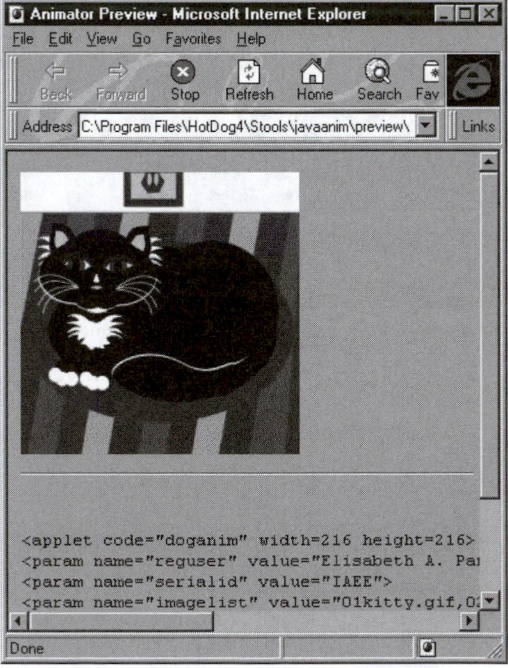

Figure 8. Animation with applet source code previewed in a browser.

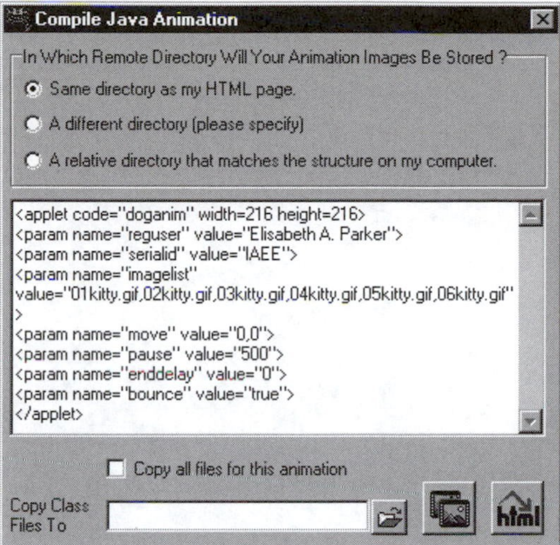

Figure 9. When the **Compile Java Animation** dialog box appears, you can select options to ensure correct relative path names.

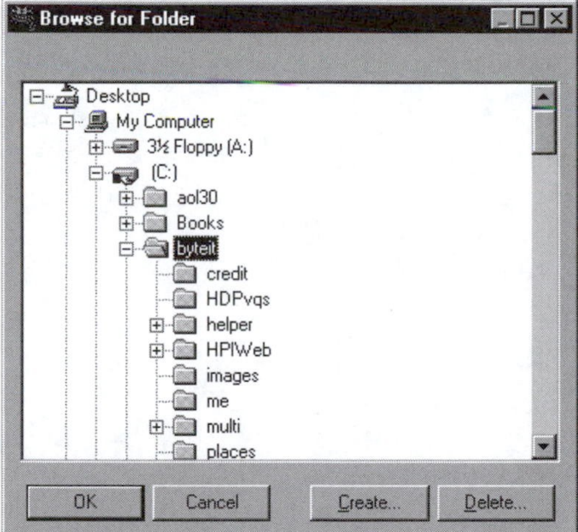

Figure 10. When the **Browse for Folder** dialog box appears, select your Web site folder, or a folder inside of your Web site folder to copy your Java animation .CLASS file into.

✔ Tips

- The **Compile Java Animation** dialog box helps generate correct relative path names. This ensures that your applet can locate and load the data files (image and sound) once you upload the HTML document, .CLASS file, and data files to your server. If your relative path names are not correct, the Java animation will not work properly.
- If your data files are located in the same folder as the HTML document that loads the animation applet, select the **Same directory as my HTML page** radio button.
- If your data files are located in a folder outside of your Web site folder, select the **A different directory** radio button.
- If your data files are stored in a folder inside of your Web site folder, and you have a corresponding folder on your Web server (for example, an **Images** folder), select the **A relative directory that matches the structure on my computer** radio button.
- When you specify a folder to copy your .CLASS file into, pick your Web site folder, or a folder located inside of your Web site folder.
- For more information about Java, and links to Java applet-generating software for non-programmers, visit the Gamelan Web site at *www.gamelan.com*.

11

JavaScript Special Effects

HotDog Pro's **JavaScript Tools** might very well become your favorite SuperTool. With **JavaScript Tools** you can generate sophisticated JavaScript scripts that make your Web pages more interesting and useful. For example, you can create a search pad so users can enter key words to search the Web. Or you can set your Web page up to launch a separate window that pops up automatically and makes an announcement. JavaScript is a programming language that makes it easy for non-programmers to generate scripts that make Web pages more exciting and interactive. In Web parlance, Java and JavaScript-enhanced pages are referred to as *dynamic* HTML. Unlike Java animations (as discussed in Chapter 10), you insert JavaScript code directly into your HTML document. Or the **JavaScript Tools** do it for you. If you know a bit about JavaScript, you can also use the **JavaScript Language Editor** SuperTool to edit and customize JavaScript scripts. To learn more about JavaScript and interesting shareware and freeware scripts that you can use, visit Gamelan at www.gamelan.com.

JavaScript Tools

HotDog Pro's **JavaScript Tools**, as shown in Figure 1, are pre-made JavaScript scripts that you can add to your Web pages. Select an item from the list, click the **Next** button, and follow the easy instructions to place an item in your HTML document. You can also preview an item to see what it does by selecting the item and clicking the **Preview** button. If you know a little about how JavaScript works, you can also customize a JavaScript script's behavior with the **JavaScript Language Editor**.

To insert a JavaScript script in your HTML document

1. Place your cursor at the insertion point of your HTML document.
2. Select **JavaScript Tools** from the **SuperToolz** menu.
3. When the **JavaScript Tools** application window appears, as shown in Figure 1, select an item from the scrolling list and click the **Next** button.
4. When the dialog box or series of dialog boxes appear, follow the instructions. Click the **Next** button to display more options, or click the **Finished** button.

To preview a JavaScript script

1. Select an item from the **JavaScript Tools** scrolling list.
2. Click the **Preview** button.
3. If you've selected more than one browser in your **Browser** Preferences, a pop-up list appears so you can select a browser.

When your browser launches, a window appears and displays a preview of the JavaScript script.

Figure 1. You can preview and select pre-made JavaScript scripts and add them to your pages from the **JavaScript Tools** application window.

✔ Tips

- When the **JavaScript Tools** insert JavaScript scripts in your HTML document, HotDog Pro displays them in a different color from the rest of your HTML and text to set them apart.
- If you're not sure what an item from the **JavaScript Tools** scrolling list does, you can preview it.
- You can choose how you want to preview scripts by selecting an item from the **Preview Mode** list. The **As whole page** option displays the selected script as its own Web page in the current browser window. The **As separate frame** option displays the selected script as its own Web page in a separate browser window. The **All as buttons** option displays a Web page with a list of scripts. You can display each script by clicking the buttons.

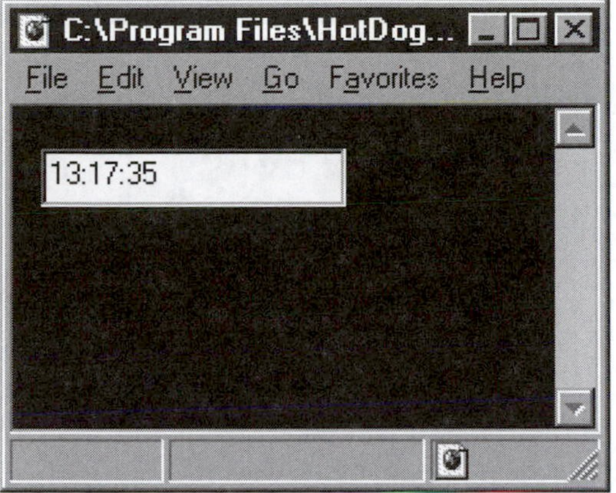

Figure 2. You can create a JavaScript clock that appears in your Web page, loads automatically in a separate window, or displays a button that users can click to display the clock in a separate window.

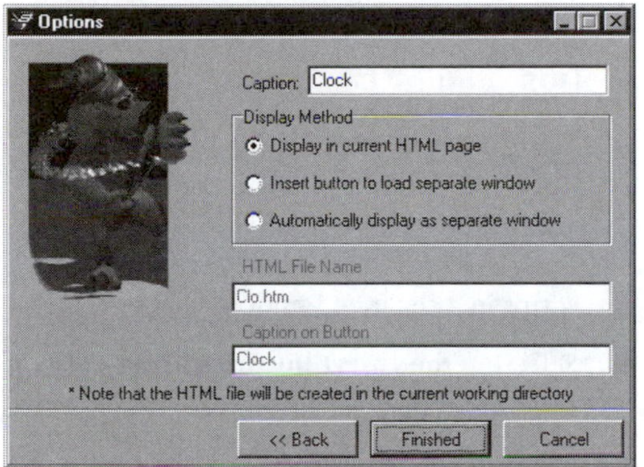

Figure 3. You can select options for displaying your clock from the **Options** dialog box.

Creating a Clock

You can add a simple digital clock to your page like the one shown in Figure 2. With JavaScript clocks, you don't have to worry about what time zone the user lives in. The clock automatically sets itself to the clock on your visitor's computer system.

To create a clock

1. Select **Clock** from the **JavaScript Tools** scrolling list, then click the **Next** button.

2. When the **Options** dialog box appears, as shown in Figure 3, enter a caption (such as **The time now is**) in the **Caption** text field.

3. Select an option from the **Display Method** list by clicking a radio button. You can choose to display your clock in the Web page (**Display in current HTML page**), insert a button that users can click to launch a separate Web page that displays the clock (**Insert button to load separate window**), or to automatically display the clock in a separate Web page (**Automatically display as separate window**).

   A. If you choose the **Display in current HTML page** option, go to step 5.

   B. If you choose the **Insert button to load separate window** option from the **Display Method** list, enter a name for the new HTML file in the **HTML File Name** text field. Click the **Next** button.

(continued)

c. If you choose the **Insert button to load separate window** from the **Display Method** list, enter a name for the new HTML file in the **HTML File Name** text field. Enter the text you want to appear on the button (such as "Click to display the time") in the **Caption on Button** text field. Click the **Next** button.

4. When you select one of the separate window display options, the second **Options** dialog box appears, as shown in Figure 4. You can specify the separate window's dimensions by entering pixel measurements in the **Width** and **Height** text fields, and determine which browser interface elements to display by selecting items from the **Separate Window Options** list.

5. Click the **Finished** Button.

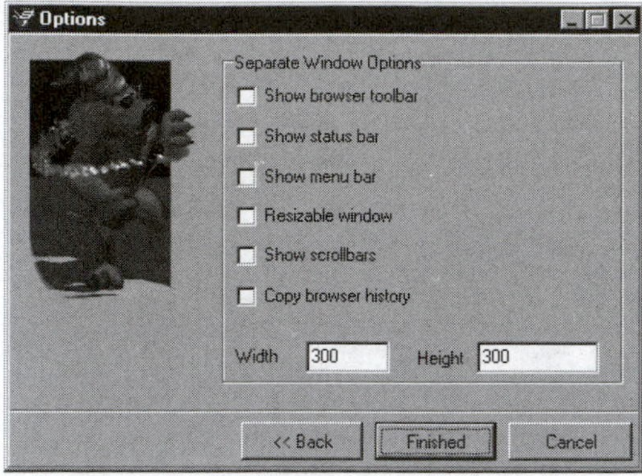

Figure 4. The second **Options** dialog box appears if you choose to run the JavaScript in a separate window. It lets you determine the separate window's size and select which (if any) browser interface elements you want to display.

✔ Tips

- You can set up most of the **JavaScript Tools** scripts to display in a separate window. Or you can provide users with a button that they can click to run your script in a separate window.
- Selecting the **Insert button to load separate window** option leaves your Web pages less cluttered, and lets visitors decide whether to run the script or not.
- A **separate window** is a regular Web page. You can open it in HotDog Pro and add a color scheme, background, and images as you would with any other HTML document.
- The **JavaScript Tools** application creates the new Web page in the same folder as the current HTML document.

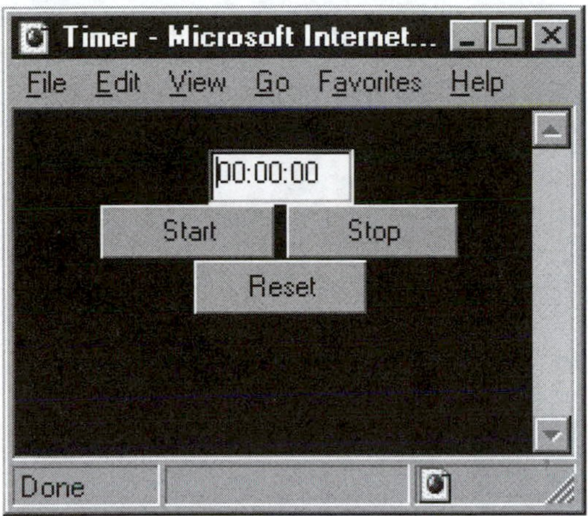

Figure 5. You can give visitors a timer so they can keep track of how long they surf the Web.

✔ Tips

- When you choose to run a JavaScript script in your HTML document, the text displays according to your HTML document's default color scheme settings.
- When you choose to run a JavaScript script in a separate window, elements display according to the browser's defaults. You can open a separate window HTML document in HotDog Pro and specify a new color scheme.
- By default, separate window documents do not display any browser *interface* elements—such as the toolbar, menu bar, and status bar. This gives the separate window a neater appearance.
- The word *interface* refers to the look and feel of an application. Toolbar buttons, menus, icons and other objects that appear in an application window are *interface elements*.
- If you set up the timer to display in a separate window, users can even keep it running while they surf other Web sites.

Making a Timer

You can set up a timer that your visitors can use to time how long they're spending on your page or on the Web in general. The timer, as shown in Figure 5, provides buttons for starting, stopping, and resetting the timer..

To make a Timer

1. Select **Timer** from the **JavaScript Tools** scrolling list, then click the **Next** button.
2. When the **Options** dialog box appears, enter a caption (such as, **Time Your Web Surfing!**) in the **Caption** text field.
3. Select an option from the **Display Method** list.
   - **A.** If you choose the **Display in current HTML page** option, go to step 5.
   - **B.** If you choose the **Automatically display as separate window** option, enter the name of the new HTML document in the **HTML File Name** text field. Click the **Next** button.
   - **C.** If you choose the **Insert button to load separate window** option, enter the name of the new HTML document in the **HTML File Name** text field. Enter the text that you want to appear on the button in the **Caption on Button** text field. Click the **Next** button.
4. If you choose one of the separate window options, the second **Options** dialog box displays. Here, you can select check boxes from the **Separate Window Options** list and enter **Width** and **Height** measurements.
5. Click the **Finished** Button.

Launching a Search Pad

A search pad, as shown in Figure 6, lets visitors access popular search engines straight from your Web page. From the search pad, they can enter a keyword or words in the **Enter search terms here** text field, select a search engine from the pull-down list, and click the **Search Now** button.

Figure 6. Launch your own Search Pad so visitors can search topics on popular search engines.

To create a Search Pad

1. Select **Search Pad** from the **JavaScript Tools** scrolling list, then click the **Next** button.
2. When the **Options** dialog box appears, enter a caption (such as, **Welcome to my Search Pad!**) in the **Caption** text field.
3. Select a **Display Method** list option.
   - **A.** If you choose the **Display in current HTML page** option, go to step 5.
   - **B.** If you choose the **Automatically display as separate window** option, enter the name of the new HTML document in the **HTML File Name** text field. Click the **Next** button.
   - **C.** If you choose the **Insert button to load separate window** option, enter the name of the new HTML document in the **HTML File Name** text field. Enter the text that you want to appear on the button in the **Caption on Button** text field. Click **Next**.
4. If you choose one of the separate window options, the second **Options** dialog box displays. Here, you can select check boxes from the **Separate Window Options** list and enter **Width** and **Height** measurements.
5. Click the **Finished** Button.

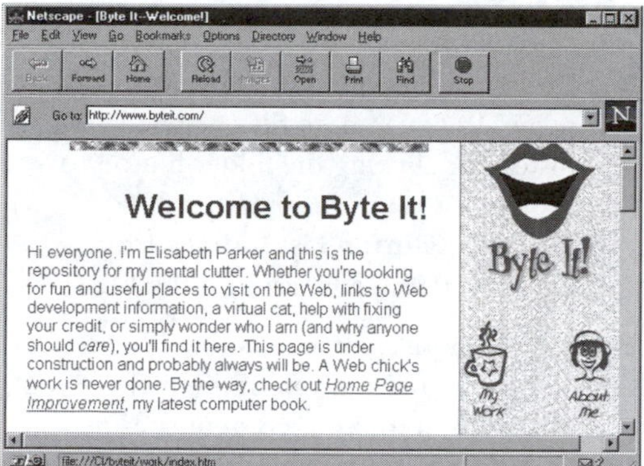

Figure 7. The Byte It! Web page at **www.byteit.com** uses animated navigational graphics. They're purple, but they turn green when the user passes the mouse button over them.

Figure 8. The **Animated Button List Builder** helps you create a list of animated buttons.

Setting Up Animated Navigation Buttons

If you use graphics as navigation buttons that users can click on to visit different parts of your Web site, try animating them. When a user passes the cursor over an animated navigation button, the image changes. For example, Byte It!'s **My Work** and **About Me** navigational graphics (shown in Figure 7) are purple. When the user passes the cursor over a navigational graphic, it turns green.

You can try this too. It's easy. First, you create a substitute image for each navigational graphic displayed on your Web page. The second image should look different in some way from the original. For example, each one of Byte It!'s purple graphics has a corresponding green one. Then, you use the **JavaScript Tools** to generate a JavaScript script that switches the images.

To create animated navigation buttons

1. Select **Animated Buttons** from the **JavaScript Tools** scrolling list, and click the **Next** button.

2. When the **Animated Button List Builder** dialog box appears, as shown in Figure 8, create a list of images that you want substituted by doing the following:

   A. Enter the path name to an image in the **Default Image** text field. The *default* image refers to the graphic that first displays in the browser.

   B. Enter the path name to the replacement image in the **MouseOver Image** text field. *MouseOver* is JavaScript-ese for "passing over an area with the cursor."

C. Enter explanatory text in the **Image Text** field. This text displays in the browser's status bar when the image changes.

D. Enter the URL or document you want to link to in the **URL Target** text field.

E. Click the **Add Button to List** button (it looks like a coffee cup with a page inside of it).

F. When the button name appears on the **Buttons** list, repeat steps A-E until you have added all the images to the **Buttons** list.

3. You can choose to display a dialog box that tells Internet Explorer users to try your page with Netscape Navigator by selecting the **Suggest to IE 3.0 users to change browser?** This JavaScript only works with Netscape Navigator.

4. Click the **Next** button.

5. When the **Options** dialog box appears, select the **Display in current HTML page** radio button and click the **Finished** button.

✔ Tips

- I advise you to enter the directory path names to your image files manually, instead of clicking the folder button to browse for files. This prevents the **Animated Button List Builder** from entering *absolute path names* for the files.
- An *absolute path name* points to a file on your computer by listing all of the path information for your computer, as in: C:\MyWebSite\Images\image.gif. A *relative path name* points to files by listing path information relative to your Web folder, as in: Images/image.gif.
- You need to use relative path names because your Web server does not have the same directory structure as your computer.
- If you would rather not enter relative path names, remember to set your **Publishing AutoReplace Preferences** to search and replace your absolute path names with relative ones.
- If, like many Web page authors, you keep your HTML files in the main Web directory and your images in a subdirectory called **Images**, then the correct relative path name to your image file is: Images/image.gif.

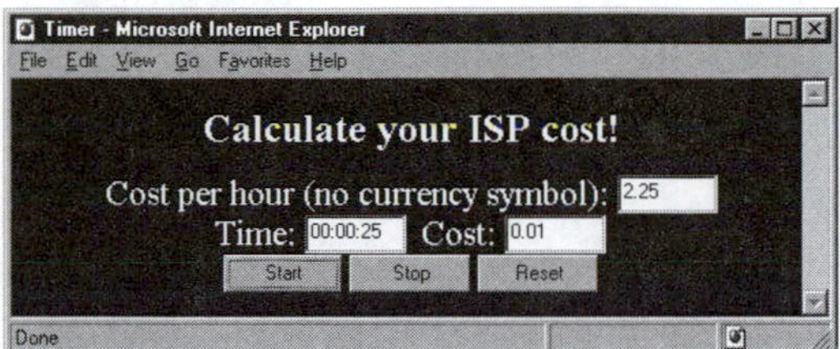

Figure 9. You can offer visitors an ISP Cost Calculator so they can keep track of their online charges.

Building an ISP Cost Calculator

If you and your page's visitors use an Internet service provider (ISP) that charges an hourly rate, you can add an ISP cost calculator to your Web site (as shown in Figure 9). The user enters their ISP's hourly charge in the **Cost per hour** text field and clicks the **Start** button. The ISP Cost Calculator starts ticking and displays the amount of time spent on the Internet and the cost incurred. As with the **Timer** script, the ISP cost calculator can display in a separate window so users can continue viewing it after they leave your Web site.

To create an ISP Cost Calculator

1. Select **ISP Cost Calculator** from the **JavaScript Tools** scrolling list, then click the **Next** button.
2. When the **Options** dialog box appears, enter a caption (such as, **Calculate your ISP cost!**) in the **Caption** text field.
3. Select a **Display Method** list option.
   - **A.** If you choose the **Display in current HTML page** option, go to step 5.
   - **B.** If you choose the **Automatically display as separate window** option, enter the name of the new HTML document in the **HTML File Name** text field. Click the **Next** button.

c. If you choose the **Insert button to load separate window** option, enter the name of the new HTML document in the **HTML File Name** text field. Enter the text that you want to appear on the button in the **Caption on Button** text field. Click the **Next** button.

4. If you choose one of the separate window options, the second **Options** dialog box displays. Here, you can select check boxes from the **Separate Window Options** list and enter **Width** and **Height** measurements.

5. Click the **Finished** Button.

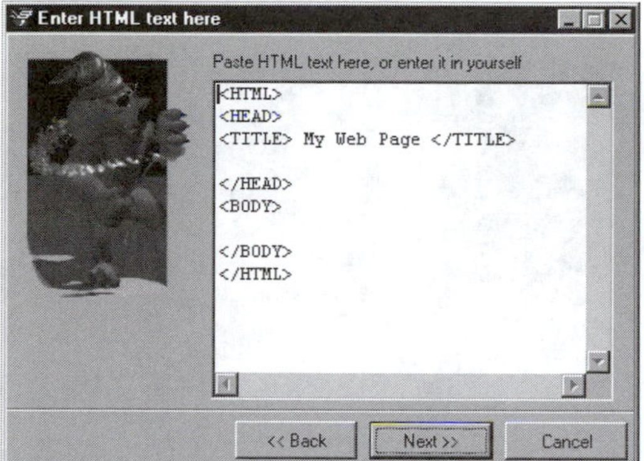

Figure 10. When the **Enter HTML text here** dialog box appears, paste text from a new HTML document in the text area to set up your separate window Web page. You can also enter additional text.

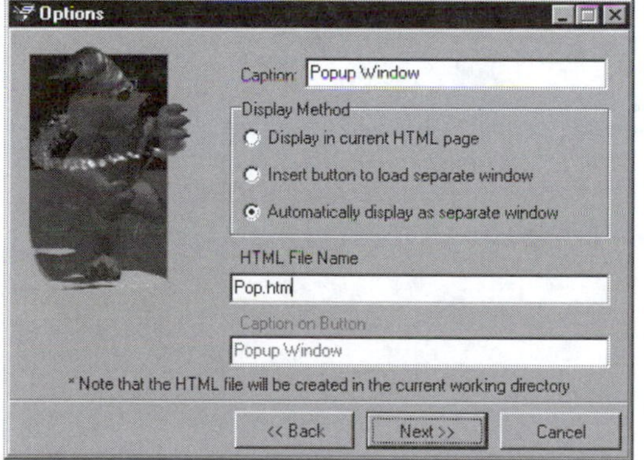

Figure 11. When the **Options** dialog box appears, select the **Automatically display as separate window** radio button and give the new HTML document a file name.

Setting Up a Pop-Up Window

You can create a pop-up Window that launches when people visit your Web page. This gives you a great way to provide updates and make important announcements without having to drastically change your page design. You may have seen commercial Web pages use this technique to advertise new products. When your regular Web page loads in the user's browser, the pop-up window automatically displays. After viewing the pop-up window's contents, users can close it and continue exploring your Web site.

Think of pop-up windows as small Web pages. Once **JavaScript Tools** helps you generate the script and the HTML document, you can update the pop-up window HTML document's content any time you want.

To set up a Pop-Up Window

1. Return to the HotDog Pro application window, open a new HTML document, select all the text and copy it to the clipboard using the **CTRL+C** key combination.
2. Select **Pop-Up Window** from the **JavaScript Tools** scrolling list, then click **Next**.
3. When the **Enter HTML text here** dialog box appears, as shown in Figure 10, use the **CTRL+V** key combination to paste the HTML document text into the text area. You can also enter any text you wish to include.

4. Click the **Next** button.

5. When the **Options** dialog box appears, as shown in Figure 11, select the **Automatically display as separate window** radio button, enter a file name for the separate window in the **HTML File Name** text field, and click the **Next** button.

6. When the second **Options** dialog box appears, as shown in Figure 12, you can specify the separate window's dimensions in the **Width** and **Height** text fields. You can also choose to display browser interface elements, such as scrollbars, by selecting checkboxes from the **Separate Window Options** list.

7. Click the **Finished** button to place the code for launching a separate pop-up window from the current HTML document.

Figure 12. When the second **Options** dialog box appears, enter height and width measurements for the pop-up window.

Figure 13. A jump list gives visitors an easy way to find their way around your site.

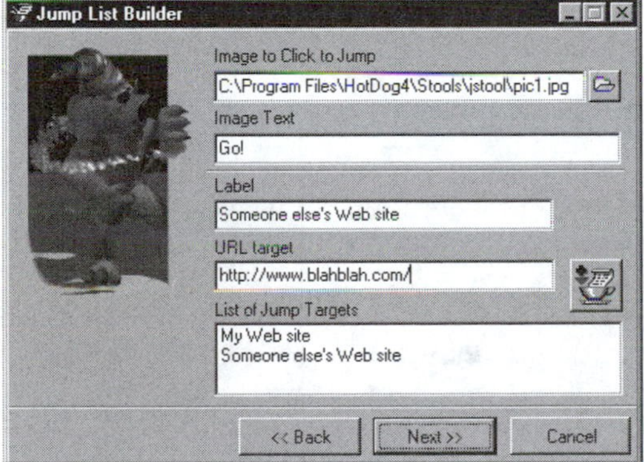

Figure 14. The **Jump List Builder** helps you generate a list of links.

Making a Jump List

Jump lists, like the one shown in Figure 13, give your visitors a handy way to navigate your Web page. **JavaScript Tools** helps you create a pull-down list with links. Users can select items from the pull-down list and click the **Go!** button to jump to the link. While jump lists are ideal for large Web sites with lots of sections and pages, they look slick and professional on any Web site.

To make a jump list

1. Select **Jump List** from the **JavaScript Tools** list.
2. When the **Jump List Builder** dialog box appears, as shown in Figure 14, you can create your list of links.
   - **A.** Enter the relative path name to your **Go!** button image in the **Image to Click to Jump** text field.
   - **B.** Enter alternative text for the **Go!** button image in the **Image Text** text field.
   - **C.** Enter the text you want to display as a list item in the **Label** text field.
   - **D.** Enter the HTML document name or URL you want to link to in the **URL target** text field.
   - **E.** Click the **Add Jump Target to List** button to add the current item to the **List of Jump Targets** (it looks like a coffee cup with a piece of paper inside of it).
   - **F.** Repeat steps A-E to add more items to the **List of Jump Targets**.
3. Click the **Next** button.

4. When the **Options** dialog box appears, as shown in Figure 15, enter a caption for your jump list in the **Caption** text field, and select an item from the **Display Method** list.

   A. If you choose the **Display in current HTML page** option, go to step 6.

   B. If you choose the **Automatically display as separate window** option, enter the name of the new HTML document in the **HTML File Name** text field. Click the **Next** button.

   C. If you choose the **Insert button to load separate window** option, enter the name of the new HTML document in the **HTML File Name** text field. Enter the text that you want to appear on the button in the **Caption on Button** text field. Click the **Next** button.

5. If you choose one of the separate window options, the second **Options** dialog box displays. Here, you can select check boxes from the **Separate Window Options** list and enter **Width** and **Height** measurements.

6. Click the **Finished** button.

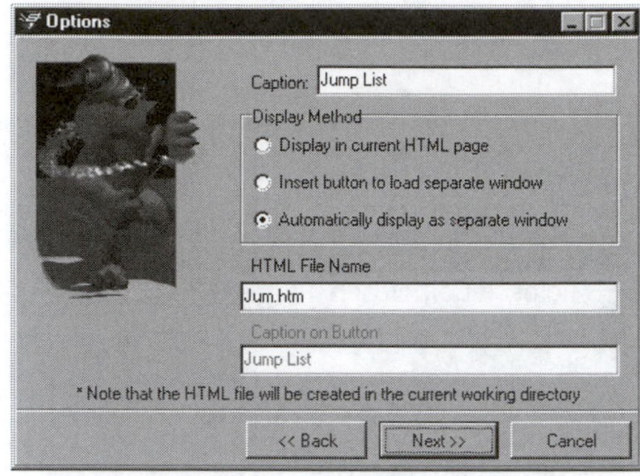

Figure 15. You can choose how to display your jump list by selecting items from the **Options** dialog box.

✔ Tips

- You can use any image you want as the **Go!** button for your jump list.
- Try to avoid adding more than 10 items to your jump list.
- Some of your visitors may not be used to using pull-down lists to navigate Web sites. Consider including some quick instructions on your page.

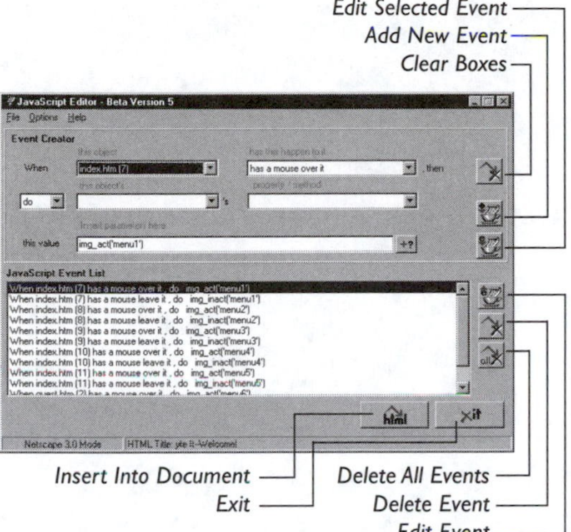

Figure 16. The **JavaScript Editor** makes it easy for JavaScript-savvy users to edit JavaScript scripts.

✔ Tips

- The **JavaScript Language Editor** is not designed for beginners—in order to make use of this tool, you need a basic knowledge of how JavaScript works.
- If you can learn HTML, then you can easily learn JavaScript. A good introductory book, like the *JavaScript for the World Wide Web Visual QuickStart Guide* by Tom Negrino and Dori Smith, can help you get up and running in no time.
- You can find lots of links to tutorials, ready-made JavaScript scripts, and other JavaScript resources at EarthWeb's Gamelan site (*www.gamelan.com*).
- When you generate scripts with **JavaScript Tools** and add them to your HTML documents, launch the **JavaScript Language Editor** and take a peek at your script. While this may not make you an expert, you can get a glimpse of how JavaScript works.

Customizing JavaScript with the JavaScript Language Editor

Do you know a little JavaScript? If so, take a look at the **JavaScript Language Editor**, as shown in Figure 16. The **JavaScript Language Editor** helps you edit and customize JavaScript scripts that you generate with **JavaScript Tools**, download from the Web (with the author's permission, of course!), or create yourself. If you don't know JavaScript yet, never fear. It's designed for non-programmers and isn't hard to learn.

JavaScript scripts consist of pairs of *events* and *events handlers*. Events occur as users interact with your Web pages. Events handlers tell the browser what happens when a visitor triggers an event—for example, when a user clicks the "Start" button (the event), a timer starts running (as instructed by the event handler).

The **JavaScript Editor** displays all editable JavaScript events in the current HTML document. You can make changes by selecting items from the **JavaScript Event List**, then choosing options from the pull-down lists. The top row of lists displays the selected event and the object it applies to (such as a button or image), and the bottom rows of lists provide options for specifying events handlers.

To launch the JavaScript Language Editor

1. Open an HTML document that contains a JavaScript script.
2. Select **JavaScript Language Editor** from the **SuperToolz** menu.

To edit a JavaScript event

1. Select an event from the **JavaScript Event List**.
2. Click the **Edit Event** button.
3. When the event's components appear as items in the **Event Creator** pull-down lists, you can make edits by selecting permissible items from the pull-down lists, or by entering new text.

To add a new JavaScript event

1. Click the **New Event** button.
2. Select permissible items from the pull-down lists.

To remove a JavaScript event

1. Select an item from the **JavaScript Event List**.
2. Click the **Delete** button.

To add changes to the HTML document

1. Click the **Compile HTML** button.

12

Setting Up Style Sheets

Do you want your Web pages to look more like the kind of page layouts you can design with your desktop publishing program or word processor? With Cascading Style Sheets (CSS), you can create pages with margins, borders, and other sophisticated formatting attributes. And best of all—even if you don't want to get that fancy—you can create style sheets that automatically apply font styles so you don't have to format all of the text yourself. When you want to change the look of your Web pages, you can simply change the styles instead of tediously reformatting text. HotDog Pro makes it easy for you to set up styles.

So what's the catch? Netscape Navigator doesn't support as many CSS (style sheet) attributes as Internet Explorer—so you have to preview pages to make sure they look good in both browsers. In addition, older browsers (pre-Internet Explorer 3.0 or Netscape Navigator 4.0) can't display CSS formatting at all. So you have to design your pages so they would still look good without the CSS style sheets applied. Nonetheless, it's fun to be ahead of the game—and style sheets can definitely save you time. For links to more information about style sheets, visit the Cascading Style Sheets page at weber.u.washington.edu/~rells/css/index.html.

Creating Styles

With HTML, you format text—such as headings, paragraphs, and list items—by enclosing the text with the appropriate HTML tag. With style sheets, you can create default text formatting attributes for each tag and apply them to your HTML documents. These lists of tags with text formatting attributes are *styles*. You can either select the styles you create and insert them directly into an HTML document, or create a style sheet document with the **.CSS** file name extension, and link your HTML documents to it. When you open styled HTML documents in a browser, the text displays with the styles applied.

HotDog Pro's user-friendly **Edit Styles** dialog boxes make it easy for you to attach styles to different HTML tags. You can then select styles from the CSS Style Sheets toolbar's pull-down list to apply them to a document. Before you begin, display the CSS Style Sheets toolbar by selecting **Toolbars** from the **View** menu, and then selecting **CSS Style Sheets** from the pull-down list.

To create a new style

1. Click the **Edit Styles** button on the CSS Style Sheets toolbar, as shown in Figure 1.
2. When the **Style Sheets** dialog box appears, read the explanatory text and click **OK**. You can also click the **Don't show me this screen again** check box if you don't want this dialog box to display in the future.
3. When the **Edit Styles** dialog box appears, as shown in Figure 2, click the **New** button.
4. When the next **Edit Styles** dialog box appears, as shown in Figure 3, enter a name for your new style in the **Name** text field.

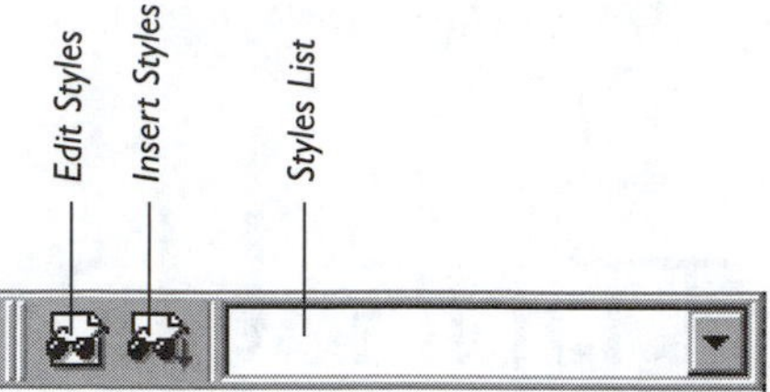

Figure 1. Click the **Edit Styles** CSS Style Sheets toolbar button to display the **Style Sheets** dialog box.

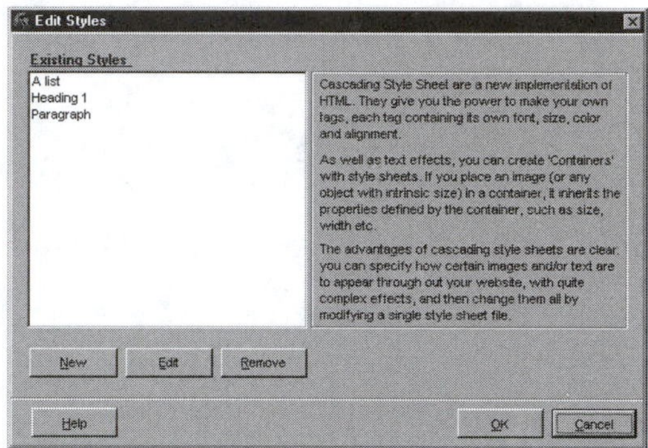

Figure 2. The first **Edit Styles** dialog box displays a list of **Existing Styles** that you can select and edit. Or you can click the **New** button to create a new style.

✔ Tips

- You can specify properties for as many, or as few, style sheet parameters as you wish. *Parameters* is computerese for sets of variables. As this chapter explains, style sheet parameters include text, effects, borders, and more.
- You can create as many styles for an HTML tag as you want. However, you can't use two different styles for the same tag in the same HTML document.
- To display the expanded list of style parameters, as shown in Figure 3, click the **+** signs next to the **Text** and **Container** list items.

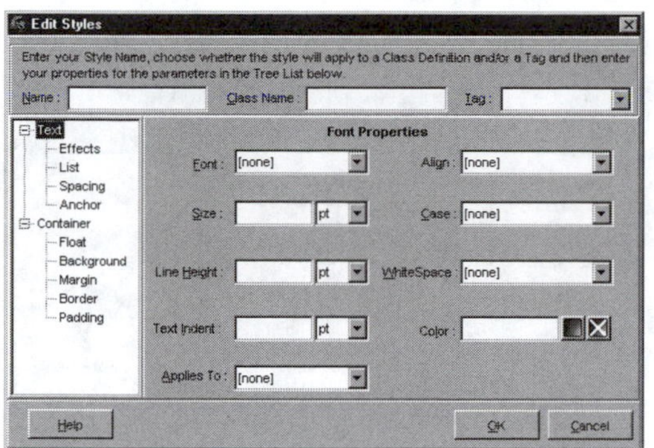

Figure 3. The second **Edit Styles** dialog box displays options so you can name a style, select the HTML tag you want to apply it to, and select parameters to specify properties for.

5. You can either apply a style to an entire class of tags by entering the class name in the **Class Name** text field, or you can select a specific tag from the **Tag** list.

6. Select parameters from the list area and enter properties settings (the rest of the chapter explains how to set different types of parameters in greater detail).

7. Click **OK** to return to the first **Edit Styles** dialog box.

8. From the first **Edit Styles** dialog box, you can create additional styles, click **OK** to save your new styles and return to the HotDog Pro application window, or click **Cancel** to return to the HotDog Pro application window without saving your changes.

9. When you create new styles, they appear in the first **Edit Styles** dialog box's **Existing Styles** list, and as items on the CSS Style Sheets toolbar's **Insert Style** list.

Specifying Text Parameters

Text parameters are easy to incorporate into your style sheets and Web page designs. They change the appearance and style of your fonts, but do not affect the positioning of page elements (as *container* parameters do). If a visitor has Internet Explorer 3.0 or Netscape Navigator 4.0 or higher, your pages look fabulous. If a visitor has an older browser, your pages still look fine and they won't know what they're missing.

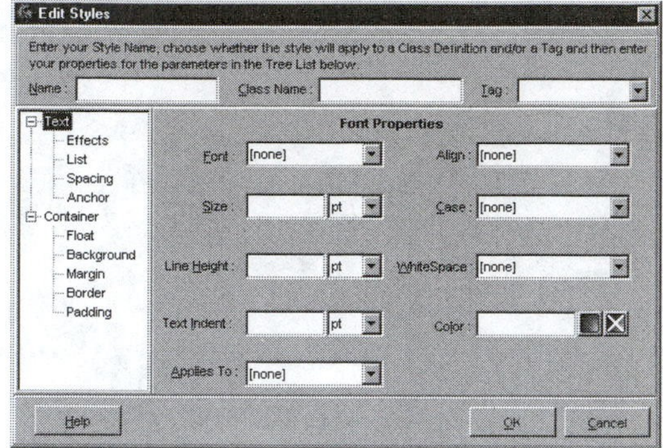

Figure 3a. To specify properties for text parameters, select **Text** from the **Edit Styles** dialog box and choose options.

Text parameter categories

- **Text:** For specifying basic text parameters, such as the font, font size, alignment, and indentation. To specify basic text parameters, select **Text** from the **Edit Styles** list, then enter settings in the **Edit Styles—Text** dialog box (shown in Figure 3a).
- **Effects:** For specifying basic font styles, such as bold and italicized text. To specify parameters for font effects, select **Effects** from the **Edit Styles** list, then enter settings in the **Edit Styles—Effects** dialog box (shown in Figure 4).
- **List:** For specifying bullet styles and indenting. To specify List parameters, select **List** from the **Edit Styles** list, then enter settings in the **Edit Styles—List** dialog box (shown in Figure 5).
- **Spacing:** For specifying space between letters and words (shown in Figure 6).
- **Anchor:** For applying styles to unvisited, visited, and active links (shown in Figure 7).

✔ Tips

- The WhiteSpace style parameter is tricky. Use it with caution. For example, the **NoWrap** option prevents your text from automatically wrapping. Unless you insert line breaks, text extends beyond the browser's display area.
- If you select an item from the **Applies To** list (to apply a style to only the first letter or line of text that is formatted with a particular HTML tag), you'll need to create an additional style to apply to the rest of the text that appears within the same HTML tag. This is an exception to the "only one style per tag in one HTML document" rule.

Text parameter properties

For specifying basic text parameters, such as the font, font size, alignment, and indentation, as shown in Figure 3a.

- **Font:** To pick a font, select it from the **Font** list.
- **Size:** To specify a font size, enter a number in the **Size** text field. You can also choose a unit of measurement by selecting it from the drop-down list.
- **Line Height:** To specify the distance between lines of text, enter a number in the **Line Height** text field. You can also choose a unit of measurement by selecting it from the drop-down list.
- **Text Indent:** To specify how far text should indent, enter a number in the **Text Indent** text field. You can also choose a unit of measurement by selecting it from the drop-down list.
- **Applies To:** You can also apply a style to the first letter or line of text within a tag by selecting an item from the **Applies To** list.
- **Align:** To specify whether the text aligns to the middle, right, or left, select an item from the **Align** list.
- **Case:** To display text in all uppercase or all lowercase, select an item from the **Case** list.
- **WhiteSpace:** You can select settings to determine how the browser handles text wrapping and line breaks by selecting an item from the **WhiteSpace** list.
- **Color:** You can specify a color for the text by clicking the **Color** selection box to display the **Colors** palette dialog box.

Effects parameter properties

For specifying basic font styles, such as bold and italicized text, as shown in Figure 4.

- **Bold:** To bold text, click the **Bold** checkbox.
- **Italic:** To italicize text, click the **Italic** checkbox.
- **Strikethrough:** To display text with a line through the middle of it (so it looks like someone crossed it out) select the **Strikethrough** checkbox.
- **Blink:** To make the text blink on and off, select the **Blink** checkbox.
- **Underline:** To underline text, select the **Underline** checkbox.
- **Overline:** You can display a line above the text by selecting the **Overline** checkbox.

List parameter properties

For specifying list styles and formatting, as shown in Figure 5.

- **List Style:** When specifying styles for bulleted and numbered lists, you can pick the types of bullets or numbers you want to use by selecting an item from the **List Style** list.
- **URL:** For bulleted lists, you can also choose to use an image as a bullet, instead of a character by entering the image's file name and directory path in the **URL** text field.
- **List Position:** You can choose how to indent your lists by selecting an option from the **List Position** list. **Inside** wraps text beneath the list number or bullet. **Outside** indents text from the list number or bullet.

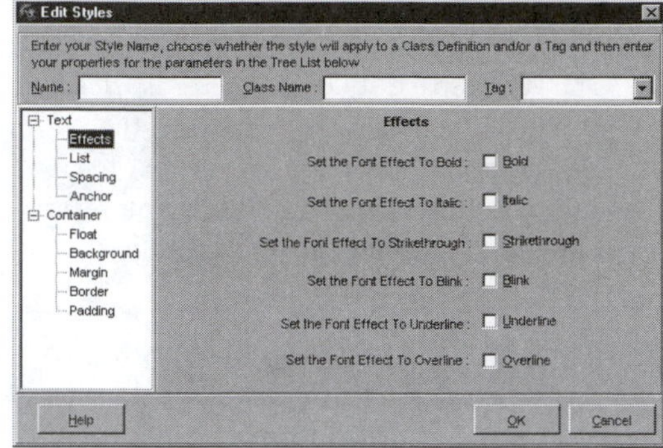

Figure 4. You can specify font effects properties in the **Edit Styles—Effects** dialog box.

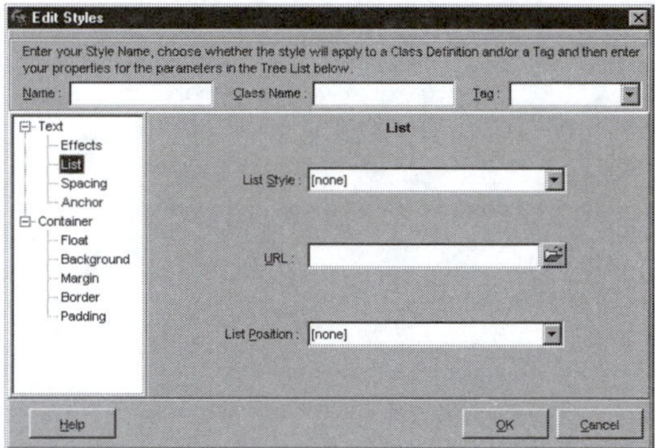

Figure 5. You can specify list properties in the **Edit Styles—List** dialog box.

✔ Tips

- Use the **Blink** property sparingly. It distracts visitors from the other content on your Web page.
- Be careful if you choose to underline text—people may mistake underlined text for links!

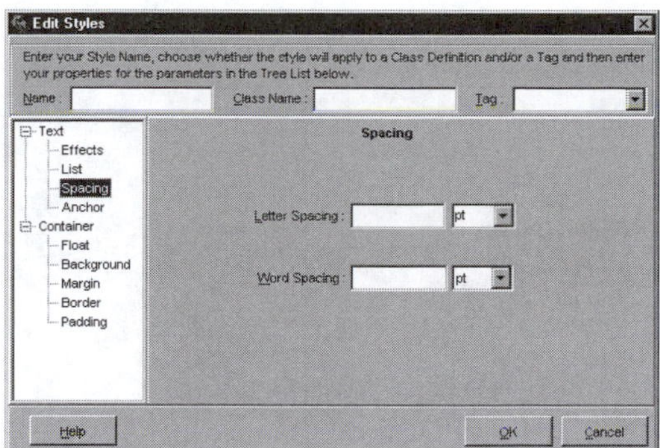

Figure 6. You can specify spacing properties in the **Edit Styles—Spacing** dialog box.

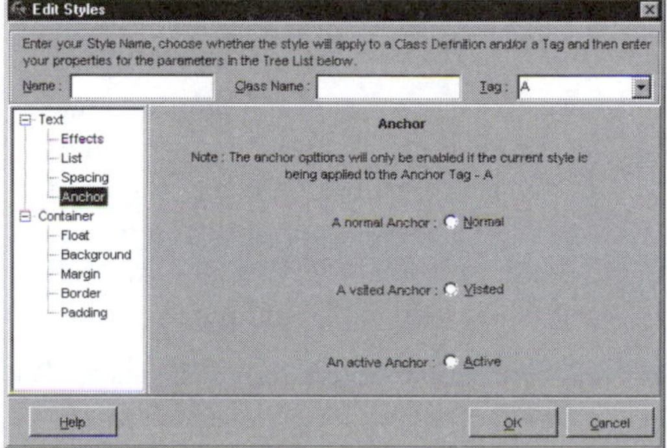

Figure 7. You can specify anchor tag properties for linked text in the **Edit Styles—Anchor** dialog box.

✔ Tip

■ If you select a radio button to apply a style to a normal, visited, or active anchor, then you need to create additional style sheets for the other types of anchors. This is an exception to the "only one style per tag in one HTML document" rule.

Spacing parameter properties

For specifying spacing between letters and words, as shown in Figure 6.

- **Letter Spacing:** You can specify an amount of space to display between letters by entering a number in the **Letter Spacing** text field. You can also choose a unit of measurement by selecting it from the drop-down list.
- **Word Spacing:** You can specify an amount of space to display between words by entering a number in the **Word Spacing** text field. You can also choose a unit of measurement by selecting it from the drop-down list.

Anchor parameter properties

For applying styles to normal, visited, and active links, as shown in Figure 7.

- **A Normal Anchor:** When creating a style for an anchor (link) tag, you can select the **Normal** radio button to specify a style for how links appear before the user clicks on it.
- **A Visited Anchor:** When creating a style for an anchor tag, you can select the **Visited** radio button to specify a style for how links appear after the user clicks on it.
- **An Active Anchor:** When creating a style for an anchor tag, you can select the **Active** radio button to specify a style for how links appear while the user clicks on it.

Specifying Container Parameters

Style sheets can also help you create impressive page layouts. You can set *container* parameters to determine the positioning of text in relation to other text and page elements. Container parameters enable text to behave more like an image or other page element. For example, you can set text up to display in a box with its own background and borders, and determine how text flows around the container.

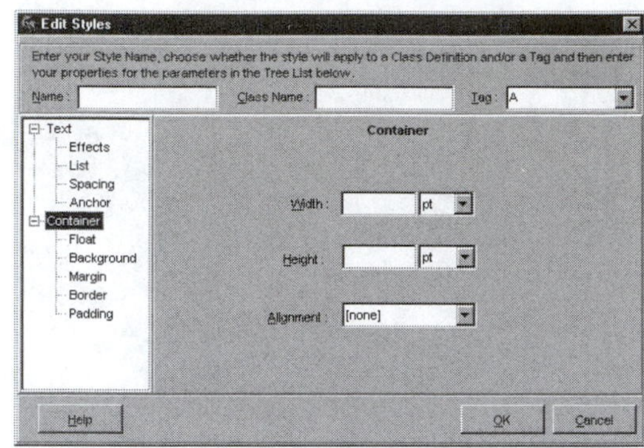

Figure 8. You can specify container properties in the **Edit Styles—Container** dialog box.

Container parameters

- **Container:** For specifying the width, height, and alignment of the container (as shown in Figure 8).
- **Float:** For specifying how text wraps around the container (as shown in Figure 9).
- **Background:** For specifying a background color or image for your container (as shown in Figure 10).
- **Margin:** For specifying the amount of space that appears between the container and external page elements (as shown in Figure 11).
- **Border:** For specifying border width and style (as shown in Figure 12).
- **Padding:** For specifying the amount of space that appears between the edges of the container and the text inside of the container (as shown in Figure 13).

Container parameter properties

For specifying the size and alignment of the container, as shown in Figure 8.

- **Width:** To specify a width for your container, enter a number in the **Width** text field. You can also choose a unit of measurement by selecting it from the drop-down list.

✔ Tips

- When you specify colors for style parameters, a series of numbers separated by commas appear in the text field. These are RGB color values. RGB stands for red, green, and blue—computers combine these three colors to create all of the other colors you see on the computer screen.
- Backgrounds for containers (as well as Web pages and tables) are generated from a single, small image. The image *tiles* across the Web page, table, table cell, or container to form a patterned background. *Tiling* means repeating an image over and over again until it fills a space, the same way you would place tiles on a kitchen or bathroom floor until the floor is covered.

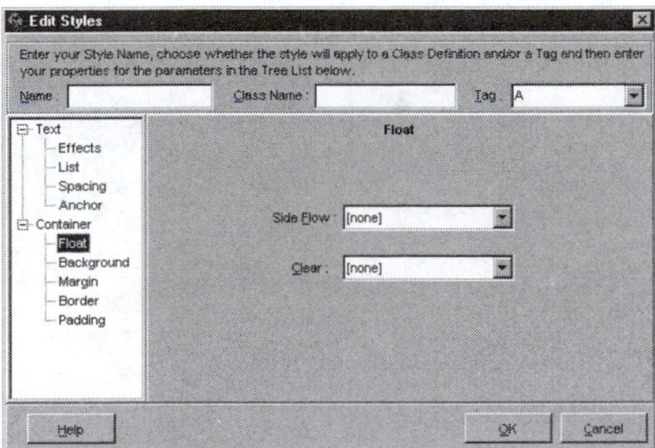

Figure 9. You can specify float properties in the **Edit Styles—Float** dialog box.

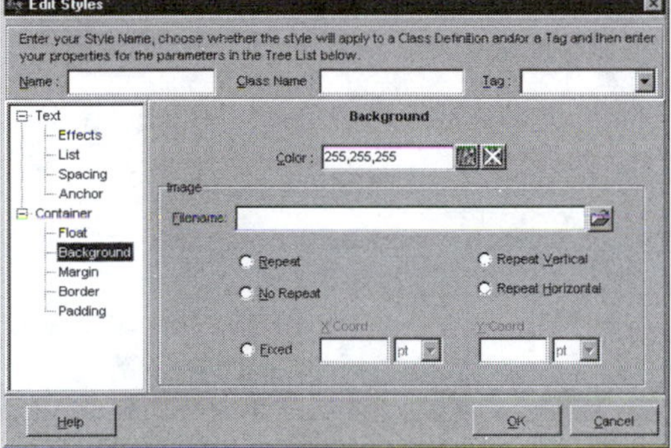

Figure 10. You can specify background properties in the **Edit Styles—Background** dialog box.

- **Height:** To specify a height for your container, enter a number in the **Height** text field. You can also choose a unit of measurement by selecting it from the drop-down list.
- **Alignment:** To specify whether the container aligns to the left, center, or right side of the page, select an option from the **Alignment** list.

Float parameter properties

For specifying how text flows around the container, as shown in Figure 9.

- **Side Flow:** You can choose to have text flow along the left, right, or both sides of the container by selecting an option from the **Side Flow** list.
- **Clear:** You can choose to exclude text from flowing along the left, right, or both sides of the container by selecting an option from the **Clear** list.

Background parameter properties

For specifying how the container's background displays, as shown in Figure 10.

- **Color:** To specify a background color for your container, click the **Color** selection button. When the **Color** palette dialog box appears, pick a color and click **OK** to return to the **Edit Styles** dialog box. When you select a color, the series of numbers that represents the color appears in the **Color** text field.
- **Image:** You can also specify a background image for the container by entering the file name and directory path in the **Filename** text field. To determine how your background image *tiles* (repeats itself) across the container to create the pattern, you can select one of the **Repeat** options by clicking a radio button.

Margin parameter properties

For specifying the amount of space between the container and the surrounding text, as shown in Figure 11.

- **Top:** To specify the amount of space that appears between the top of the container and the text above it, enter a number in the **Top** text field. Select a unit of measurement from the list.
- **Right:** To specify the amount of space that appears between the right side of the container and the text to the right of it, enter a number in the **Right** text field. Select a unit of measurement from the list.
- **Bottom:** To specify the amount of space that appears between the bottom of the container and the text below it, enter a number in the **Bottom** text field. Select a unit of measurement from the list.
- **Left:** To specify the amount of space that appears between the left side of a container and the text to the left of it, enter a number in the **Left** text field. Select a unit of measurement from the drop-down list.

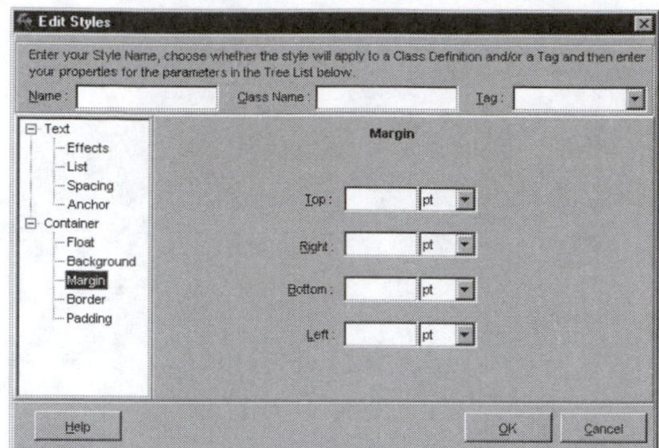

Figure 11. You can specify margin properties in the **Edit Styles—Margin** dialog box.

Border parameter properties

For specifying border properties, as shown in Figure 12.

- **Left:** You can specify a thin, medium, or thick border for the left side of the container by selecting an option from the **Left** list in the **Size** column. Choose a border style from the **Left** list in the **Style** column.
- **Right:** You can specify a thin, medium, or thick border for the right side of the container by selecting an option from the **Right** list in the **Size** column. Choose a border style from the **Right** list in the **Style** column.

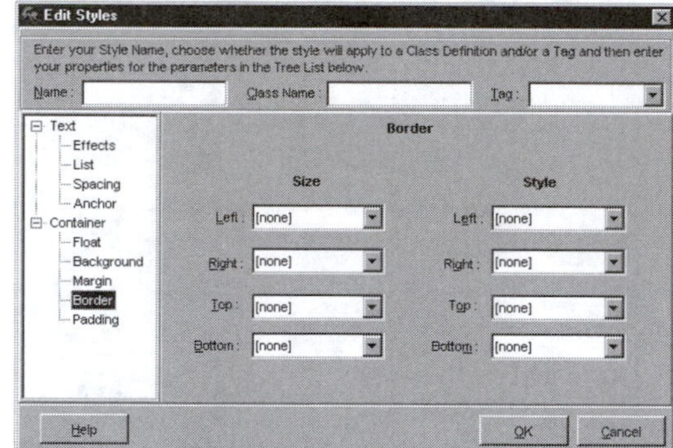

Figure 12. You can specify border properties in the **Edit Styles—Border** dialog box.

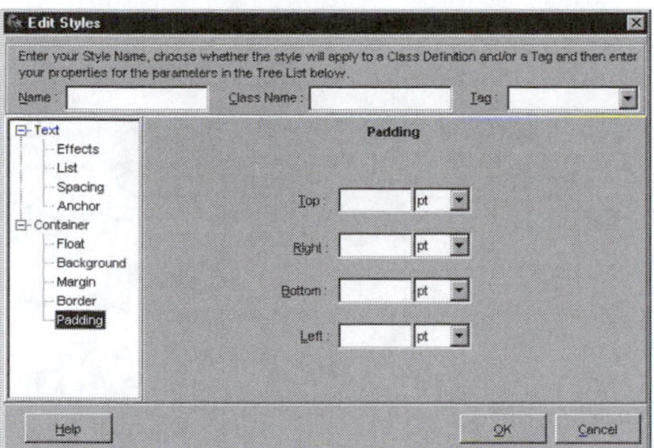

Figure 13. You can specify padding properties in the **Edit Styles—Padding** dialog box.

✔ Tips

- If you specify properties for your style's container parameters, be sure to preview pages in multiple browsers. Older browsers don't support styles. Even the latest versions of Netscape Navigator and Internet Explorer don't interpret style sheets in exactly the same way. Because container settings affect the positioning of page elements, you need to make sure that your pages look acceptable to all of your visitors.
- For best results with borders, you should enter the same size and style for each side of the container when specifying **Border** properties.

- **Top:** You can specify a thin, medium, or thick border for the top side of the container by selecting an option from the **Top** list in the **Size** column. Choose a border style from the **Top** list in the **Style** column.
- **Bottom:** You can specify a thin, medium, or thick border for the bottom side of the container by selecting an option from the **Bottom** list in the **Size** column. Choose a border style from the **Bottom** list in the **Style** column.

Padding parameter properties

For specifying space between the container borders and the text inside the container, as shown in Figure 13.

- **Top:** To specify the amount of space that appears between the top of the container and the text inside the container, enter a number in the **Top** text field. Select a unit of measurement from the list.
- **Right:** To specify the amount of space that appears between the right side of the container and the inside of the container, enter a number in the **Right** text field. Select a unit of measurement from the list.
- **Bottom:** To specify the amount of space that appears between the bottom of the container and the text inside of the container, enter a number in the **Bottom** text field. You can also choose a unit of measurement by selecting it from the drop-down list.
- **Left:** To specify the amount of space that appears between the left side of a container and the text inside of the container, enter a number in the **Left** text field. You can also choose a unit of measurement by selecting it from the drop-down list.

Applying Styles to HTML Documents

Once you create a set of styles, you can begin using them in your Web pages. There are two ways to apply styles to your HTML documents with HotDog Pro. You can either insert styles directly into the current document, or you can create a style sheet document and link HTML documents to the style sheet.

To apply styles to the current document

1. From the HotDog application window, click the **Insert Style Sheet** toolbar button.
2. When the **Insert Styles** dialog box appears, as shown in Figure 14, click the **Insert a Style into the current document** button.
3. When the second **Insert Styles** dialog box appears, as shown in Figure 15, select the styles you want to apply from the **Available Styles** list.
4. Click the **Add to List** button to display selected styles in the **Current Styles in Document** list.
5. Click **OK** to insert the style sheet (list of styles, parameters, and properties) in your HTML document and return to the HotDog Pro application window.

When you enclose text and page elements with styled tags, the styles are automatically applied. You can also highlight text and select styles from the CSS Style Sheets toolbar's pull-down Styles list.

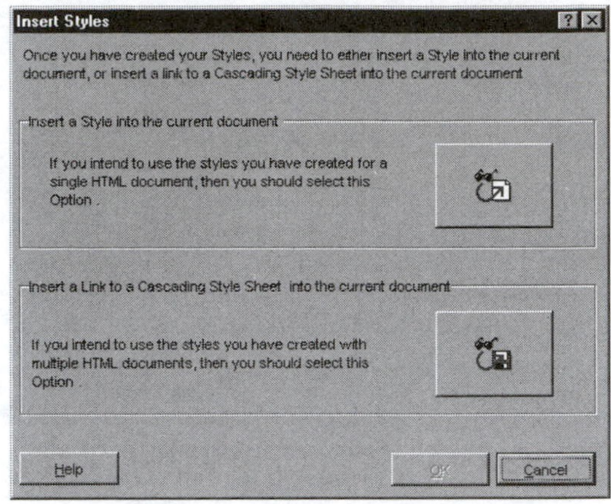

Figure 14. When the **Insert Styles** dialog box appears, click the **Insert a Style into the current document** button to add a style sheet directly to an HTML document.

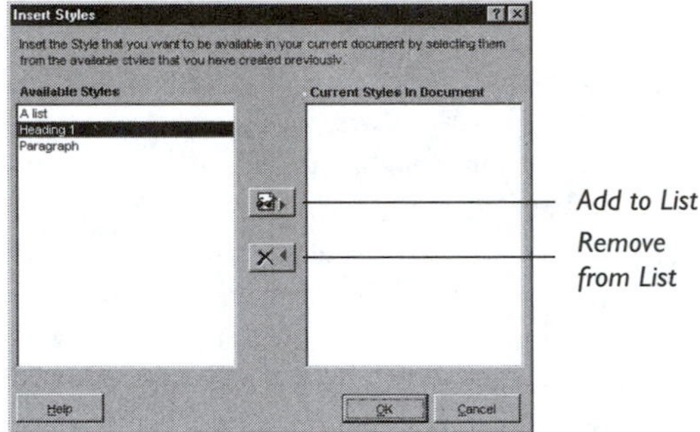

Figure 15. When the second **Insert Styles** dialog box appears, you can select items from the **Available Styles** list and copy the styles to the **Current Styles in Document** list.

✔ Tips

- Creating style sheet (**.CSS**) documents and linking your HTML files to them can save you lots of time and effort.
- You can create a style sheet document and link all of your HTML files to it. When it's time to give your Web site a new look, you'll only need to change one document.

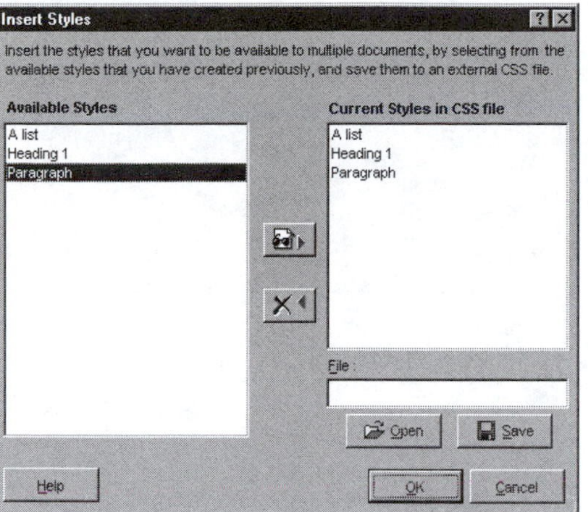

Figure 16. When the second **Insert Styles** dialog box appears, select the styles you want to include in the style sheets document from the **Available Styles** list, then click the **Save** button.

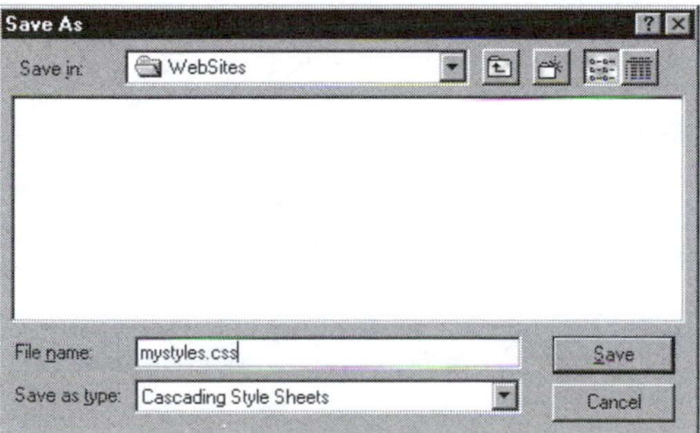

Figure 17. When the **Save As** dialog box appears, you can name and save your style sheets document.

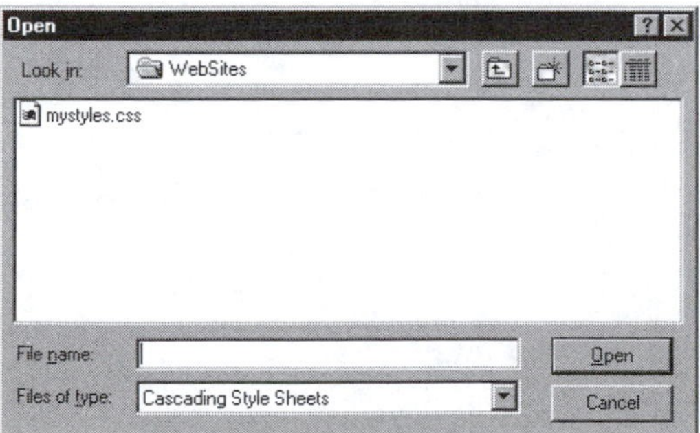

Figure 18. When the **Open** dialog box appears, you can browse for a style sheet (**.CSS**) document.

To create a cascading style sheet (CSS) document

1. From the HotDog Pro application window, click the **Insert Style Sheet** toolbar button.
2. When the **Insert Styles** dialog box appears, click the **Insert a link to a Cascading Style Sheet into the current document** button.
3. When the second **Insert Styles** dialog box appears, as shown in Figure 16, select the a style from the **Available Styles** list.
4. Click the **Add to List** button to add the selected style to the **Current Styles in CSS file** list.
5. When you finish adding styles to the **Current Styles in CSS File** list, click **Save**.
6. When the **Save As** dialog box appears, as shown in Figure 17, browse for a folder and name your file. Style Sheets documents use the **.CSS** file name extension.
7. Click the **Save** button to return to the **Insert Styles** dialog box, then click **OK**.

To link the current HTML file to a CSS document

1. From the HotDog application window, click the **Insert Style Sheet** toolbar button.
2. When the **Insert Styles** dialog box appears, click the **Insert a link to a Cascading Style Sheet into the current document** button.
3. When the second **Insert Styles** dialog box appears, click the **Open** button.
4. When the **Open** dialog box appears, as shown in Figure 18, browse for a style sheet document with the **.CSS** file name extension, then click **Open**.
5. When you return to the **Insert Styles** dialog box, click **OK** to link your document to the style sheet.

Editing Styles

You can edit styles quickly and easily. If you edit a .CSS document, the changes automatically apply to all Web pages that link to the .CSS document. If you apply styles to individual documents, as explained in the "To apply styles to the current document" section, then you'll need to delete existing style information and insert the edited styles.

To edit a style

1. Click the Edit Style button on the CSS Style Sheets toolbar.
2. When the **Style Sheets** dialog box appears (if you haven't disabled it by selecting the **Don't show me this screen again** check box), click the **OK** button.
3. When the **Edit Styles** dialog box appears, select a style from the **Existing Styles** list, then click the **Edit** button.
4. When the second **Edit Styles** dialog box appears, make your changes, then click **OK** to return to the first **Edit Styles** dialog box.
5. You can edit or create more styles, click **OK** to save your changes and return to the HotDog Pro application window, or click **Cancel** to return to the HotDog Pro application window without saving your changes.

To remove a style from the Current Styles in CSS file list

1. Select a style from the **Current Styles in CSS file** list.
2. Click the **Remove** button.

Creating Text Effects

Make some news! The **Text Effects** SuperTool helps you generate exciting Java text effects for special announcements, news, and information updates, like the **Wavy** effect shown in Figure 1. Whether you want your text to scroll, bounce, wave, or gently undulate across the screen, your page can feature attention-grabbing text that moves. Text effects are Java applets, which Chapter 10 explains in greater detail. When you generate Java text effects, the **Text Effects** SuperTool generates a Java applet **CLASS** file and inserts the appropriate HTML code in your current document. Text effects applets can run in any Java-enabled browser.

You can select from a variety of text effects, and preview them to see how they look. When you select a text effect, the **Text Effects** SuperTool provides you with additional options for customizing the text effect, along with a brief explanation about how the text effect behaves.

To create a text effect

1. From the HotDog Pro application window, place your cursor at the insertion point of an HTML document, and select **Text Effects** from the **SuperToolz** menu.
2. When the **Text Effects** application window appears, as shown in Figure 2, enter text in the text area.
3. You can select text formatting options, along with text and background colors by selecting a font style and size from the pull-down lists, and clicking the **Bold**, **Italic**, **Text Color**, or **Background Color** buttons.
4. Specify size and alignment options for your text effect by clicking the **Applet Size Info** button and entering information when the **Applet Size Information** dialog box appears, as shown in Figure 3.
5. Select the effect you want to apply by clicking on one of the text effect tabs.
6. When the options for the selected effect appear, you can select items and fill information in the appropriate text boxes.
7. When you finish, click the **Compile HTML** button to add the text effect to your document.

To preview a text effect

1. Enter your text.
2. Pick a text effect.
3. When the text effect options appear, enter parameters or select items from the radio buttons, check boxes, and lists.
4. Click the **Preview** button. If you have selected more than one browser in your **Preferences**, a cascading menu appears so you can select which broswer to display the applet in.

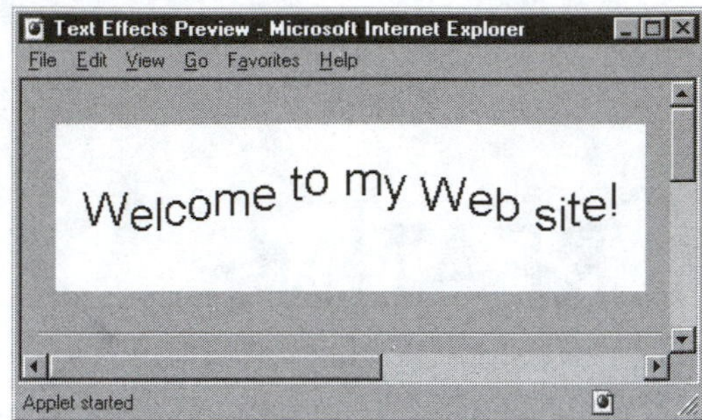

Figure 1. The **Text Effects** SuperTool helps you add animated text effects to your Web pages.

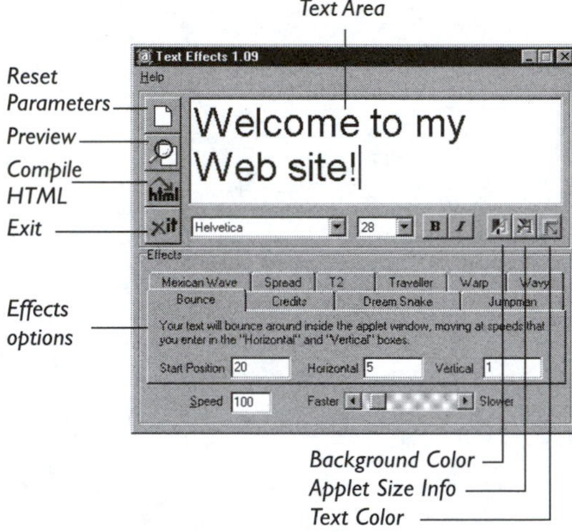

Figure 2. The **Text Effects** application window provides lots of text effects to choose from.

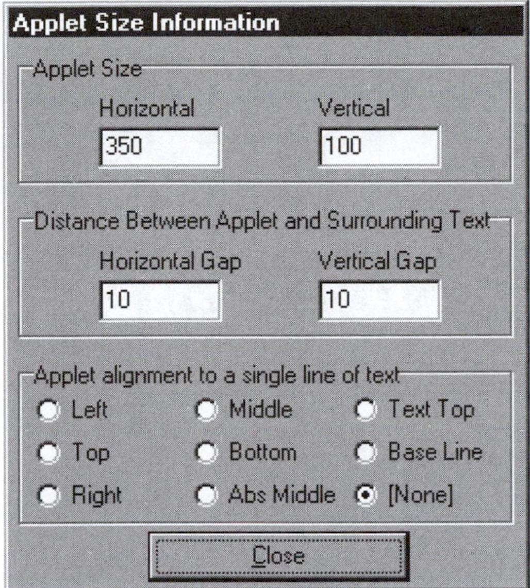

Figure 3. You can specify horizontal and vertical dimensions for your applet, a buffer between the applet and surrounding page elements, and alignment options in the **Applet Size Information** dialog box.

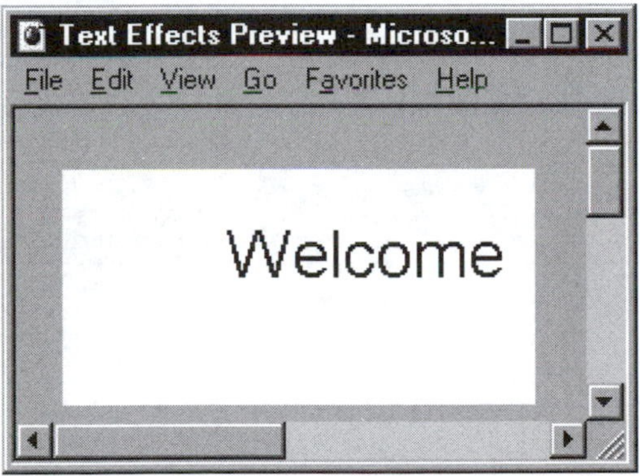

Figure 3a. The **Bounce** text effect.

Bounce

The Bounce effect moves text upwards while it bounces and zig zags from side to side across the applet area, as shown in Figure 3a. You can specify where the applet appears and how frequently the text bounces up and down.

To apply a Bounce text effect

1. From the **Text Effects** window, select font styles, text color, and background color options, and an applet size for the text, then select the **Bounce** option.

2. When the **Bounce** options appear, as shown in Figure 2, enter a number in pixels for where you want the text to begin appearing in the **Start Position** text field to determine where the text first appears.

3. Enter a width measurement for the right and left margins of the text area by entering a number of pixels in the **Horizontal** text field.

4. Enter a height measurement for the top and bottom margins of the text area by entering a number of pixels in the **Vertical** text field.

5. Enter a number for the speed (in milliseconds) at which you want the text to move across the applet area in the **Speed** text field. You can also use the slider to adjust speeds from **Faster** to **Slower**.

6. Click the **Compile HTML** toolbar button to add the effect to your HTML document.

Credits

The Credits effect works like film credits that you see in the movie theater, as shown in Figure 4. Text scrolls upwards from the bottom of the applet area. To separate items, you can press the **Enter** key between entries. The **Credits** effect is ideal for displaying a list of people who contributed content to your Web site.

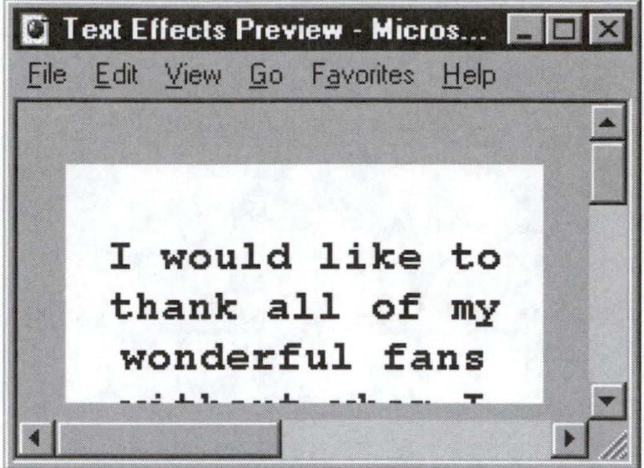

Figure 4. The **Credits** text effect scrolls text upwards like movie credits.

To apply a Credits text effect

1. Enter a list of text items in the text area, select font, text color, and background options, and an applet size for the text, then click the **Credits** tab to display the **Credits** option, as shown in Figure 4a.
2. Enter a number for how fast you want credits to scroll in the **Scroll Speed** text field, or use the **Faster ... Slower** slider to determine how fast lines of text scroll up the applet area.
3. Click the **Compile HTML** toolbar button to add the effect to your HTML document.

Figure 4a. Text **Credits** effect options.

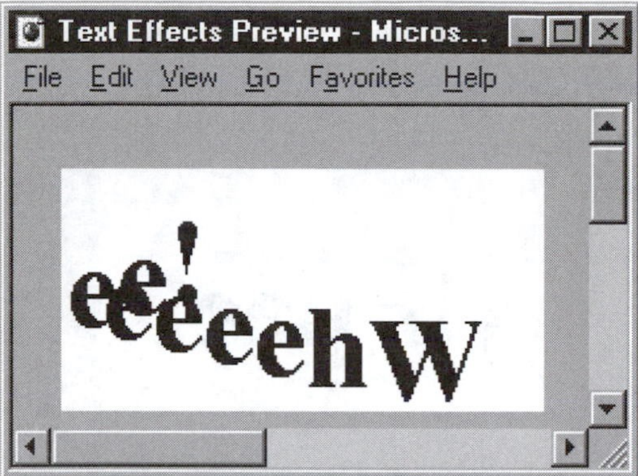

Figure 5. The **Dream Snake** text effect whirls around the applet area.

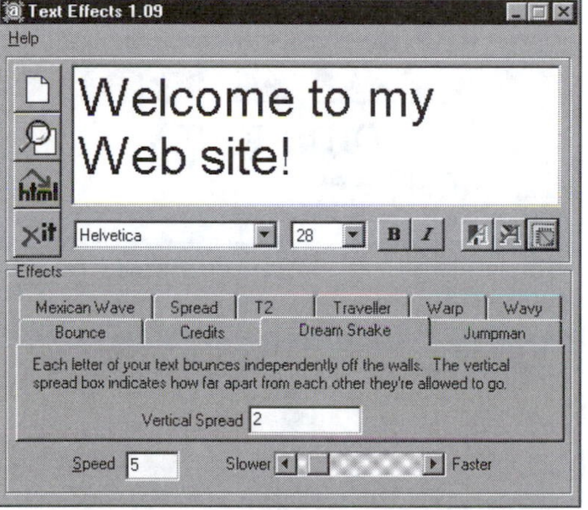

Figure 5a. Settings for the **Dream Snake** text effect.

Dream Snake

The Dream Snake, as shown in Figure 5, works like a perpetual motion gadget. The text moves from right to left and bounces up and down like the **Bounce** effect. But **Dream Snake** text also snakes around, reverses itself, and then bounces backwards from left to right, then wraps around again and repeats.

To apply a Dream Snake text effect

1. Enter text in the text area, and select font, text color, and background color options, and an applet size for the text.
2. Click the **Dream Snake** tab to display the **Dream Snake** options, as shown in Figure 5a.
3. Enter a number for how fast you want the letters to move up and down in the **Vertical Speed** text field.
4. You can also use the **Faster ... Slower** slider to adjust how fast your text moves from right to left.
5. Click the **Compile HTML** toolbar button to add the effect to your HTML document.

Jumpman

With Jumpman, each letter jumps up and down independently of the others, as shown in Figure 6. The letters move up and down at random intervals.

To apply a Jumpman text effect

1. Enter your text in the text area, select font, text color, and background color options, and an applet size for the text.
2. Click the **Jumpman** tab to display **Jump Man** options, as shown in Figure 6a.
3. Enter a number for the maximum jump height in the **Height** text field.
4. Enter a number to determine increments for text jumps in the **Step Size** text field.
5. You can also use the **Faster ... Slower** slider to determine the speed at which text moves across the applet area, or enter a number (in milliseconds) in the **Speed** text field.
6. Click the **Compile HTML** toolbar button to add the effect to your HTML document.

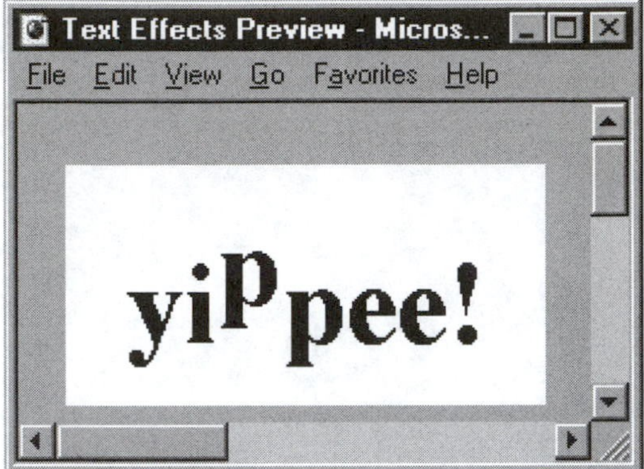

Figure 6. The **Jumpman** text effect bounces each letter up and down.

Figure 6a. Settings for the **Jumpman** text effect.

Figure 7. The **Mexican Wave** text gently bounces while sloping upwards, then bounces back down.

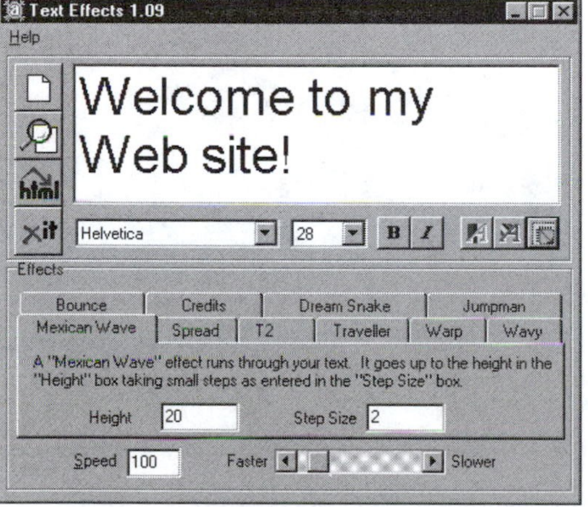

Figure 7a. Settings for the **Mexican Wave** text effect.

Mexican Wave

With the **Mexican Wave** effect, text slopes up, rises, then gently bounces down, as shown in Figure 7. You can determine the maximum height of the text and the step size (how steeply the text rises).

To apply a Mexican Wave text effect

1. From the **Text Effects** window, select font styles, text color, and background color options, then select the **Mexican Wave** option.
2. When the **Mexican Wave** options appear, as shown in Figure 7a, enter a number in the **Height** text field to determine the highest point text rises to.
3. Enter a number to determine the increments in which text rises and descends from the maxium height in the **Step Size** text field.
4. Enter a number for the speed (in milliseconds) at which you want the text to move across the applet area in the **Speed** text field. You can also use the slider to adjust speeds from **Faster** to **Slower**.
5. Click the **Compile HTML** toolbar button to add the effect to your HTML document.

Spread

The Spread effect makes text expand outward, as shown in Figure 8, then contract inward again.

To apply a Spread text effect

1. Enter your text in the text area, select font, text color, and background color options, and an applet size for the text.
2. Click the **Spread** tab to display the **Spread** options, as shown in Figure 8a.
3. Enter a number for the maximum amount of space the text expands to fill in the **Spread Distance** text field.
4. You can also use the **Faster ... Slower** slider to determine the speed at which text moves across the applet area, or enter a number (in milliseconds) in the **Speed** text field.
5. Click the **Compile HTML** toolbar button to add the effect to your HTML document.

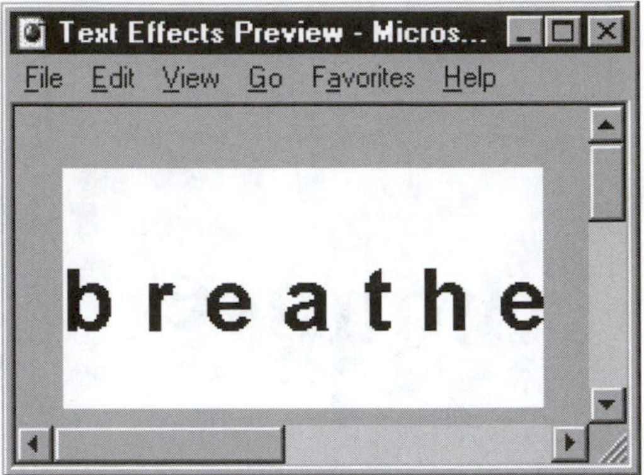

Figure 8. Text with the **Spread** effect applied expands and contracts.

Figure 8a. Settings for the **Spread** text effect.

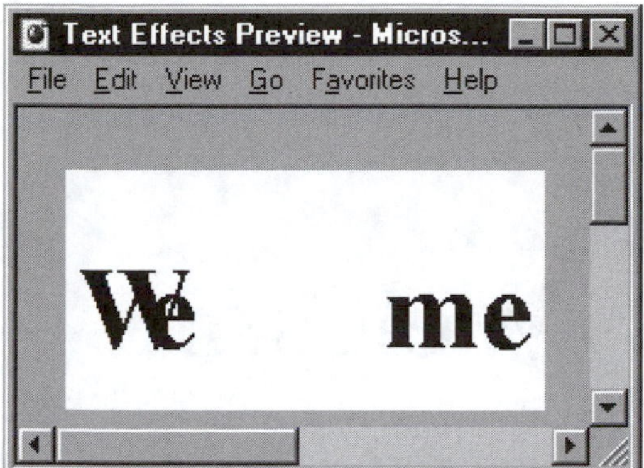

Figure 9. When you apply the **T2** effect to text, letters move into place alternately from the left and the right.

Figure 9. Settings for the **T2** text effect.

T2

Letters move into place alternately from left to right to form the words you enter in the text field, as shown in Figure 9. The T2 effect looks neat, but you should use it with only a few words and high speeds, or else your visitors may lose patience.

To apply a T2 text effect

1. Enter your text in the text area, select font, text color, and background color options, and an applet size for the text.
2. Click the **T2** tab to display **T2** options, as shown in Figure 9a.
3. Enter a number to determine how quickly each letter moves into place in the **Character Speed** text field.
4. You can also use the **Faster … Slower** slider to determine the speed at which text appears in the applet area, or enter a number (in milliseconds) in the **Speed** text field.
5. Click the **Compile HTML** toolbar button to add the effect to your HTML document.

Traveller

Text appears, then the letters fade from right to left and appear again, as shown in Figure 10. You don't need to enter any parameters, however, the people at Sausage Software recommend entering low speeds so your visitors can better appreciate the effect.

To apply a Traveller text effect

1. Enter your text in the text area, select font, text color, and background color options, and an applet size for the text.
2. Click the **Traveller** tab to display **Traveller** options, as shown in Figure 10a.
3. Use the **Faster ... Slower** slider to determine the speed at which text moves across the applet area, or enter a number (in milliseconds) in the **Speed** text field.
4. Click the **Compile HTML** toolbar button to add the effect to your HTML document.

Figure 10. With the **Traveller** text effect, letters fade in and fade out.

Figure 10a. Settings for the **Traveller** text effect.

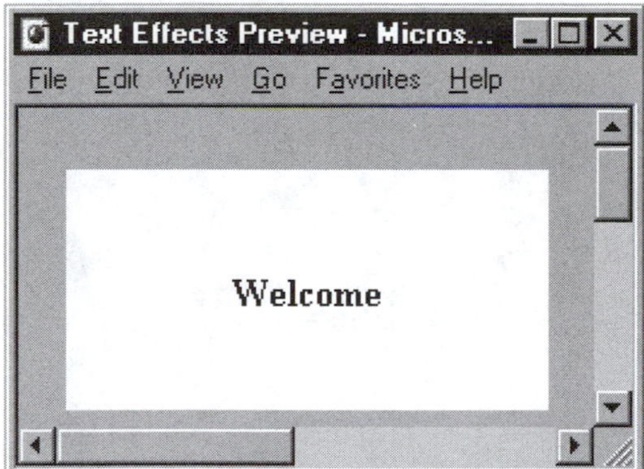

Figure 11. Text with the **Warp** effect applied expands and shrinks.

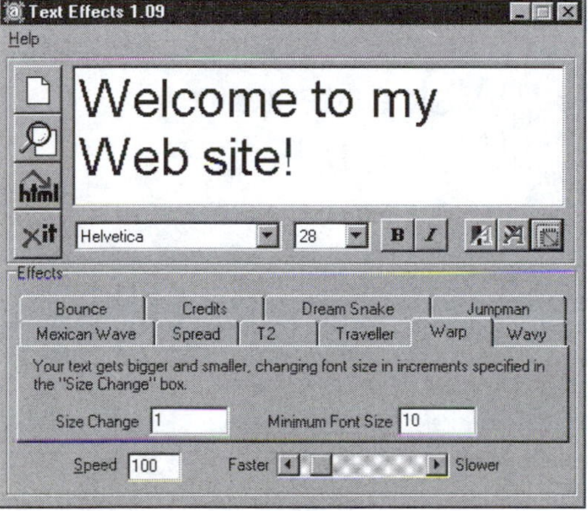

Figure 11a. Settings for the **Warp** text effect.

Warp

Text appears, recedes to a smaller point size (as shown in Figure 11), then gradually expands again. You can specify how quickly the font sizes change.

To apply a Warp text effect

1. Enter your text in the text area, select font, text color, and background color options, and an applet size for the text.
2. Click the **Warp** tab to display **Warp** options, as shown in Figure 11a.
3. Enter a number to determine the incremental font size changes in the **Size Change** text field, and enter a number to determine the smallest font size in the **Minimum Font Size** text field.
4. You can also use the **Faster ... Slower** slider to determine the speed at which text moves across the applet area, or enter a number (in milliseconds) in the **Speed** text field.
5. Click the **Compile HTML** toolbar button to add the effect to your HTML document.

Wavy

Wavy text undulates up and down, and back and forth in a continuous wave. You can specify the speed and height of the waves.

To apply a Wavy text effect

1. Enter your text in the text area, select font, text color, and background color options, and an applet size for the text.
2. Click the **Wavy** tab to display **Wavy** options, as shown in Figure 12a.
3. Enter a maximum height to determine how high the wave rises in the **Height** text field, and enter a number to determine the increment for how quickly text rises and falls in the **Step Size** text field.
4. You can also use the **Faster ... Slower** slider to determine the speed at which text moves across the applet area, or enter a number (in milliseconds) in the **Speed** text field.
5. Click the **Compile HTML** toolbar button to add the effect to your HTML document.

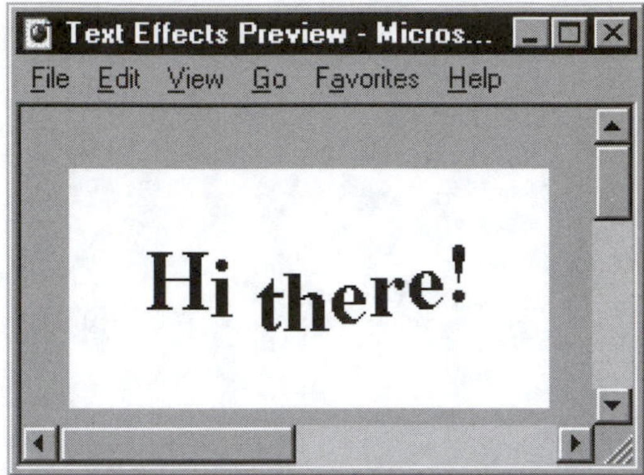

Figure 12. When you apply the **Wavy** text effect, text undulates in a continuous wave.

Figure 12a. Settings for the **Wavy** text effect.

14

Setting Up Online Forms

Electronic forms give you an easy way to get feedback from your visitors. You can ask people questions such as who they are, what they think of your site, and where they like to surf the net. Forms can include text fields, radio buttons, checkboxes, and lists of items. When the visitor finishes filling out the form, they can click the **Submit It!** Button to send their information, or the **Reset** button to cancel their information and start over again. The forms data gets sent to you via email.

Online forms can also help you do business. If you have a secure server (or subscribe to a service that does), you can let your customers order products online by credit card. Even if you aren't ready for online order-taking just yet, visitors can still fill out forms to request information. For more about how HotDog Pro can help you do business online, see Chapter 18.

Form Elements and Form Elements Properties

Online forms, like the one shown in Figure 1, can contain a variety of elements. You can display text fields and text areas so that visitors can type responses. You can also display options as lists, or text items accompanied by radio buttons or checkboxes, so visitors can select items. HotDog Pro's **Form Wizard** helps you create a form, and specify properties for each form element. Properties determine how form elements display, and how form data appears when visitors submit forms to you by email. Table 1 explains the HTML code that the **Form Wizard** generated for the form shown in Figure 1.

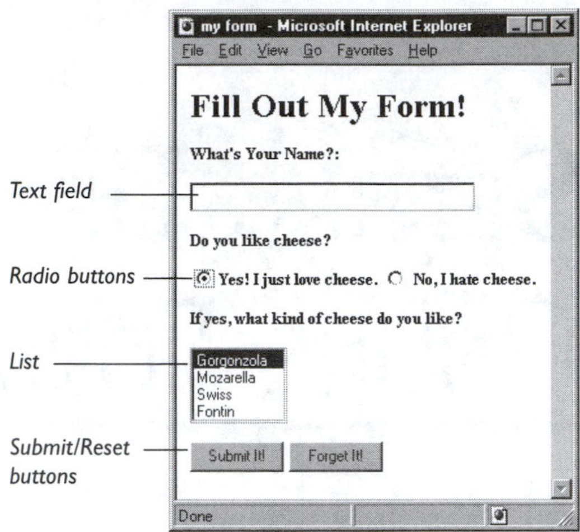

Figure 1. An electronic form with a text field, radio buttons, a list, and submit and reset buttons (Submit It!/ Forget It!).

Form Elements

- **Form declaration:** Forms are enclosed by the **<FORM>...</FORM>** opening and closing tags. The Form Wizard also helps you generate specifications for the **METHOD** and **ACTION** form tag attributes, which tell the server how to process the form when the user clicks the **Submit** button.
- **Checkbox:** Displays a checkbox that users can select to indicate a yes or no response.
- **Radio Button:** Displays a radio button. Radio buttons are ideal for allowing users to select one item from a list of choices.
- **Textbox:** Displays a text entry field so users can type a single line of text, such as a name or address.
- **Hidden Box:** Contains notes and comments about the form for your use only. Hidden Box elements do not display in the browser.

HTML Code for a Form

FORM HTML CODE	WHAT IT MEANS
<H1>Fill Out My Form!</H1>	You can give your form a heading.
<FORM METHOD="POST" ACTION="MAILTO:myself@ myisp.com">	Begins form and specifies how the form gets sent.
<B>What's Your Name?:</B> <P>	You can include text with form elements to prompt users.
<INPUT TYPE="text" NAME= "Name" SIZE="40" VALUE=""> <P>	Specifies a text field that prompts the user to enter their name.
<B>Do you like cheese?</B> <P>	Text prompt for selecting a radio button.
<INPUT TYPE="radio" <B>Yes! I just love cheese.</B>	Text label for the **Yes** radio button.
<INPUT TYPE="radio" NAME="LikesCheese" VALUE="No">	Displays a radio button that indicates **No**.
<B>No. I hate cheese.</B> <P>	Text prompt for the **No** radio button.
<B>If yes, what kind of cheese do you like?</B><P>	Text prompt for selecting an item from the list box.
<SELECT NAME="CheeseType" SIZE="4">	Begins a list box with types of cheeses.
<OPTION VALUE="Gorgonzola" SELECTED>Gorgonzola	Displays Gorgonzola as the default list selection.
<OPTION VALUE="Mozzarella"> Mozzarella	Displays Mozzarella.
<OPTION VALUE="Swiss" >Swiss	Displays Swiss.
<OPTION VALUE="Fontina"> Fontina	Displays Fontina.
</SELECT>	Ends list box.
<P><INPUT TYPE="submit" NAME="Submit" VALUE="Submit It!">	Displays a Submit button that users can click to send you their data.
<INPUT TYPE="reset" VALUE="Forget It!">	Displays a reset button so users can click to cancel.
</FORM>	Ends the form.

Table 1. Code for a typical online form.

- **Password:** Displays a text field so you can have users enter a password. Users cannot submit the form without entering a valid password in the text field.
- **Text Area:** Displays a large text area so users can enter comments and suggestions.
- **List Box:** Displays a list of items that users can select from. A List Box allows users to select more than one choice from the list.
- **Submit Button:** Displays a button that users can click to submit their form data.
- **Reset Button:** Displays a button that users can click to reset the form.
- **Image:** Displays an image that you can display in place of the **Submit** button.

Form Element Properties

- **Input Type:** Specifies a type of form element (such as a text box or radio button).
- **Name:** Assigns a name to the element. When you receive form data by email, the form element's name appears, followed by the value selected or entered by the user.
- **Size:** Determines the size of a text field, text area, or list box.
- **Value:** Specifies a default value for a radio button or check box (such as **Yes** or **No**), or a list item (such as **Gorgonzola**). When you receive form data by email, the form element's value appears preceded by the name associated with that value.

To create a form

1. From the HotDog Pro application window, place your cursor at the insertion point of your document and click the **Form** button on the **Insert** toolbar.
2. When the **Form Wizard** dialog box appears, as shown in Figure 2, read the instructions and click the **Next** button.
3. When the **Form Wizard—Form Element Wizard** dialog box appears, as shown in Figure 3, select a form element from the button bar to display it on the form elements list.
4. When the instructions and options appear for the selected form element, you can specify properties for that element.
5. Repeat Steps 3 and 4 to add other form elements and specify properties for them.
6. When you finish adding form elements, click the **Next** button (the following sections explain form elements in greater detail).
7. When the next **Form Wizard** dialog box appears, as shown in Figure 4, select the **Send all form details to an email address** radio button to have forms data emailed to you. If your server requires you to process forms through a CGI script located on the server, select the **Send form details to a URL**. Click the **Next** button.
8. When the next **Form Wizard** dialog box appears, as shown in Figure 5, enter an email address or a URL in the text field. Click the **Finish** button.
9. When the **Form Wizard** finishes generating the HTML form code in the current HTML document, you can enter text to explain or label each form element.

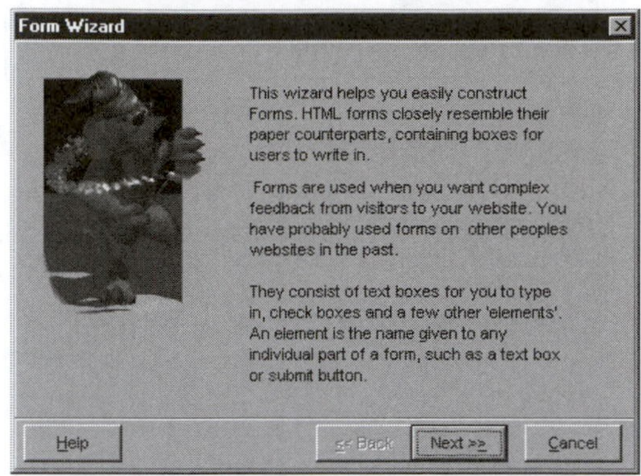

Figure 2. To create a form, click the **Insert Form** toolbar button to launch the **Form Wizard.**

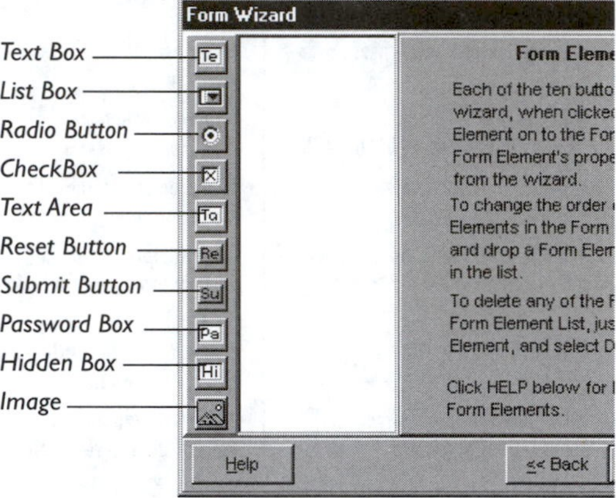

Figure 3. When the **Form Wizard—Form Element Wizard** dialog box appears, you can select form elements and specify properties for them.

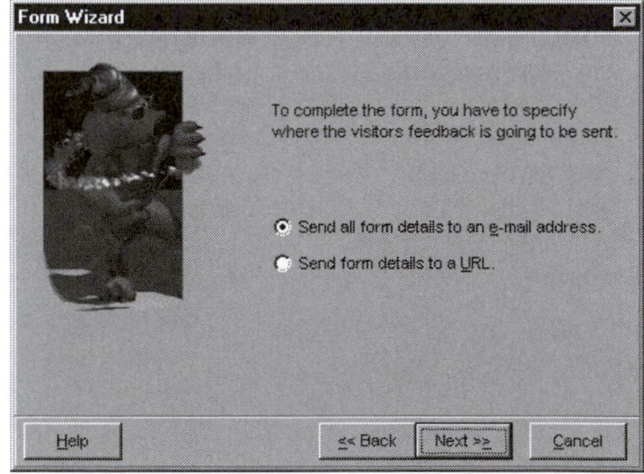

Figure 4. You can have forms data sent directly to your email address, or enter the URL of a CGI script on your server that can process the forms data.

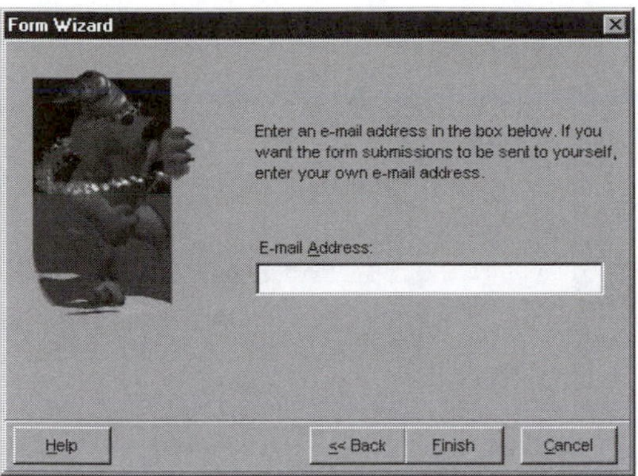

Figure 5. Enter your email address or a URL in the text field and click the **Finish** button.

✔ Tips

- You must include a **Submit** and **Reset** button in your form.
- You can select and enter properties for form elements now, then arrange your form and enter explanatory text when you return to the HTML document. Forms can include text and images.
- Before you select a **Form Wizard** option to send form details to an email address, or send form details to a URL (see Figure 4), ask your ISP, Web hosting company, or server administrator for instructions. Form processing differs from server to server.

What Happens When a User Submits a Form?

When a user fills out the form shown in Figure 1 and clicks the **Submit It!** Button, the form data gets sent to you as an email message. Email messages generated from forms contain a list of the values associated with your form elements, alongside the data entered or selected by the user.

When you receive forms data via email, the message looks similar to the one shown below:

Name: Jerry the Mouse

LikesCheese: Yes

CheeseType: Gorgonzola

Adding and Specifying Properties for Form Elements

When you select form elements from the **Form Wizard** dialog box, the properties options for the selected element appears. You can specify properties by entering text in the text fields and selecting options, then selecting the next form element. The following sections explain form element options in greater detail.

To create a Text Box

1. Select the **Text Box** button from the **Form Wizard** button bar.
2. When the **Text Box** options appear, as shown in Figure 6, enter a name for the element in the **Name** text field. The name should relate to the information users enter in the text box.
3. Enter a number of characters in the **Text Element Size** text field. This number determines the width of the text box.
4. You can limit the number of characters a person can enter in the **Maximum Number of Characters** text field.
5. You can enter default text in the **Default Text to Appear** text field. Default text automatically displays in the text box.

When you finish making your text field, you can select another element to add to your form. If you've added all of your form elements, you can click the **Next** button to finish generating the form.

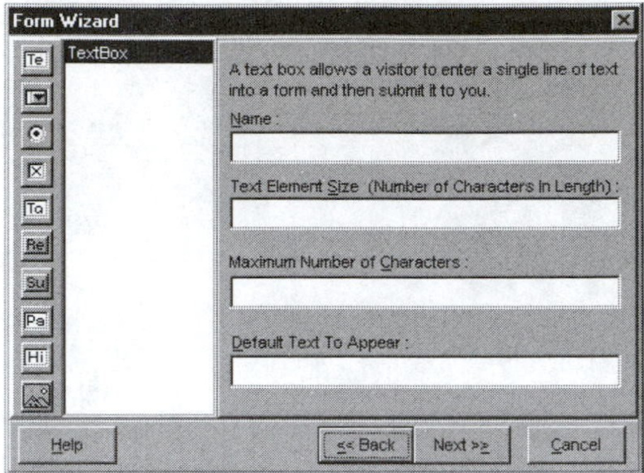

Figure 6. Options for creating a **Text Box**.

✔ Tips

- When specifying names and values, use alphanumeric characters without spaces, punctuation, or special characters like **&**. You can separate words with the _ sign (as in **Likes_Cheese**). You should specify the same name for all radio buttons within the same series.
- Each radio button in the series should have a different value.
- A radio button name should remind you of the question it goes with (such as **LikesCheese** for **Do you like cheese?**), and the radio button values should indicate responses (such as **Yes** or **No**).

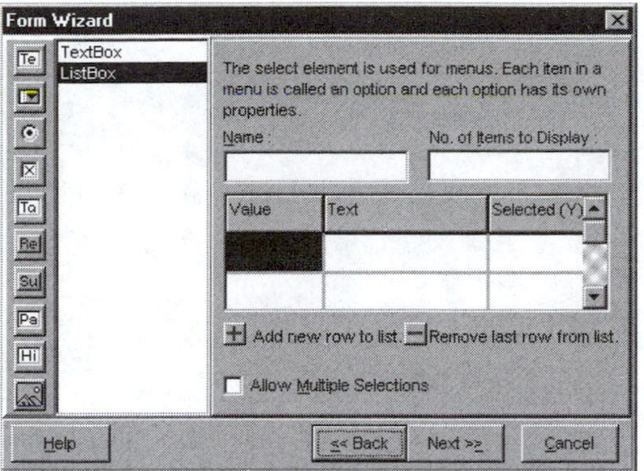

Figure 7. Options for creating a **List Box**.

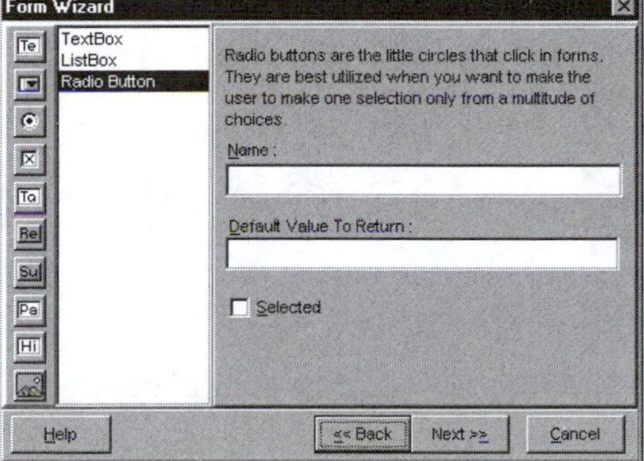

Figure 8. Options for creating a **Radio Button**.

To create a List Box

1. Select the **List Box** button from the **Form Wizard** button bar.
2. When the **List Box** options appear, as shown in Figure 7, enter a name for your list in the **Name** text field and specify how many items to include on the list in the **Number of Items to Display** text field.
3. Enter a value for the first list item in the **Value** column, and enter the text that you want to display in the list in the **Text** column.
4. Repeat Step 3 for each list item.
5. You can add a new row to the list by clicking the **+** sign, or remove the last row from the list by clicking the - sign.
6. You can also select a list item to display as a default selection by entering **Y** in the **Selected (Y)** column.
7. To allow users to select multiple selections, click the **Allow Multiple Selections** checkbox. Select another element to add to your form, or click the **Next** button.

To create a Radio Button

1. Select the **Radio Button** button from the **Form Wizard** button bar.
2. When the **Radio Button** options appear, as shown in Figure 8, enter a name for your radio button in the **Name** text field.
3. Enter a default value to return.
4. You can also specify that a radio button appear as the default selection by clicking the **Selected** checkbox. Select another element to add to your form, or click the **Next** button.

To create a CheckBox

1. Select the **CheckBox** button from the **Form Wizard** button bar.
2. When the **CheckBox** options appear, as shown in Figure 9, enter a name for your radio button in the **Name** text field.
3. Enter a default value to return.
4. You can also specify that a checkbox appear as the default selection by clicking the **Checked** checkbox. Select another element to add to your form, or click the **Next** button.

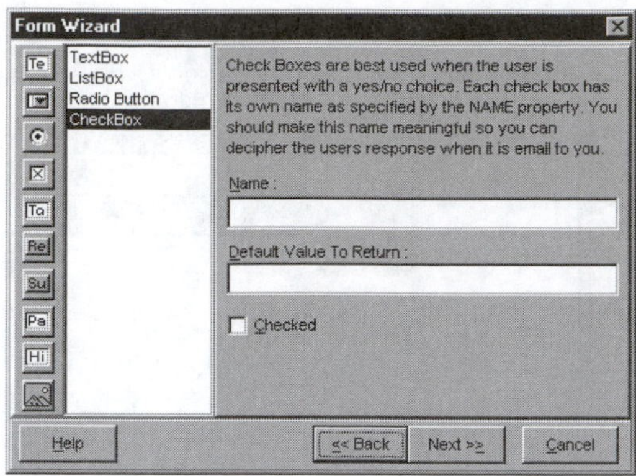

Figure 9. Options for creating a **CheckBox.**

To create a Text Area

1. Select the **Text Area** button from the **Form Wizard** button bar.
2. When the **Text Area** options appear, as shown in Figure 10, enter a name for the element in the **Name** text field. The name should relate to the information users enter in the text area.
3. Enter a number in the **Rows** text field to determine the height of the text area.
4. Enter a number of characters in the **Number of Characters Long** text field. This number determines the text area width.
5. You can enter default text in the **Default Text To Appear** text field. Default text automatically displays in the text area. Select another element to add to your form, or click the **Next** button.

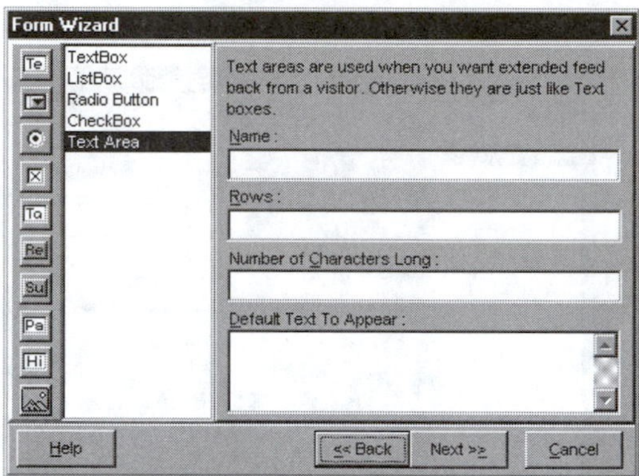

Figure 10. Options for creating a **Text Area.**

To create a Reset Button

1. Select the **Reset Button** button from the **Form Wizard** button bar.
2. When the **Reset Button** options appear, as shown in Figure 11, enter the text that you want to appear on the button (as in, **Forget It!**) in the **Caption** text field.

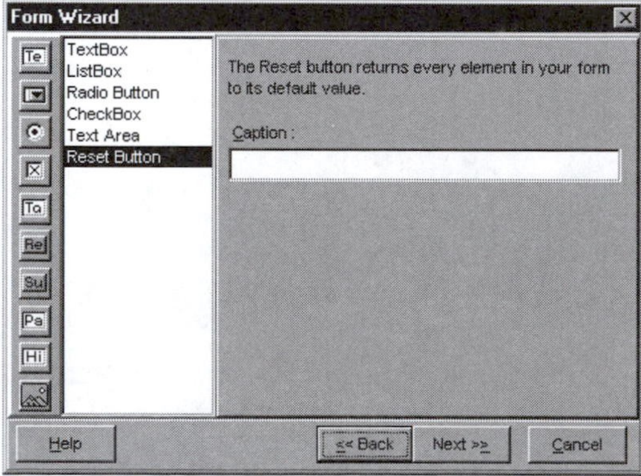

Figure 11. Options for creating a **Reset Button.**

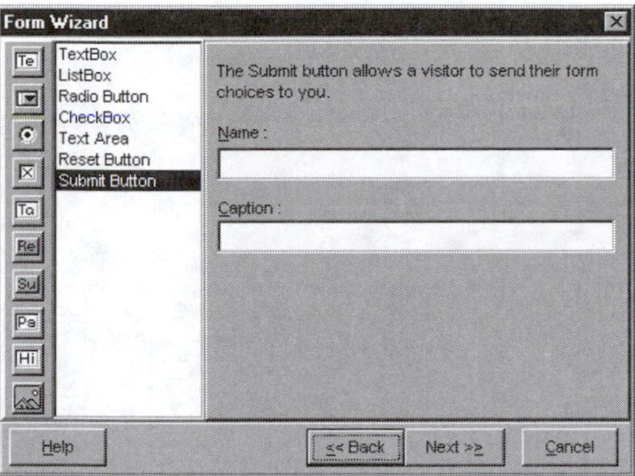

Figure 12. Options for creating a **Submit Button**.

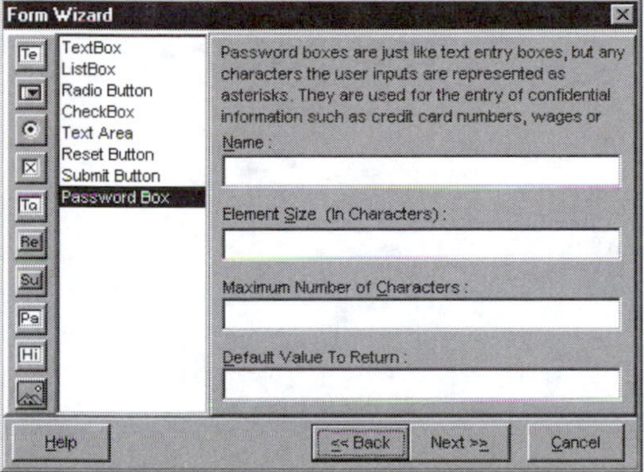

Figure 13. Options for creating a **Password Box**.

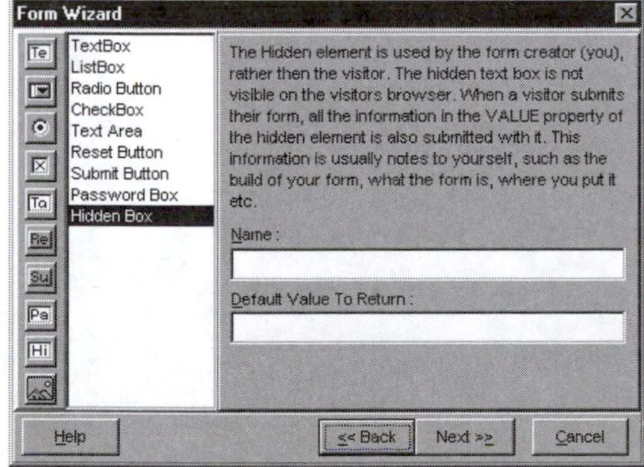

Figure 14. Options for creating a **Hidden Box**.

To create a Submit Button

1. Select the **Submit Button** button from the **Form Wizard** button bar.
2. When the **Submit Button** options appear, as shown in Figure 12, enter the text that you want to appear on the button (as in, **Submit It!**) in the **Caption** text field. Select another element to add to your form, or click the **Next** button.

To create a Password Box

1. Select the **Password Box** button from the **Form Wizard** button bar.
2. When the **Password Box** options appear, as shown in Figure 13, enter a name for the element in the **Name** text field. The name should relate to the information users enter in the Password Box.
3. Enter a number of characters in the **Element Size** text field. This number determines the width of the Password Box.
4. You can limit the number of characters a person can enter in the **Maximum Number of Characters** text field.
5. You can enter default text in the **Default Value To Return** text field. Default text automatically displays in the Password Box. Select another element to add to your form, or click the **Next** button.

To create a Hidden Box

1. Select the **Hidden Box** button from the **Form Wizard** button bar.
2. When the **Hidden Box** options appear, as shown in Figure 14, enter a name for the element in the **Name** text field. The name should relate to the information users enter in the Hidden Box.

(continued)

3. Enter a value in the **Default Value To Return** text box. The text entered here appears in your forms email message. Select another element to add to your form, or click the **Next** button.

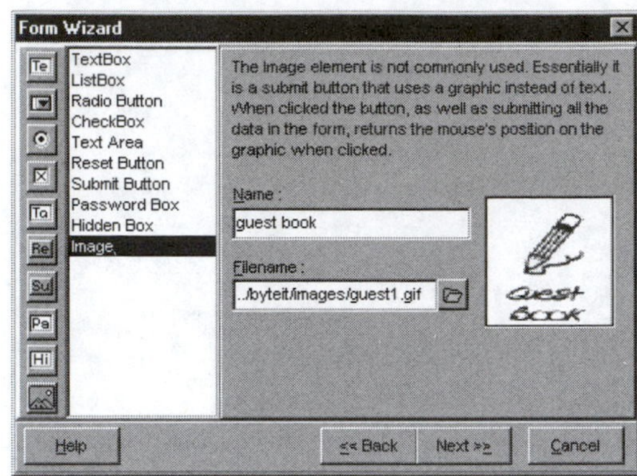

Figure 15. Options for using an image as your **Submit** button.

To use an image for your Submit button

1. Select the **Image** button from the **Form Wizard** button bar.
2. When the **Image** options appear, as shown in Figure 15, enter a name for the image element in the **Name** text field.
3. Enter the file name and directory path for the image you want to use in the **Filename** text field.

To remove form elements from the List

1. Select an item from the **Form Wizard** list by clicking on it with the right mouse button.
2. When the pop-up menu appears, select **Delete Form Element**.

WEB SITE MANAGEMENT

15

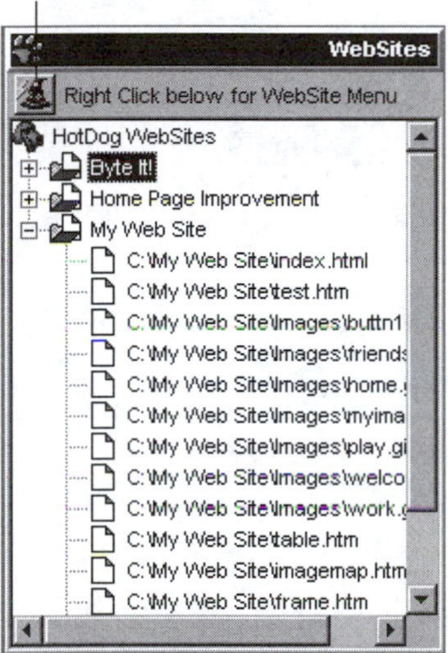

Figure 1. The **WebSites Manager** helps you keep track of your Web sites and your files.

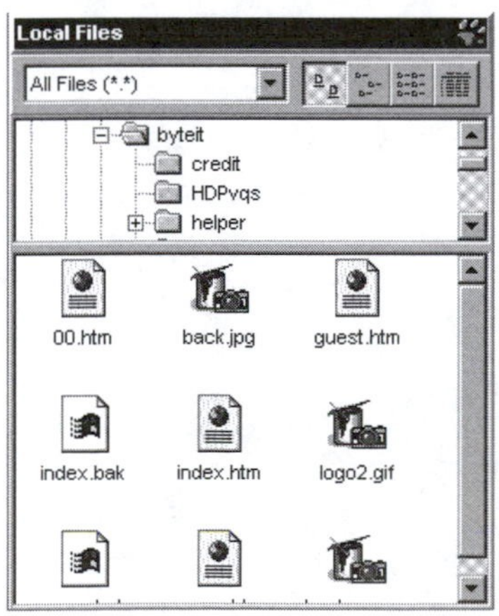

Figure 2. The **WebSites Manager** looks similar to the **Local Files** resource (which lets you drag and drop files into the current document), but they serve very different purposes.

Once you create your Web site, HotDog Pro helps you keep track of it. The **WebSites Manager,** as shown in Figure 1, displays a list of your HotDog Pro Web sites. At first glance, the **WebSites Manager** looks similar to the **Local Files** resource, shown in Figure 2. The **Local Files** resource displays files in the current folder so you can drag and drop items into your document to insert images or create links.

The **WebSites Manager**, on the other hand, displays a list of HotDog Pro WebSites that you've created and added to the list, along with your files and directory paths. When you click the **+** sign next to a folder, a list of files and file locations appear. When you double-click an HTML document, HotDog Pro opens the document. The WebSites Manager automates a variety of Web-related tasks, displays file locations so you can enter directory paths more easily, and makes it easy to keep track of multiple Web sites. Chapter 3 tells you how to create a HotDog Pro WebSite with the **WebSite Wizard**. This chapter explains the **WebSites Manager** in greater detail.

To display the WebSites Manager

1. Select **Resource Manager** from the **View** menu.
2. Select **WebSites** from the cascading list.

Managing Your Web Site

The **WebSites Manager** only displays files that you add to the list yourself. This spares you the confusion of sorting through distracting file clutter—such as experimental pages and back up files—every time you want to open a document. However, you have to remember to add documents to the list when you create them, and to remove files that you don't use. You can add and delete files, WebSites, and SubSites (a WebSite within a WebSite) from the list, as needed. Deleting files from the list does *not* remove files from your actual Web folder.

To add a WebSite to the WebSites Manager

1. Click the **WebSite Wizard** button (it looks like a little Wizard hat).
2. When the **WebSite Wizard** dialog box appears, follow the instructions. Chapter 3 explains how to use the **WebSite Wizard** in detail.
3. After you create the new WebSite, you can add files to it, as explained in the "To add files to a WebSite" section.

To create a SubSite (for a Web site subdirectory)

1. Click a WebSite folder with the right mouse button.
2. When the pop-up menu appears, as shown in Figure 3, select **Create SubSite**.
3. When the **New SubSite** dialog box appears, as shown in Figure 4, enter a name for the SubSite, and click **OK**.
4. When the new SubSite folder appears on the list, you can add files to it, as explained in the following section.

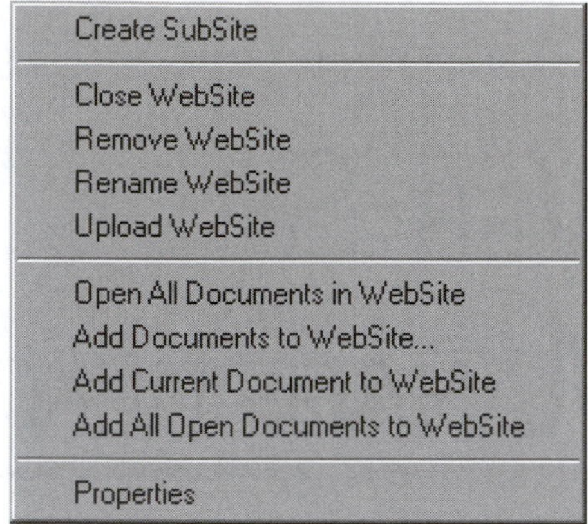

Figure 3. When you click your right mouse button on a site on the **WebSites** list, a pop-up menu appears. To create a SubSite, select **Create SubSite** from the list.

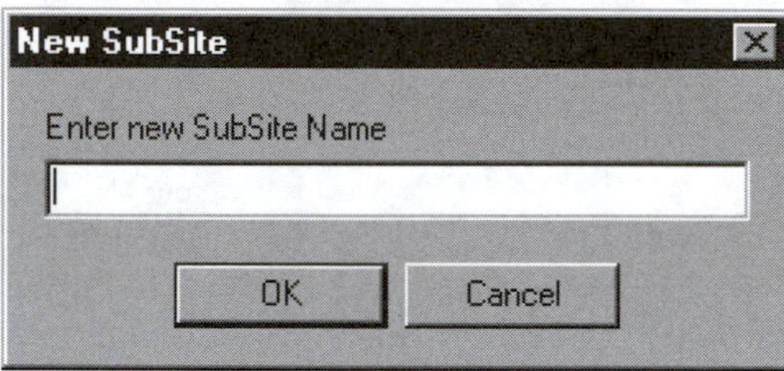

Figure 4. When the **New SubSite** dialog box appears, enter a name for your SubSite.

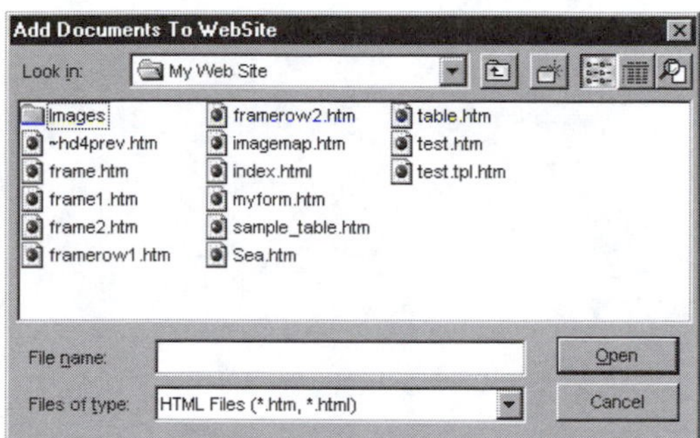

Figure 5. You can add multiple files to your HotDog Pro WebSite from the **Add Documents to WebSite** dialog box.

To add files to a WebSite

1. Click the WebSite or SubSite with the right mouse button and select **Add Documents to WebSite** from the pop-up menu.
2. When the **Add Documents to WebSite** dialog box appears, as shown in Figure 5, select the file or files you want to add, and click the **Open** button.

To add the current document to a WebSite

1. Click the WebSite or SubSite with the right mouse button.
2. Select **Add Current Document to WebSite** from the pop-up menu.

The document will appear at the bottom of the WebSites list.

To add all open documents to a WebSite

1. Click the WebSite or SubSite with the right mouse button.
2. Select **Add All Open Documents to WebSite** from the pop-up menu.

The documents will appear at the bottom of the WebSites list.

To open all documents in a WebSite

1. Click the WebSite or SubSite with the right mouse button.
2. Select **Open All Documents in WebSite** from the pop-up menu.

To rename a WebSite

1. Click the WebSite or SubSite with the right mouse button.
2. Select **Rename WebSite** from the pop-up menu.

   The name of the WebSite appears highlighted on the list so you can enter a new name for it.

To remove a WebSite

1. Click the WebSite or SubSite with the right mouse button.
2. Select **Remove WebSite** from the pop-up menu.
3. When the **Confirm** dialog box appears, click the **Yes** button.

To upload a WebSite

1. Click the WebSite or SubSite with the right mouse button.
2. Select **Upload WebSite** from the pop-up menu.
3. When the **Confirm** dialog box appears, click **Yes**. For more details on uploading your WebSite, see Chapter 17.

✔ Tips

- If your Web site has many directories, you can create SubSites to display files and folders in the WebSite Manager as they appear in your Web site folder. Give the SubSites the same names as your Web site directories. You can then add files from the real folders to the corresponding SubSite.
- In addition to HTML documents, you can add images and other types of files to a HotDog Pro WebSite. However, you can only open HTML files from the WebSite Manager.

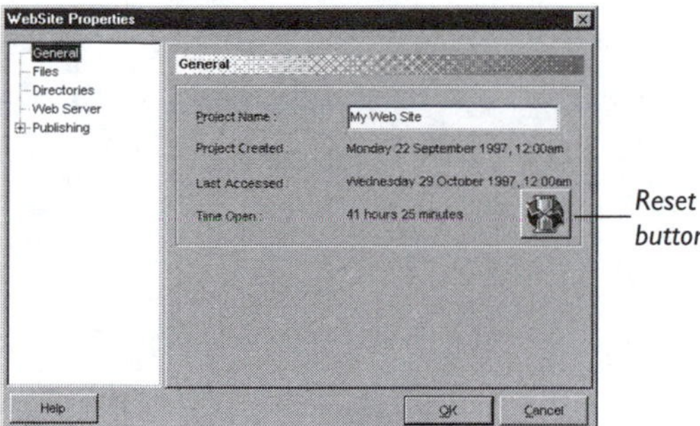

Figure 6. You can enter customized settings for individual HotDog Pro WebSites in the **WebSite Properties** dialog boxes.

Specifying WebSite Properties

You can enter customized properties settings for individual HotDog Pro WebSites. WebSites properties override HotDog Pro's default application preferences (as explained in Chapter 2) when you work on documents included in the WebSite. You can specify a default working directory, and enter server information to automate file uploads. In addition, you can specify Publishing properties to replace absolute file names with relative file names so your pages, images, links, and Java applets display and interact the same way on the server as they do on your computer.

To specify WebSite Properties

1. Click a WebSite with the right mouse button.
2. Select **Properties** from the pop-up menu.
3. When the **WebSite Properties—General** dialog box appears, as shown in Figure 6, you can select categories from the list and enter or edit settings.
4. When you finish, click **OK**.

General Properties

The **WebSite Properties—General** dialog box, shown in Figure 6 (on the previous page), displays the WebSite project name and other basic information.

General Properties options

- You can change the name of your WebSite by entering a new name in the **Project Name** field.
- You can also view project information, including the creation data, last access date, and the total number of hours spent working on the site.
- To reset the timer to zero, click the **Reset** button (it looks like an hourglass).

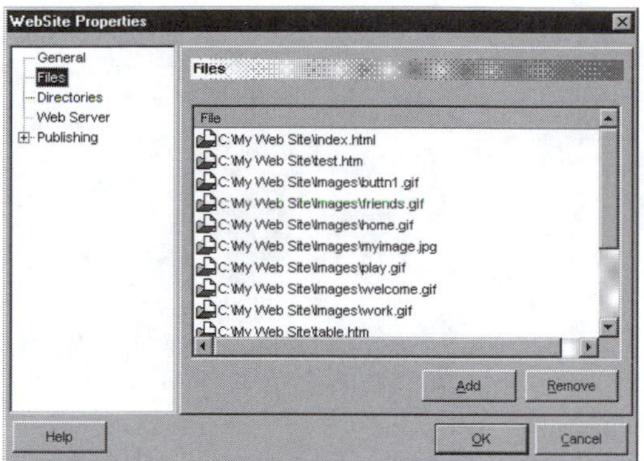

Figure 7. You can add and remove files in the **WebSite Properties—Files** dialog box.

Files Properties

The **WebSite Properties—Files** dialog box, shown in Figure 7, displays a scrolling list of files included in the project.

Files Properties options

- To add a file to the list, click the **Add** button.
- To remove a file from the list, click the **Remove** button.

Local Directories Properties

You can specify default document and image folders in the **WebSite Properties—Local Directories** dialog box, as shown in Figure 8. This means less browsing for files when you open, save, and insert files while working on the WebSite.

To specify Local Directories Properties

1. Enter a directory path in the **Documents** text field to specify a default local directory for HTML documents within the selected WebSite. You can also click the folder icon to browse for a directory.

2. Enter a directory path in the **Graphic Images** text field to specify a default local directory for images within the selected WebSite. You can also click the folder icon to browse for a directory.

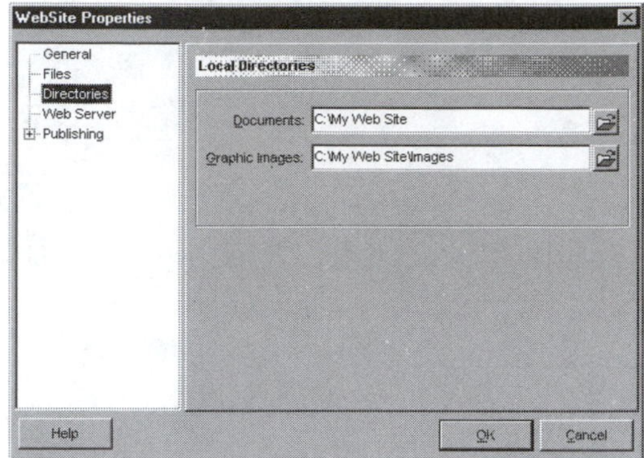

Figure 8. You can specify default directories in the **WebSite Properties—Local Directories** dialog box.

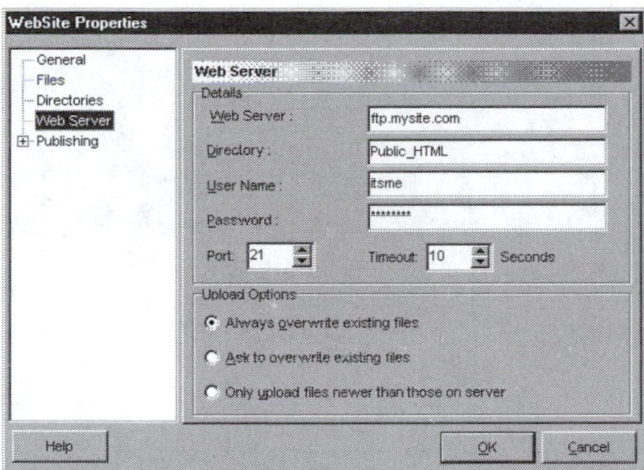

Figure 9. To upload pages to your WebSite, enter your server's settings in the **WebSite Properties—Web Server** dialog box.

Web Server Properties

You can enter your server settings in the **WebSite Properties—Web Server** dialog box, as shown in Figure 9. This information enables HotDog Pro to upload pages from the selected Web site quickly and easily.

To specify Web Server Properties

1. Enter an FTP address or Web site address in the **Web Server** text field.
2. Enter your server directory name in the **Directory** text field.
3. Enter your account user name in the **User Name** text field.
4. Enter your password in the **Password** text field.
5. You can specify a new port number in the **Port** text field if the server administrator tells you to do so.
6. Enter the number **120** in the **Timeout** text field.
7. You can select an option for how the WebSite Manager should handle overwriting old files with updated versions by clicking a radio button from the **Upload Options** list.

Publishing Properties

The **WebSite Properties—Publishing** dialog box, as shown in Figure 10, provides options for automatically reformatting documents, removing carriage returns, converting special characters to HTML, and searching and replacing directory path elements when you publish Web pages to the server.

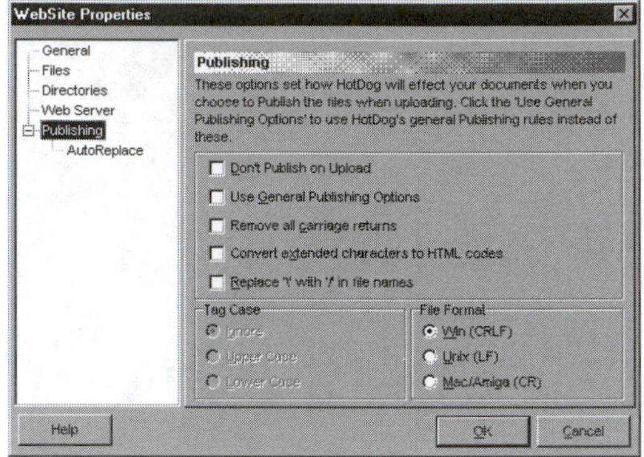

Figure 10. You can enter settings for how HotDog Pro publishes your Web site to the server in the **WebSite Properties—Publishing** dialog box.

Publishing Properties options

- **Don't Publish on Upload:** Select this option to tell the WebSites manager not to make changes to documents when you upload them to the server.
- **Use General Publishing Options:** Select this option to use the **Publishing** options specified in the HotDog Pro application preferences (see Chapter 3).
- **Remove all carriage returns:** Removes all carriage returns from HTML documents.
- **Convert extended characters to HTML codes:** Searches for special characters, like **&** ampersands, and replaces them with the correct HTML code.
- **Replace '\' with '/' in file names:** Replaces all backslashes used in directory paths for local files with the forward slashes required by the server.

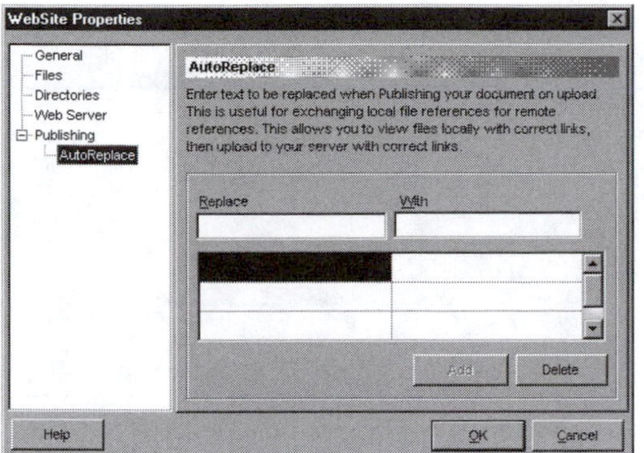

Figure 11. The **WebSite Properties—Publishing: AutoReplace** dialog box lets you specify text for the WebSite Manager to automatically search and replace while uploading documents to the server.

Publishing: AutoReplace Properties

The **WebSite Properties—Publishing: AutoReplace** dialog box, as shown in Figure 11 lets you search and replace text that recurs throughout your Web site. This is ideal for changing absolute directory path names for local files with relative path names so your Web pages work properly on the remote server. For example, you can tell the **WebSite Manager** to replace all occurrences of the local file directory path **C:\MyWebSite\Images** with the correct **Images/** relative path. For more information about setting up your local WebSite so it mirrors the directory structure on your server, select **Contents** from the **Help** menu, and look up **WebSite Manager**.

To specify Publishing: AutoReplace Properties

1. Enter the text you want to replace in the **Replace** text field.
2. Enter the replacement text in the **With** text field.
3. Click the **Add** button to add your automatic search and replace specifications to the list.
4. Repeat steps 1-3 to add more items to the list.

When you finish, you can edit other preferences, or click **OK** to exit the dialog box and save your changes.

Importing HotDog Pro 3.0 Projects

If you've upgraded from HotDog 3.0, you can import your HotDog Projects into the **WebSites Manager**.

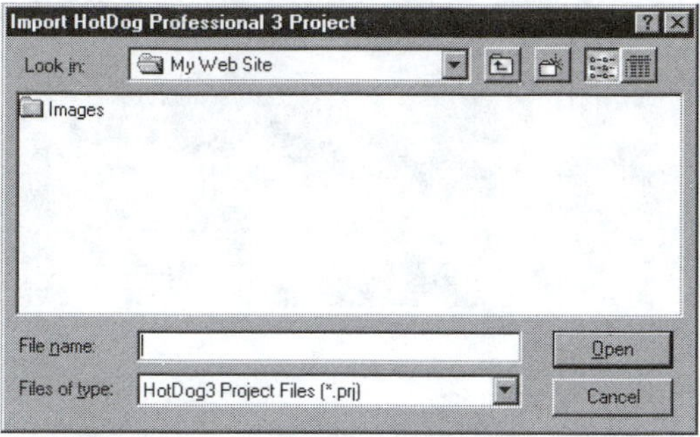

Figure 12. If you've upgraded from HotDog Pro 3.0, you can import your projects into the **WebSites Manager**.

To import a HotDog Pro 3.0 Project into the WebSites Manager

1. From the **WebSites Manager**, click the **HotDog WebSites** dog icon with the right mouse button.
2. When the pop-up list appears, select **Import HotDog3 Project**.
3. When the **Import HotDog Professional 3 Project** dialog box appears, as shown in Figure 12, browse for your project (with the **.PRJ** file name extension).
4. Select the project file then click the **Open** button.

Your HotDog3 Project will appear on the **WebSite Manager** list as a WebSite with all of your files. You can now manage your Web pages the way you always have—and take advantage of HotDog Pro's new features.

Checking Your Pages

Once you've set up your Web site the way you want it, it's time to upload it, right? But wait! First, you should preview your pages, check your spelling and HTML syntax, test your links, and make sure your pages don't take too long to download. HotDog Pro gives you the tools you need to double-check your site and make your pages look professional.

Tools for perfect pages

- **Internal and external page preview:** You can preview your pages with HotDog Pro's built-in browser, **Rover**. Or, you can preview pages in a browser by clicking the **Preview** button.
- **Spell checking:** Checks your spelling and makes corrections.
- **HTML syntax checking:** Highlights incorrect HTML and JavaScript codes so you can spot potential problems easily.
- **Link Verifier:** Displays a list of links, images, and other external page elements, and tells you the status of each element.
- **BandWidth Buster:** Tells you the download time and size of the current Web page, and helps you compress image files.
- **MultiFile Find and Replace:** Makes it easy to search and replace text and HTML codes in multiple documents throughout your site.

Previewing Pages

The **Rover** resource lets you take a peek at your Web page straight from the application window, as shown in Figure 1. Or, you can launch a preview of the page in your browser by clicking the **Preview** button. **Rover** gives you a quick, easy way to view your page layouts while you work. However, **Rover**'s capabilities are limited, and it can't display and load some page elements (such as JavaScript scripts and Java applets). That's why you should also preview your Web page in a browser like Internet Explorer, Netscape Navigator, or both. You can specify your preview browsers in the **Browser** Preferences (as explained in Chapter 2).

To preview the current HTML document with Rover

1. Select **Resources** from **View** menu.
2. When the pop-up menu appears, select **Rover**.
3. When the **Rover** resource appears in the left resource window pane, you can enlarge the window pane by clicking on the right border and dragging it to the right.

To preview the current page with a browser

1. Click the **Preview** button on the standard toolbar, or select **Preview** from the **File** menu.
2. If your **Browser** Preferences specify more than one browser, a pop-up list appears, as shown in Figure 2.
3. Select an item from the pop-up list to display a preview page in the browser, as shown in Figure 3.

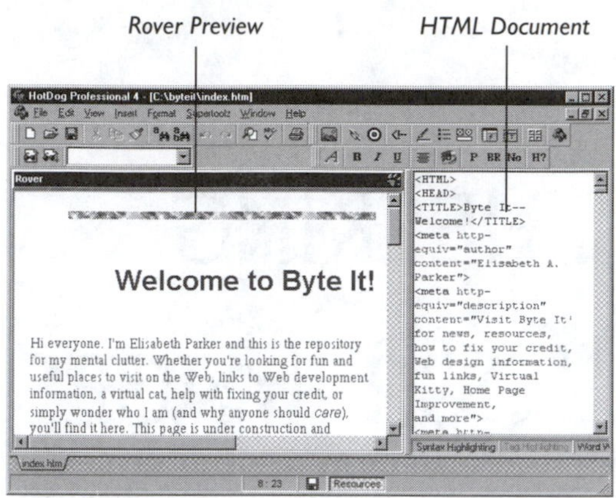

Figure 1. You can preview the current page with the **Rover** resource.

Figure 2. To preview pages, click the **Preview** button. If you have more than one browser specified in your **Browser** Preferences, a pop-up list appears so you can select a browser.

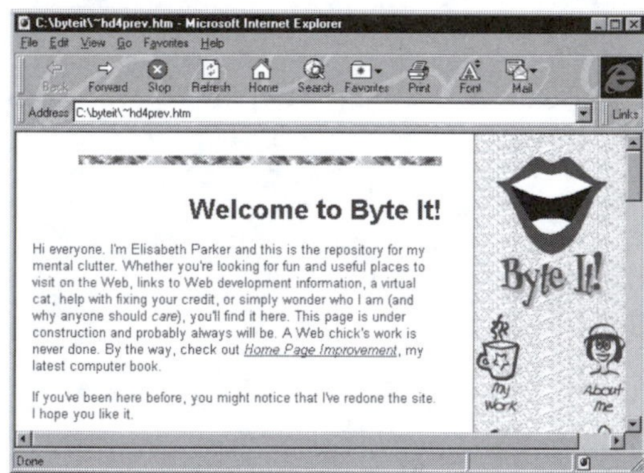

Figure 3. The browser loads a special preview page.

✔ Tip

- You can drag Rover's border across the entire application window to display a full-screen Web page preview. This temporarily hides the document window pane and the right resource window pane. To display them again, restore Rover to its normal size by dragging the border to the left.

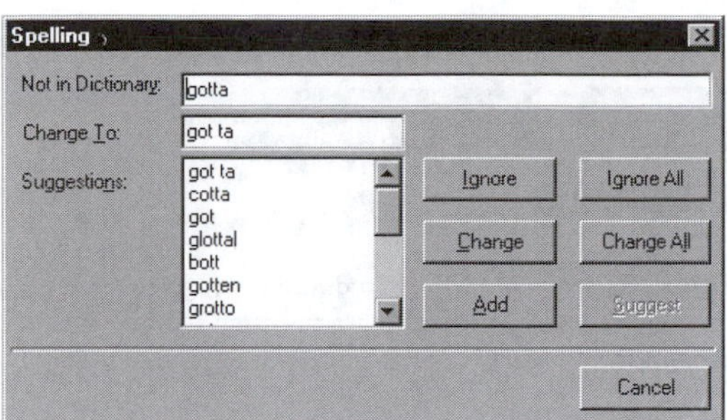

Figure 4. To check your spelling for the current document, select **Check Spelling** from the **Edit** menu to display the **Spelling** dialog box.

✔ Tips

- To preview a page in your default Web browser, you can press the **F9** shortcut key.
- It is a good idea to preview pages in both Internet Explorer and Netscape Navigator. In addition, some Web site developers also preview pages in older versions of the browsers.
- Preview page documents are located in the directory that you specify in either the **WebSite Properties—Directories** dialog box or the application's **Directories** Preferences.

Checking Spelling

You've grown accustomed to spell checking your word processing documents. So why shouldn't your Web page program have a spell checker, too? HotDog Pro's built-in spelling utility ignores those funny HTML codes and runs through the text in your document. You can also customize your spell checking list by adding words that you frequently use.

To check spelling

1. Select **Check Spelling** from the **Edit** menu, or press the **F7** shortcut key.
2. When the **Spelling** dialog box appears, as shown in Figure 4, it checks your document and queries you about words automatically.
3. When the spell checker flags a word it doesn't recognize, it displays the word in the **Not in Dictionary** text field.
   - **A.** To change the selected word, enter the new spelling in the **Change To** text field (or select a item from the **Suggestions** list), and click the **Change** button.
   - **B.** To change all instances of the selected word, enter the new spelling in the **Change To** text field (or select an item from the **Suggestions** list), and click the **Change All** button.
   - **C.** To leave the word unchanged, click the **Ignore** button.
   - **D.** To leave all instances of the selected word unchanged, click the **Ignore All** button.
   - **E.** To add the selected word to the dictionary, click the **Add** button.
4. When the **Information** dialog box appears with a message that HotDog has finished checking your spelling, click **OK**.

HTML Syntax Notification

If you have enabled the **Syntax Highlighting** feature in the application's **Appearance** Preferences, HotDog Pro highlights possible HTML errors and displays tooltips that help you determine the cause of the error. In order to check errors for the HTML specification and browser version that you had in mind while developing your pages (for example, HTML version 3.2 for Internet Explorer), you have to specify HTML filters in the **HTML Tags Manager**. For more about preferences and HTML filters, see Chapter 2.

To check HTML syntax

1. Scroll through your HTML document.
2. When HotDog Pro doesn't recognize a line of HTML or JavaScript code, it highlights the text, as shown in Figure 5.
3. Hold your cursor over the highlighted item to display a tooltip. Tooltips can help you determine the cause of the error so you can make corrections.

```
    <TD><CENTER>
<A HREF="work/index.htm"
onmouseover="img_act('menu1')"
 onmouseout="img_inact('menu1')">
<IMG SRC="images/work.gif" HEIGHT=100 WIDTH=57
NAME="menu1"
ALT="My Work" BORDER="0"></A>
```

Figure 5. When HotDog Pro doesn't recognize code that you've entered, it highlights the code so you can correct it.

✔ Tips

- A highlighted item of code doesn't *always* mean the code is incorrect. HotDog Pro simply may not recognize a newly enabled tag or attribute.
- If you're positive that there's nothing wrong with a highlighted item, check your HTML filter specifications and make sure you've set them up so that HotDog Pro checks for the HTML version and browser you use. You can also add new items to the HTML Tags Manager so that HotDog Pro will recognize new tags and attributes as you discover them.
- Designing cutting-edge pages that work in both Internet Explorer and Netscape can prove challenging. Syntax checking can help you avoid compatibility problems.

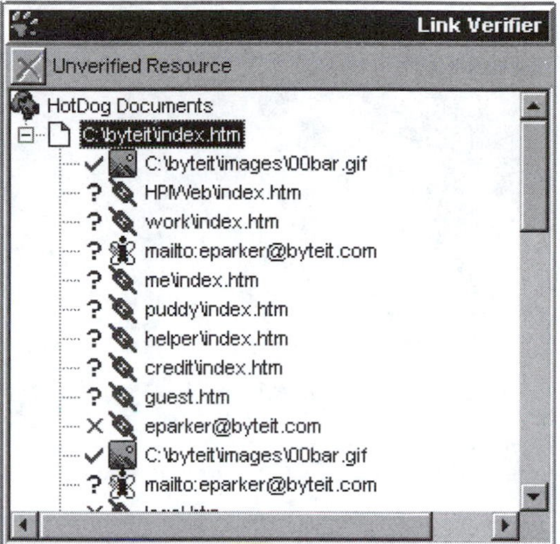

Figure 6. The **Link Verifier** checks the directory paths and URLs of the links, images, and other Web page elements specified in the current HTML document.

✔ Tips

- In order to check external links with the **Link Verifier**, you have to go online first.
- You should check your external links frequently—Web sites change constantly.
- You can still verify internal links when you're offline.

Testing Your Links with the Link Verifier

The link verifier, as shown in Figure 6, tests links for the current document and indicates their status. In addition, it also displays page elements—such as images—and tells you whether the directory paths are specified correctly. A check mark indicates that the link works, an **X** tells you that the link does not work, and a **?** means that the **Link Verifier** is unable to check the link (this happens with external links when you're offline). When you select an item from the **Link Verifier** list, the corresponding item in your HTML document highlights so you can locate it and make a correction.

To test your links

1. Open the document you want to verify and go online.
2. Select **Resource** from the **View** menu, then select **Link Verifier** when the cascading list displays.
3. When the **Link Verifier** appears, as shown in Figure 6, it lists your links, images and other elements, and displays icons that indicate whether or not they work.
4. To correct the directory path or URL for incorrectly specified links, images, and other page elements, select an item with an **X** next to it to automatically highlight the corresponding HTML code in your document. You can then easily scroll through your document to locate the item and correct it.
5. You can open additional documents and verify the links for them. When you open a document, the **Link Verifier** automatically checks the links.

Estimating Page Download Time with BandWidth Buster

As a rule of thumb, a Web page should take no longer than 30 seconds to download on a 28.8 Kbps modem. That's about how long most people can wait before getting impatient and clicking their browser's **Stop** button and going somewhere else. In most cases, you don't have to worry about download time. GIF and JPEG images are small, and simple JavaScript scripts and Java applets load almost immediately. However, pages with large images (or lots of images) and multimedia files may cause trouble.

But how can you tell how long it would take to download a page? When in doubt, use the **BandWidth Buster**. The **BandWidth Buster** displays the HTML document and associated files, and tells you the combined file size of all the files and how long the page would take to download. In addition, it provides you with options for *compressing* (or "busting") your images.

To estimate page download time

1. Select **BandWidth Buster** from the **SuperToolz** menu.
2. When the **BandWidth Buster** dialog box appears, as shown in Figure 7, read the instructions and click the **Next** button.
3. When the second **BandWidth Buster** dialog box appears, as shown in Figure 8, click the **Open** button.
4. When the **Open** dialog box appears, as shown in Figure 9, browse for your HTML document, then click the **Open** button.

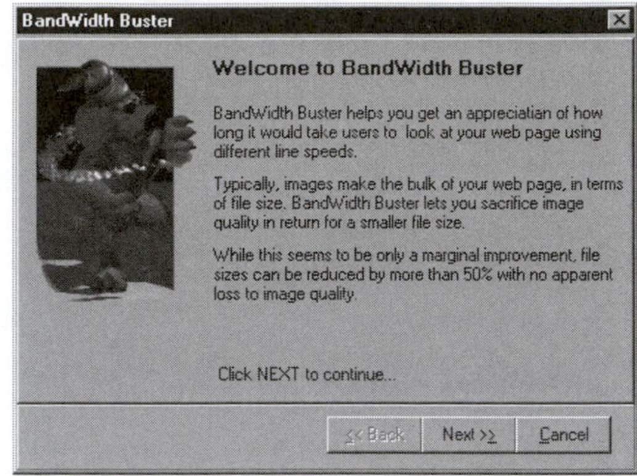

Figure 7. When the **BandWidth Buster** dialog box appears, read the instructions and click the **Next** button.

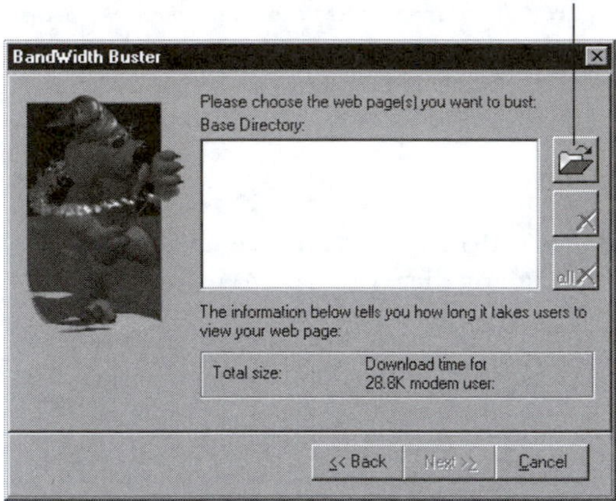

Figure 8. When the second **BandWidth Buster** dialog box appears, click the **Open** button.

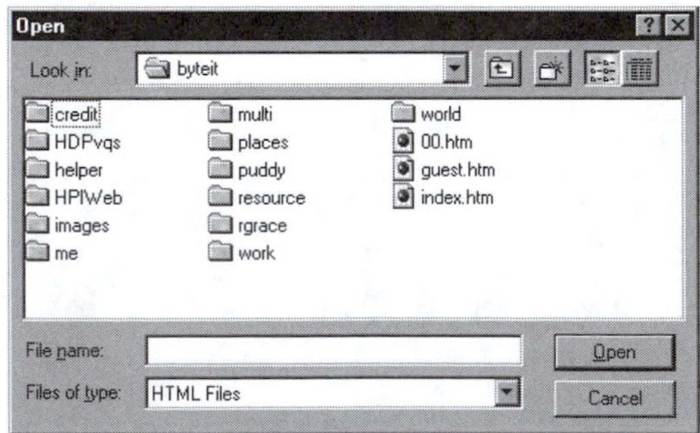

Figure 9. When the **Open** dialog box appears, browse for your file, and click **Open**.

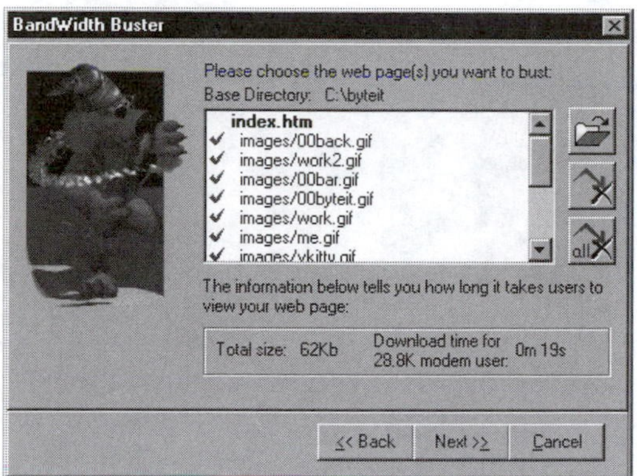

Figure 10. When the HTML document and list of associated files appear on the list, you can view information about the size of the combined files and the estimated amount of time for the page to download.

✔ Tip

- As a rule of thumb, a Web page should take no longer than 32 seconds to download with a 28.8 Kbps modem.

5. When the Web page document and associated files appear on the list (as shown in Figure 10), you can view information about your Web page. The dialog box displays the total size of the combined files and the estimated download time.
6. You can either click the **Back** button to check other pages, or you can click the **Next** button to choose options for reducing your image file sizes so your page displays more quickly.

You can now decide whether or not you need to reduce your file sizes. You can do this by including fewer images in your document. Or, you can let **BandWidth Buster** help you compress your images for smaller file sizes and shorter download times.

Compressing Images with the BandWidth Buster

If the **BandWidth Buster** indicates that your Web page may take too long to download, you can "bust" your image files to make them smaller. This can help reduce the download time for your Web page. Compressing image files reduces file sizes, but can also reduce the image quality. The **BandWidth Buster** requires you to save your images to a separate folder so you don't erase the original images. You can then "bust" the images and display what the new Web page file size would be if you replace your current images with the newly compressed ones.

To reduce image file sizes

1. After viewing your Web page and associated files and estimating your page's download time, as shown in Figure 10, click the **Next** button.
2. When the next dialog box appears, as shown in Figure 11, select a maximum value for an image size (in KB) from the list.
3. Enter the directory path for the folder you want to save "busted" images to. You can also click the **Open** button (with the folder icon) to browse for a folder. Click the **Next** button.
4. When the next dialog box appears, as shown in Figure 12, select an option by clicking a radio button, then click the **Next** button.

   A. Select the **Insert image as LOWSRC** option to create a low resolution (smaller) image that can display while the higher resolution (larger) image loads. This lets people view the page more quickly.

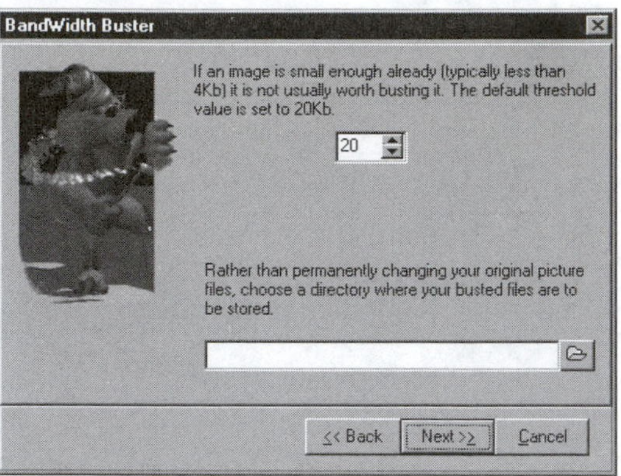

Figure 11. Specify a maximum image size value and pick a folder to store compressed image files to, so the original files are not erased.

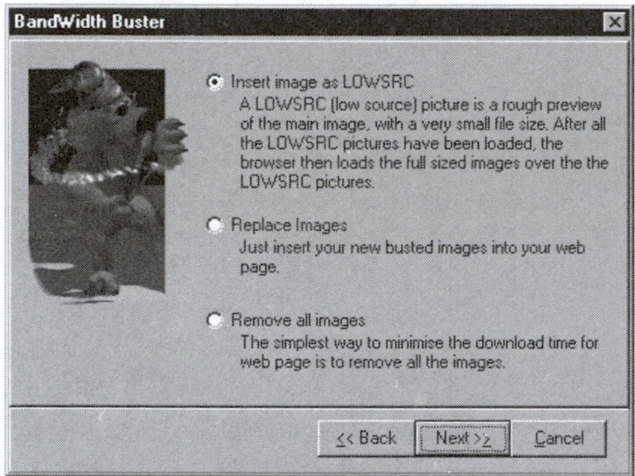

Figure 12. Select an option for "busting" your page.

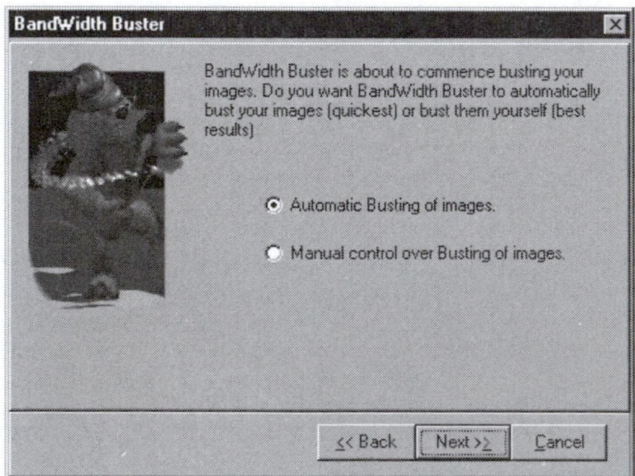

Figure 13. You can let **BandWidth Buster** compress your images, or you can choose to preview and compress images manually.

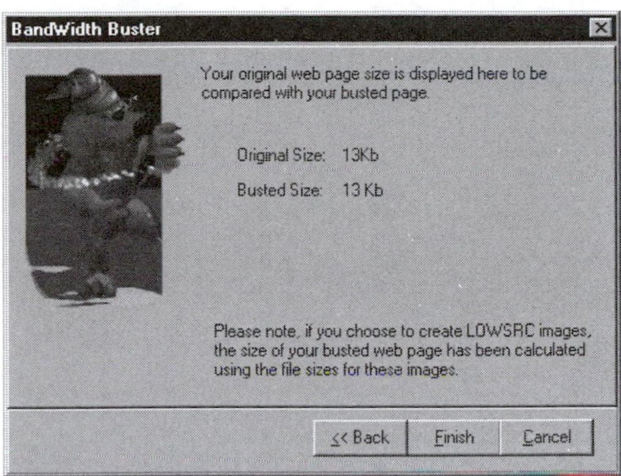

Figure 14. When the **BandWidth Buster** dialog box displays a comparison of the original and "busted" Web page sizes, you can click the **Back** button to try new options or click the **Finish** button.

✔ Tips

- The **BandWidth Buster** does not change the HTML code for the selected document or replace existing images with compressed ones. It simply displays the current Web page size, helps you compress your images, and tells you what the new file size would be if you inserted the "busted" images.
- If you choose to display a **LOWSRC** (low resolution image) before the larger image displays, the overall Web page size increases, but your Web page displays in a shorter amount of time.
- The **Image Wizard** can help you insert the HTML codes required for specifying LOWSRC and regular image files.

   B. Select the **Replace Images** option to replace old images with the new "busted" images.

   C. Select the **Remove all images** option to remove all of your images.

5. When the next dialog box appears, as shown in Figure 13, select an option, then click the **Next** button.

   A. The **Automatic Busting of images** option automatically reduces image file sizes by compressing them to lower levels. This may reduce the image's quality.

   B. The **Manual control over Busting of images** option displays a dialog box with a compression slider and image preview when you click the **Next** button. You can adjust the slider to reduce the file size, while previewing the image, then click the **Next** button.

6. When the final dialog box appears, as shown in Figure 14, you can compare the Web page's original size with the new "Busted" Web page size.

7. Click the **Back** button to choose different options for compressing your images, or click the **Finish** button.

8. Replace your old images with the newly compressed images (they are located in the folder you specified in step 3). If you specify **LOWSRC** images, rename the new images, and move them into the directory where you keep your images. You can then highlight the image source tags, launch the **Insert Image Wizard** (as explained in Chapter 5) and specify the low resolution images.

Searching and Replacing Text with MultiFile Find and Replace

Making global changes to documents on a Web site—such as replacing old contact information—used to mean lots of busy work. Now, you can search and replace text in multiple documents throughout your Web site in a few minutes with **MultiFile Find and Replace**.

To use MultiFile Find and Replace

1. Select **MultiFile Find and Replace** from the **SuperToolz** menu.
2. When the **MultiFile Find and Replace** dialog box appears, as shown in Figure 15, click the **Add a Find or Replace Item** button.
   - **A.** Enter the text you want to search for in the **Find** column, press the **Tab** key, then enter the replacement text in the **Replace** column.
   - **B.** To add additional items to the list, click the **Add a Find or Replace Item** button and repeat step A.
3. Click the **Where** tab to display the options shown in Figure 16, and select the **Do not process graphics files** checkbox.
   - **A.** To search and replace all of the files in a folder, select a folder and click the **Add the current directory or file(s) to the target list** button.
   - **B.** To search and replace individual files, select a folder, then select a document and click the **Add the current directory or file(s) to the target list** button.
   - **C.** When all of the folders or documents you want to search and replace for appear on the **Target Files & Directories** list, click the **Special** tab.

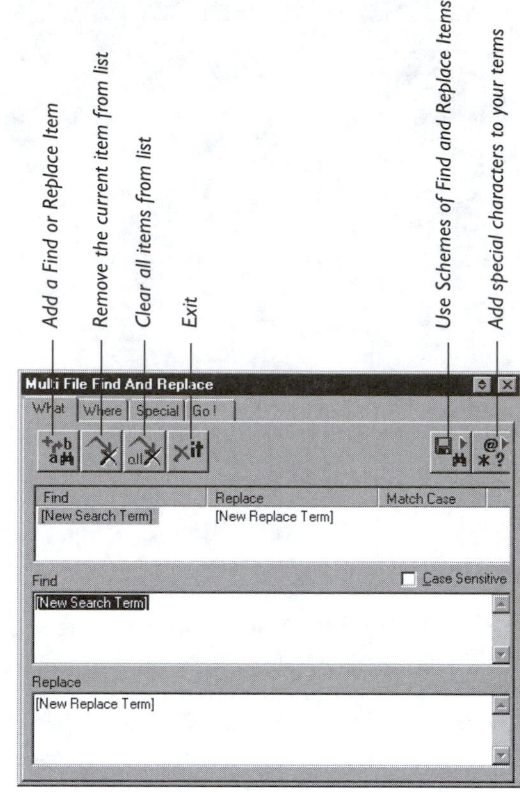

Figure 15. Enter the text you want to search for and the text you want to replace it with.

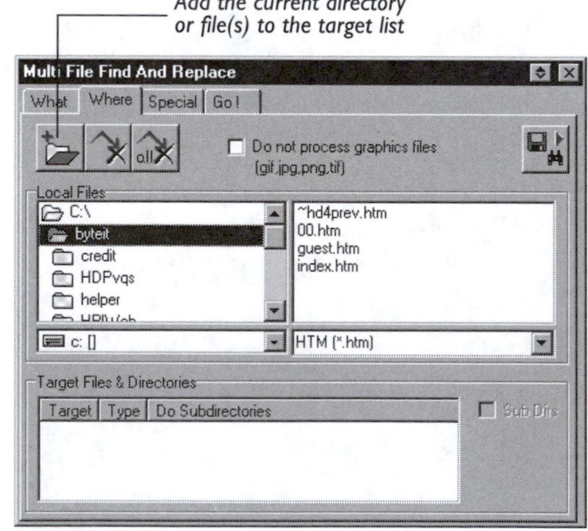

Figure 16. Select the folders and/or files you want to search.

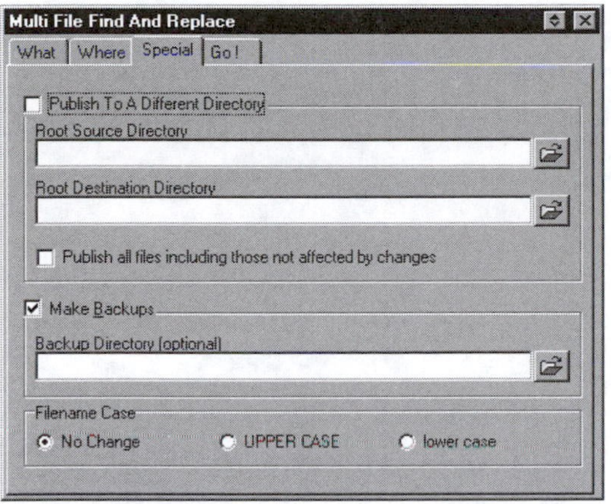

Figure 17. You can choose options for saving searched and replaced files to a different directory, or making backups of your old files.

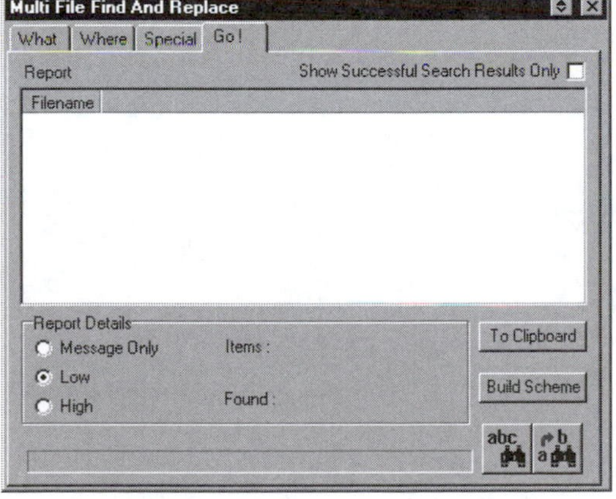

Figure 18. Click the **Go!** tab to search and replace your files. A list of files processed appears in the **Report** list.

4. When the **Special** options display, as shown in Figure 17, you can select options for leaving current files intact by publishing search and replace results to a different folder, or for making backup copies of files.

   A. To publish files with the searched and replaced text to a different directory, select the **Publish To A Different Directory** checbox.

   B. Enter the directory path to the folder that contains the files you want to search and replace in the **Root Source Directory.** You can also click the **Open** (folder) button to browse for a folder.

   C. Enter the directory path to the new documents folder in the **Root Destination Directory** text field. You can also click the **Open** button to browse for a folder.

   D. To make backups, click the **Make Backups** checkbox.

   E. You can specify a backup directory in the **Backup Directory** text field, or click the **Open** button to browse for a folder.

   F. You can also change your file names to all uppercase or all lowercase by selecting a radio button from the **Filename Case** list.

5. To search and replace your files, click the **Go!** tab, as shown in Figure 18. A list of files that have been searched, and the results appears on the **Report** list.

17 Publishing to the Server

Finally—you've set up your Web pages just the way you want them, you've checked them twice, and now you're ready to upload them to your server. This chapter tells you how to upload pages quickly and easily with the **WebSites Manager**. You can then easily view, edit, and manage pages that you've uploaded to the server with the **Internet Files** resource.

So, if we're talking about *uploading* pages to the server, why is this chapter called "*Publishing* Pages to the Server"? Because in addition to transferring pages to your server directory, HotDog Pro also automatically changes absolute path names to relative path names and other items, depending on your WebSite Properties settings (as explained in Chapter 15) or Publishing Preferences (as explained in Chapter 2).

To set up your Web Server Properties for your Web site

1. From the **WebSites Manager**, click your WebSite folder with the right mouse button.
2. When the pop-up menu appears, as shown in Figure 1, select **Properties**.
3. When the **WebSite Properties** dialog box appears, as shown in Figure 2, select **Web Server** from the list.
4. When the **Web Server** options appear, enter your server information and select options as explained in Chapter 15.
5. You can also enter properties settings for **Publishing** and **Publishing: AutoReplace** to automatically search and replace directory paths and other text and characters.

To upload a Web site

1. Connect to the Internet.
2. From the **WebSites Manager**, click the WebSite folder with your right mouse button.
3. When the pop-up list appears, select **Upload WebSite**.
4. When you select the **Always overwrite existing files** option from the **Web Server Properties** dialog box, a **Confirm** dialog box (as shown in Figure 3) appears and warns you that your upload may take a while. Click **Yes** to continue.
5. When the **Uploading Files to Web Server** dialog box appears, as shown in Figure 4, choose a publishing option, then click the **Continue** button.

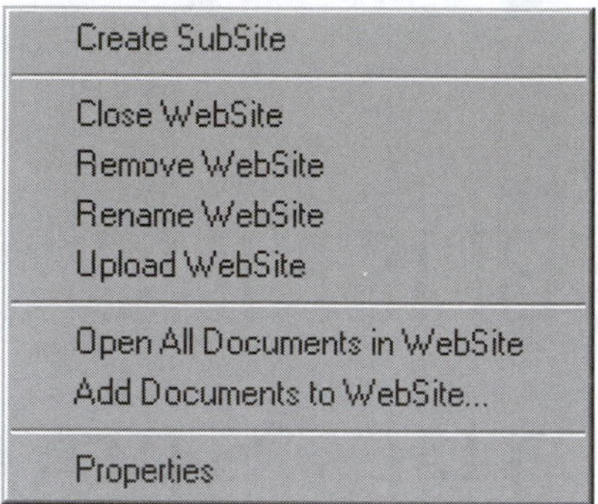

Figure 1. To edit or set up your **Web Server Properties** before uploading your Web site to the server, click your WebSite with the right mouse button and select **Properties** from the pop-up menu.

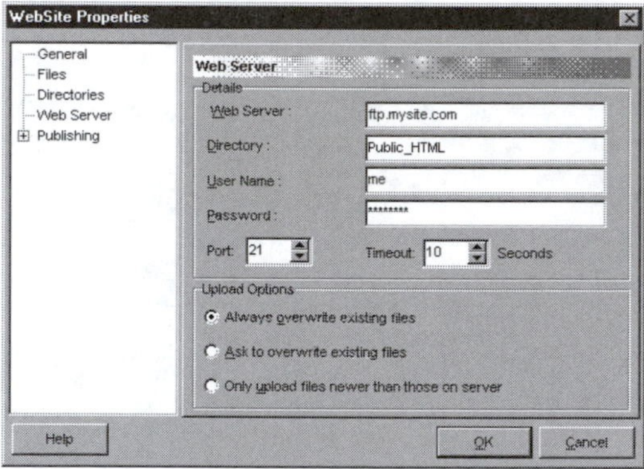

Figure 2. Before uploading your Web site, you need to specify its **Web Server Properties**.

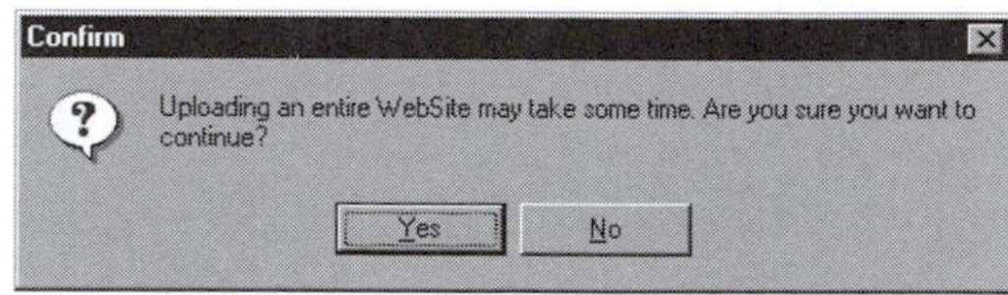

Figure 3. When you upload an entire Web site, the **Confirm** dialog box appears and asks if you want to continue.

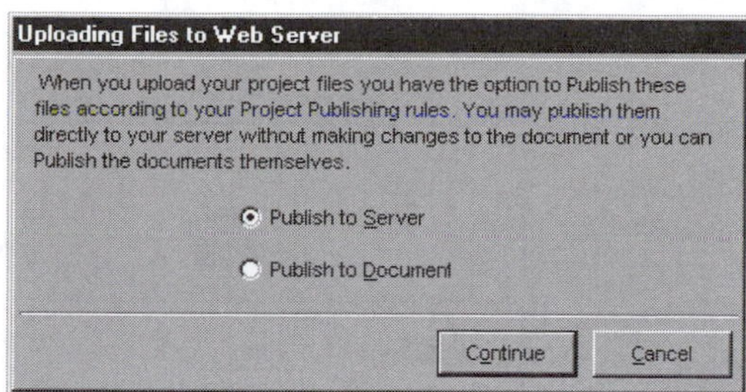

Figure 4. When the **Uploading Files to Web Server** dialog box appears, select a radio button to determine how you want the **WebSites Manager** to apply your publishing settings to remote and local files.

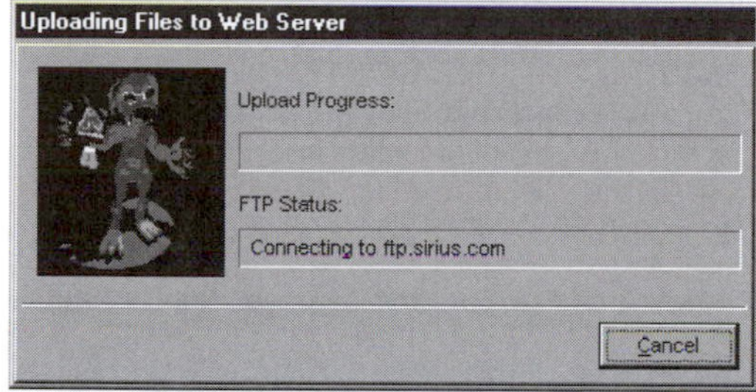

Figure 5. The second **Uploading Files to Web Server** dialog box reports the progress and status of your upload.

A. The **Publish to Server** radio button applies your WebSite's **Publishing Properties** settings to HTML files while it uploads them to the server, but leaves the local files unchanged.

B. The **Publish to Document** button applies yourWebSite's **Publishing Properties** settings to HTML files while it uploads them to the server, and also changes your local files.

6. The second **Uploading Files to Web Server** dialog box appears, as shown in Figure 5, and reports the progress and status of your upload.

✔ Tips

- You can save time during uploads by selecting the **Only upload files newer than those on server** radio button from the **Web Server Properties** options.
- The **Publishing: AutoReplace** and **Publishing** options help you replace absolute local directory paths with the relative paths used on your server. Chapter 15 talks about setting up properties for your Web site in detail.
- **WebSite Properties** settings for publishing override HotDog Pro's **Publishing Preferences**, as explained in Chapter 2.
- If you have trouble uploading pages to the server, increase the **Timeout** setting to **60** seconds in the **Web Server Properties** settings. The **Timeout** setting determines how long to keep trying to access the server before giving up. However, some servers are slower than others and require a little more time.

The Internet Files Resource

The **Internet Files** resource, as shown in Figure 6, makes working with your remote files a seamless experience. Let's say you take a peek at your Web page while you're online, and decide you want to center a heading. With the **Internet Files** resource, you can quickly access your remote directory, select a document, and edit it on the fly. When you click your browser's **Refresh** button, the new version of the document appears.

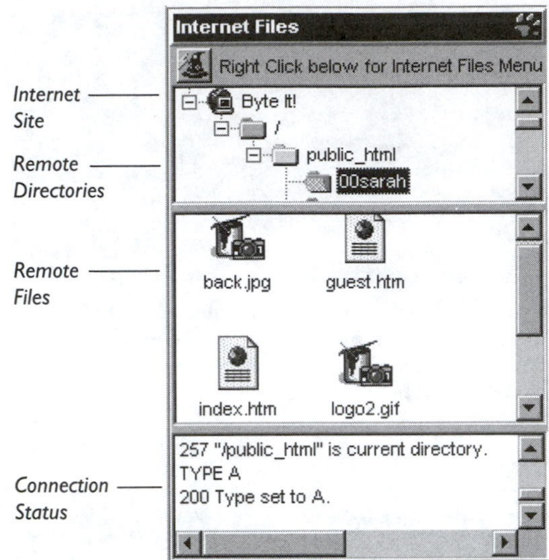

Figure 6. The **Internet Files** resource displays the contents of your Web site folder on the server.

To display the Internet Files resource

1. Select **Resources Manager** from the **View** menu.
2. Select **Internet Files** from the cascading list.

To set up an Internet site

1. From the **Internet Files** resource, click the **Wizard** button.
2. When the **Internet Site Wizard** dialog box appears, read the instructions and click the **Next** button.
3. When the second **Internet Site Wizard** dialog box appears, as shown in Figure 7, enter the name of your Web site in the **What do you want to call your server?** text field, and enter the FTP or World Wide Web address in the **What is your Server Address?** text field. Click the **Next** button.
4. When the third **Internet Site Wizard** dialog box appears, as shown in Figure 8, enter your user name in the **What is your Login name?** text field and enter your password in the **What is your Password?** text field.

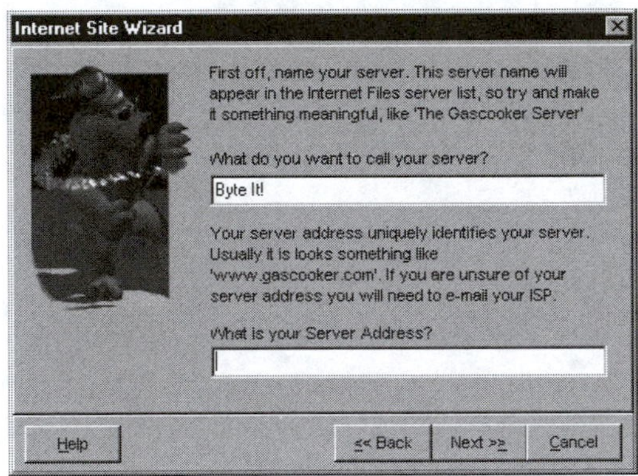

Figure 7. Enter a name for your Web site and the server's FTP or Web site address, then click the **Next** button.

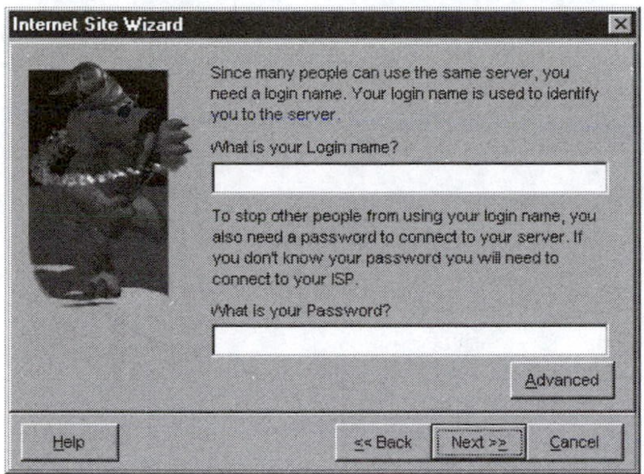

Figure 8. Enter your user name and password.

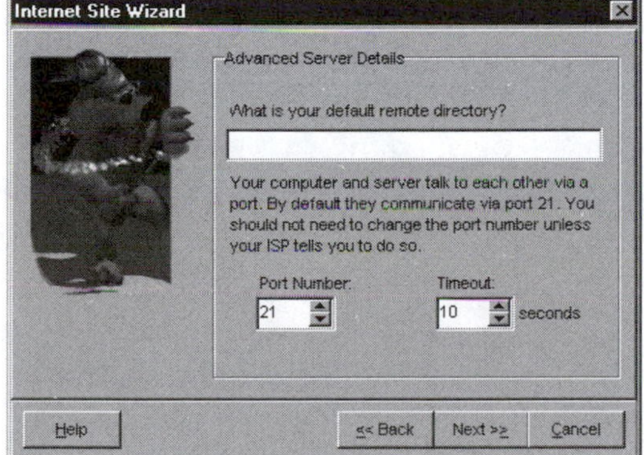

Figure 9. The **Advanced Server Details** options let you specify a default remote directory and change your timeout setting.

A. If your server requires you to log in to a remote directory, click the **Advanced** button.

B. When the **Internet Site Wizard—Advanced Server Details** dialog box appears, as shown in Figure 9, enter the name of your remote directory (for example, **public_html**). You can also change the port number (this is rarely ever necessary) and the Timeout setting.

5. Click the **Next** button.
6. When the final **Internet Site Wizard** dialog box appears, click the **Finish** button.

To view your remote file directory

1. Double-click the Internet site icon for your Web site.
2. When you're connected, you can browse through directories and view files as you would with the **Local Files** resource.

To download a remote file

1. Select a file and click your right mouse button.
2. When the pop-up menu appears, select the **Download** option.
3. When the **Save As** dialog box appears, browse for a directory, then click the **Save** button.

To edit a remote file

1. Select a file and click your right mouse button.
2. When the pop-up menu appears, select the **Edit** option.
3. When the file finishes downloading, make your changes.
4. Click the **Save** button, or select **Save** from the **File** menu to upload your changes to the server.

To remove a remote file

1. Select a file and click your right mouse button.
2. When the pop-up menu appears, select the **Delete** option.
3. When the **Confirm** dialog box appears, click **Yes**.

18 Business Tools

Are you going on the Web for business? If so, you're in the right place at the right time. The Web makes it easy for even one-person shops to look professional and offer a variety of useful services to visitors and customers. Whether you want to sell images, software, and other files online, or set your Web site up as a channel that "pushes" automatically updated content to users' browsers, you already have everything you need to get started. Or you can quickly get what you need with the SuperToolz **AutoDownloader** or from the Web.

Using the Channel Wizard

The **Channel Wizard** helps you set up your Web site as a *channel*. Channels work the same way as regular Web pages. Except that users can also subscribe to your Web site as a channel and receive automatic updates when you change the content on your page.

How does this work? The **Channel Wizard** takes you through the steps of enabling your Web page to broadcast as a channel, and inserts the HTML code for you. This includes buttons that users can click when they want to subscribe to your site. The user needs to have a browsers capable of receiving channels, like Internet Explorer 4.0, Netscape Netcaster, or PointCast.

Since the code required for enabling each of these browsers varies slightly, the **Channel Wizard** covers all your bases and helps you add buttons for each browser to your page. If a visitor finds your content compelling and wants to receive future updates, they can click the button on your page and subscribe.

To set up your WebSite as a channel

1. Place your cursor at the insertion point of your HTML document.
2. Select **Channel Wizard** from the **SuperToolz** menu.
3. When the **Channel Wizard** dialog box appears, as shown in Figure 1, read the instructions and click the **Next** button.
4. When the second **Channel Wizard** dialog box appears, as shown in Figure 2, select one or more channel viewers to enable on your Web site, then click the **Next** button.

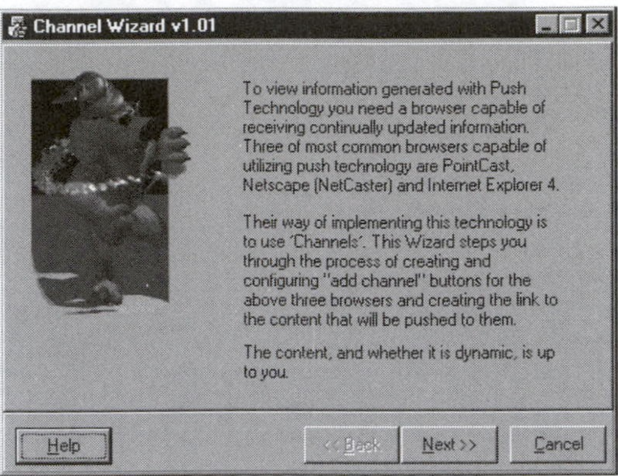

Figure 1. When the **Channel Wizard** dialog box appears, click the **Next** button.

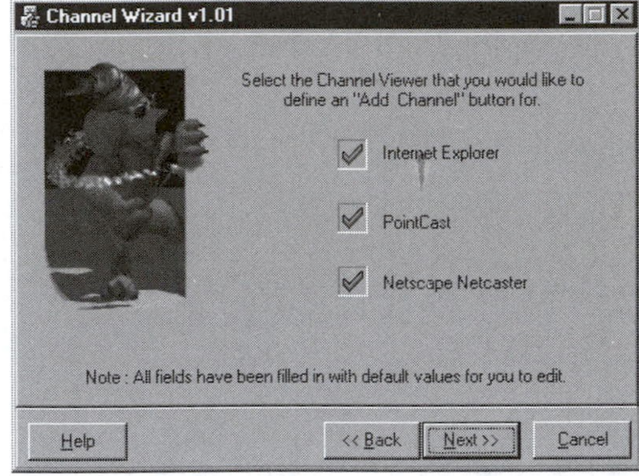

Figure 2. You can leave all three channel browsers selected to set up channel subscription buttons for Internet Explorer, Netscape NetCaster, and PointCast, or you can click check boxes to deselect items.

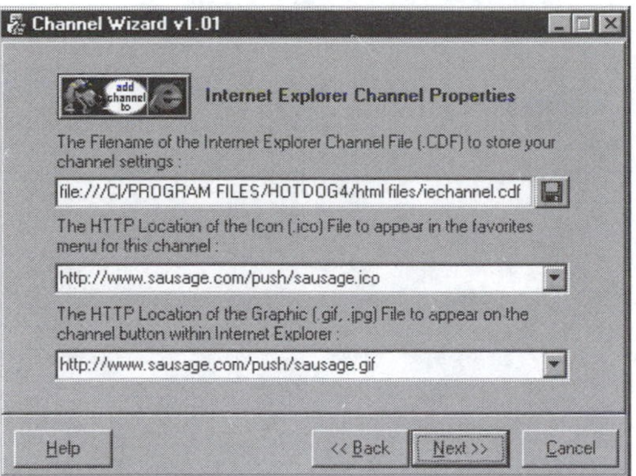

Figure 3. Enter settings for the **Internet Explorer Channel Properties**.

✔ Tips

- The small 'floppy disk' buttons shown in Figures 3 and 4 are the Save button in the Wizard for Channel Definition files.
- Broadcasting channels is called *push* technology because the data gets "pushed" to people's browsers automatically.
- When people have to actively get the data themselves the normal way (by entering a URL in their browser's location window or clicking a link), that's called *pull* technology.
- If your Web site features an online magazine, catalog, newsletter, daily announcements, or other frequently updated content, setting up a channel gives you an easy way to reach people.
- To allow as many people to subscribe as possible, you should leave all three channel browsers selected.

5. When the **Channel Wizard—Internet Explorer Channel Properties** dialog box appears, as shown in Figure 3, specify options for Internet Explorer users, then click the **Next** button.

   A. To enter a file name for the Internet Explorer Channel File (CDF), enter a directory path in the first text field, or click the **Save** (disk icon)button to browse for your Web folder. The CDF file contains the settings for your channel. You need to save it in your Web folder with the **.CDF** file name extension, and upload it to your Web site in order for your channel to work properly.

   B. To enter a location for your channel's ICO file, enter a URL in the second text field. The ICO file points to your Web site and automatically inserts an item in the user's Internet Favorites list so they can easily access your Web site. The URL should point to where you plan to store your ICO file in your remote (server) directory, and should end with the **.ICO** file name extension, for example: **http://www.myWebsite.com/channel.ico**. You can store your ICO file in the same folder as your HTML documents.

   C. You can create your own subscription graphic (the button that users click to subscribe to your Web site channel), or you can use one that Sausage Software has created for you. To define the location of a channel subscription image that you have created, enter the directory path to your image (such as **images/channel.gif**) in the third text field. To use the graphic that Sausage Software has created for you, leave the default URL selected.

6. When the **Channel Wizard—PointCast Channel Properties** dialog box appears, enter options for PointCast users, then click the **Next** button as shown in Figure 4.

   A. Enter a directory path and name for your local CDF file in the first text field, or click the **Save** (disk) icon to browse for your local directory. Save the file to your local Web site directory with the **.CDF** file name extension.

   B. In the second text field, enter the URL (remote file location) for where you plan to store your CDF file (this should correspond to your local file location).

   C. Specify a number of hours in the **Have the Channel Update Every** text field to determine the frequency of your updates. Click the **Next** button.

7. When the **Channel Wizard—Netscape NetCaster Channel Properties** dialog box appears, as shown in Figure 5, enter options for **Netscape NetCaster** users, then click the **Next** button.

   A. Specify the frequency of channel updates by selecting an option from the **Have the Channel Update every** list.

   B. To enter a location for your channel's ICO file, enter a URL in the **The HTTP Location of the Icon (ico) File to appear for this channel** text field. The ICO file points to your Web site and automatically inserts an item in the user's Bookmarks list so they can easily access your Web site. The URL should point to where you plan to store your ICO file in your remote (server) directory, and should end with the **.ICO** file name extension

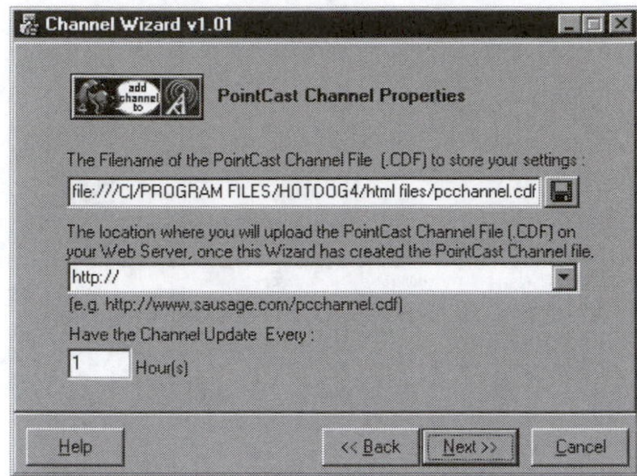

Figure 4. Enter settings for the **PointCast Channel Properties.**

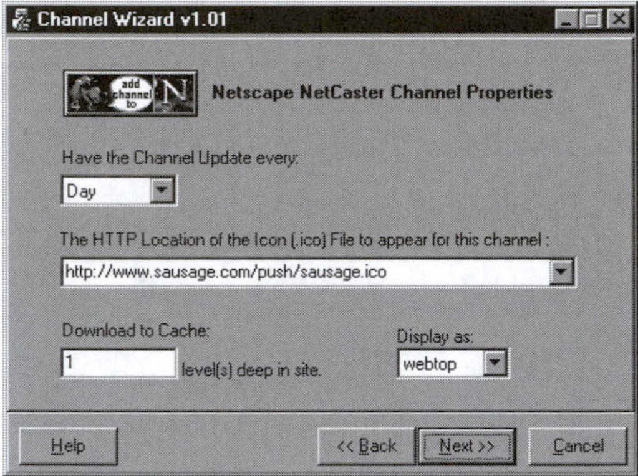

Figure 5. Enter settings for the **Netscape NetCaster Channel Properties.**

USING THE CHANNEL WIZARD

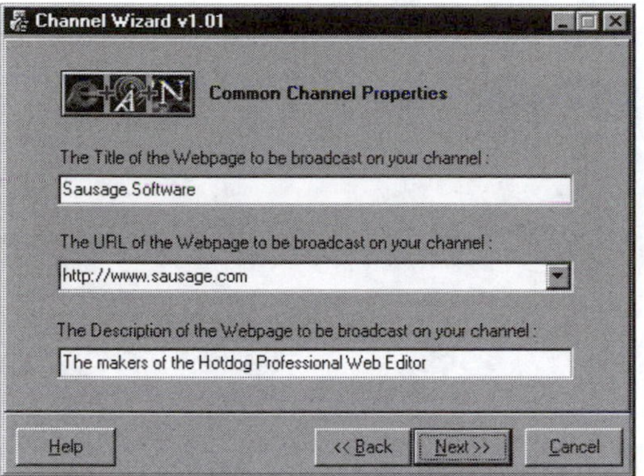

Figure 6. Enter settings for **Common Channel Properties**.

(for example, **http://ww.MyWebSite.com/channel.ico**.) You can store your ICO file in the same folder as your HTML documents.

C. Enter a number in the **Download to Cache** text field. The number should reflect the number of directory levels in your site. For example, if you have an **Images** directory inside of your Web site directory, then your Web site is **2** levels deep. If your Web site directory contains a directory that has another directory inside of it, then your Web site is **3** levels deep. To ensure that Netcaster users receive the entire content of your Web site, you need to enter the correct number of levels.

D. Select a display option from the pull-down list. **Webtop** displays your channel as part of the user's desktop and **Full Window** fills the user's entire computer screen. **Window** displays your Web site channel as a regular, resizeable browser window and is less likely to annoy users.

8. When the **Channel Wizard—Common Channel Properties** dialog box appears, as shown in Figure 6, specify a title, URL, and description for your channel, then click the **Next** button. These properties apply to channel settings for all three browsers.

A. Enter your Web page's title in the first text field.

B. Enter your Web site's URL in the second text field. To broadcast your entire site, enter the default URL (such as **http://www.isp.net/mysite/**). If you include the name of a specific document (such as **http://www.isp.net/mysite/index.html**) then your channel only broadcasts that one document.

(continued)

c. Enter a brief description of your Web site in the third text field.

9. When the final **Channel Wizard** dialog box appears, as shown in Figure 7, click the **Finish** button to place the HTML code in your document. You can also confirm your settings and click the **Back** button to make changes.

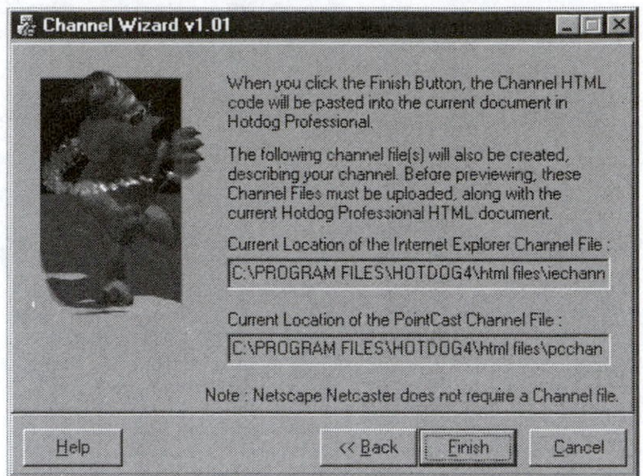

Figure 7. Confirm your settings and click the **Finish** button to generate the HTML code and files for your channels.

✔ Tips

- Why limit yourself or your visitors? Add buttons and specifications for all three channel browsers.
- You don't need to have all three channel browsers (or any of them) installed on your own computer to enable them for your users.
- Make sure to enter different file names for your Internet Explorer and PointCast CDF files (Netcaster does not require a CDF file).
- While it is very thoughtful of Sausage Software to create channel selection buttons for you, using these images instead of your own can slow down your page display. Since Sausage Software stores the buttons on their Web site, your users' browsers have to make an extra trip to their server to get the images.

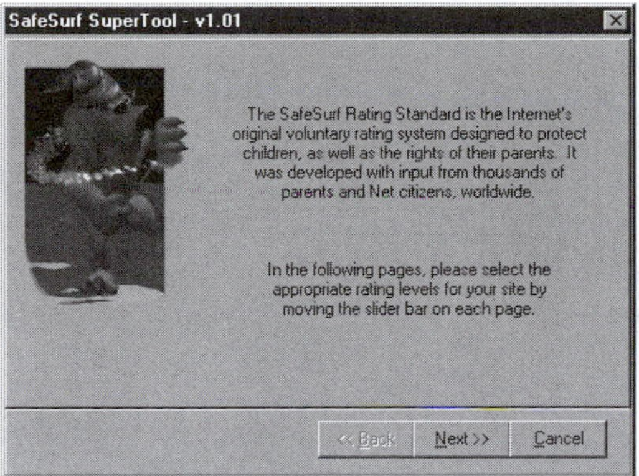

Figure 8. To begin rating your Web site, read the instructions and click the **Next** button.

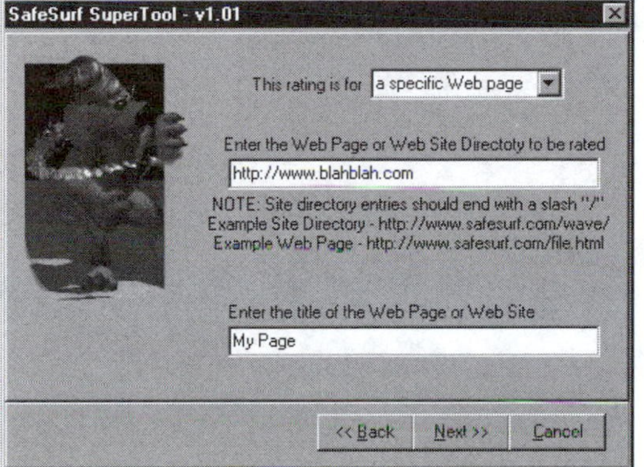

Figure 9. Enter information about the Web page or Web site you want to apply ratings to.

Rating Your Site with SafeSurf

If your Web site contains content for children, **SafeSurf** can reassure their parents about your site. If some people may find your Web site's content inappropriate, **SafeSurf** can help you avoid legal problems and save you the trouble of dealing with offended visitors. SafeSurf is an organization that helps individuals and businesses rate their sites so parents can protect their children by setting up their browsers to block certain types of content.

Web site developers can voluntarily submit their Web site URLs to **SafeSurf** for ratings. When **SafeSurf** sends notification by email, the developer can place the appropriate HTML code in their documents and display the official **SafeSurf Rated** logo. It costs nothing to rate your site.

The **SafeSurf** SuperTool guides you through the process of generating and inserting your ratings code, and helps you register your results with **SafeSurf**.

To apply SafeSurf ratings to your Website

1. Go online (the **SafeSurf** SuperTool generates an email message for you to send to SafeSurf).
2. Place your cursor at the insertion point of the HTML document you want to rate.
3. Select **SafeSurf** from the **SuperToolz** menu.
4. When the first **SafeSurf** dialog box appears, as shown in Figure 8, click the **Next** button.
5. When the second **SafeSurf** dialog box appears, as shown in Figure 9, enter information about the Web page or Web site you want to apply ratings to, then click the **Next** button.

A. Select an option for whether your rating applies to an individual Web page, or an entire directory, from the **This rating is for** pull-down list.

B. Enter the URL for your Web page or Web site directory in the **Enter the Web Page or Web Site Directory to be rated** text field.

C. Enter a title for your Web page in the **Enter the title of the Web Page or Web Site** text field.

6. When the **SafeSurf—Recommended Age Range** dialog box appears, as shown in Figure 10, use the slider to determine an appropriate age level. When you move the slider, the corresponding age level appears in the **Description** area. Click the **Next** button.

7. When the **SafeSurf—Sex, Violence and Profanity** dialog box appears, as shown in Figure 11, move the slider to adjust the level, then click the **Next** button.

   A. You can also set individual ratings for profanity, drug use, intolerance, and other specific themes by clicking the **Set Individual Ratings** button to progress through a series of dialog boxes. Individual ratings are helpful in some situations. If your Web site's content is basically inoffensive but contains some profanity, rating your site at high levels for sex, violence, *and* profanity doesn't make sense.

8. When the dialog box shown in Figure 12 appears, click the **Add Image** checkbox to display the **SafeSurf** logo on your page, then click the **Next** button.

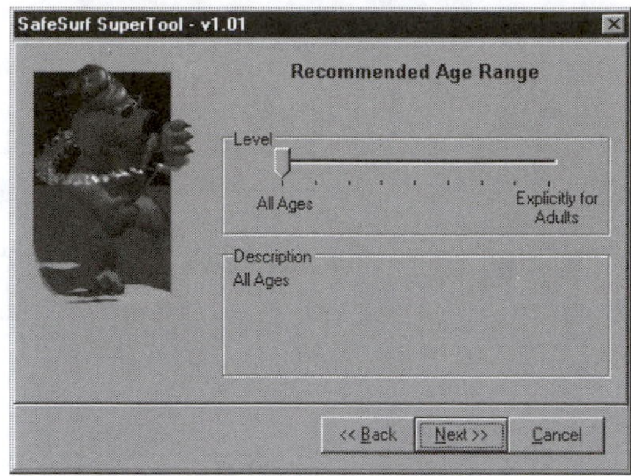

Figure 10. When the **Recommended Age Range** dialog box appears, you can adjust the slider to the appropriate age level.

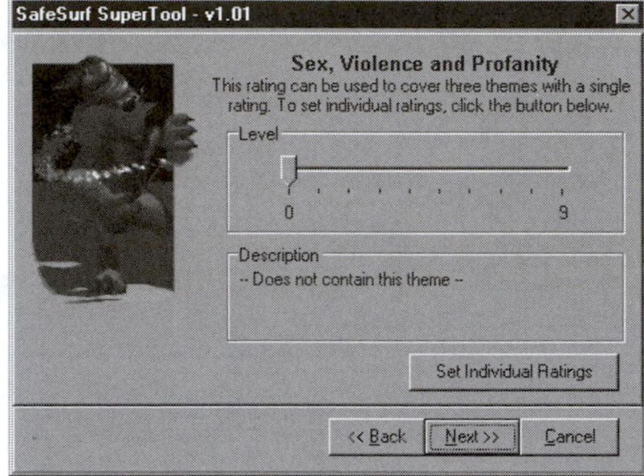

Figure 11. When the **Sex, Violence and Profanity** dialog box appears, specify a level for these themes by moving the slider. Or choose ratings for individual criteria by clicking the **Set Individual Ratings** button.

Figure 12. Select the **Add Image** checkbox to display the **SafeSurf Rated** logo on your Web page.

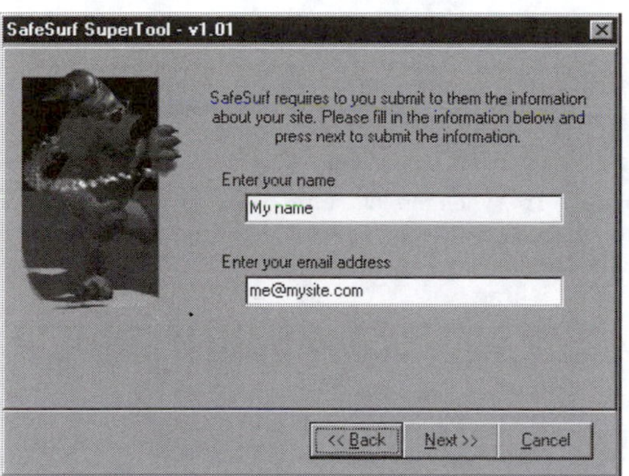

Figure 13. To begin submitting your information to SafeSurf, enter your name and email address.

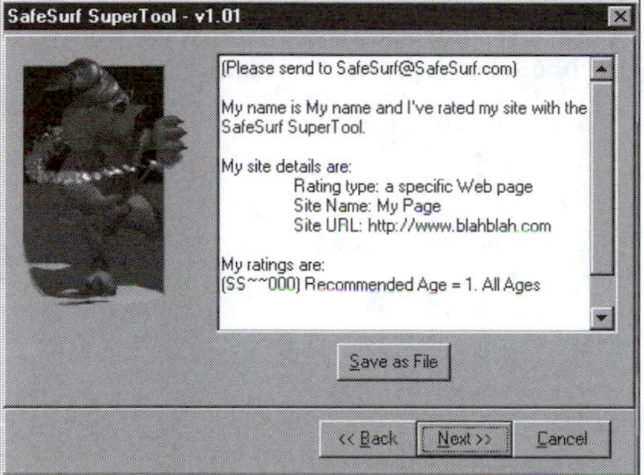

Figure 14. If you are not online, the **SafeSurf** SuperTool helps you generate a text file that you can copy and paste into an email message later.

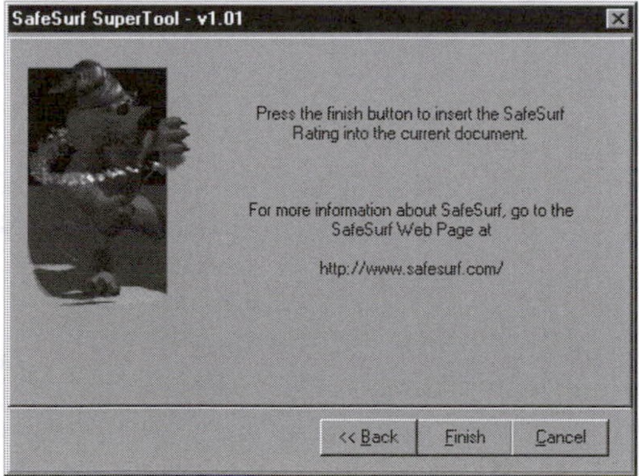

Figure 15. To generate the ratings HTML code and insert it in your document, click the **Finish** button.

9. When the dialog box shown in Figure 13 appears, enter your name and email address in the appropriate text field. SafeSurf requires you to send your page information to them. Click the **Next** button.

A. If you are online, the **SafeSurf** SuperTool generates an email message and sends off your ratings information.

B. If you are still offline, the dialog box shown in Figure 14 appears and displays a text file with your ratings information. Click the **Save as File** button to create a text file that you can later copy and paste into an email message, which you can send to **SafeSurf@SafeSurf.com**. Click the **Next** button.

10. When the final dialog box appears, as shown in Figure 15, click the **Finish** button.

Selling Web Page Content with InfoSeller

Are you an artist or writer? Or do you have valuable information to offer? Sell it on the Web. You can open an online gallery, or become your own publisher. Sell your clip art, stock photos, and Web page content for amounts as little as $2.00 a piece.

All you need to get started is some exciting page content, a valid VISA or Mastercard, and the **InfoSeller** SuperTool. InfoSeller gets you started by registering you with eVend and helping you generate "cashlets". A "cashlet" is a Java applet that displays information about your file and enables visitors to pay for the file by credit card and download it.

You don't have to worry about the day to day transactions because eVend processes the orders securely, and pays you for orders on a monthly basis. All this for about 20 or 30 cents per transaction, plus a small percentage. For more information, visit eVend's Web site at *www.evend.com*.

To download the InfoSeller

1. Go online.
2. Select **AutoDownloader** from the **SuperToolz** menu.
3. When the **AutoDownloader** dialog box appears, select the **InfoSeller** SuperTool for download (for more about downloading SuperToolz, see Chapter 1).
4. Unlike most other SuperToolz, the **InfoSeller** does not download and install automatically. The **InfoSeller** requires you to click **OK** to continue installing when the **Warning** dialog box displays, as shown in Figure 16.

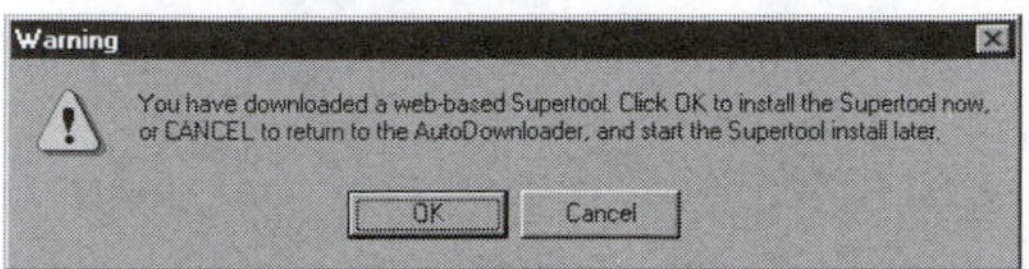

Figure 16. When the **Warning** dialog box appears to let you know the InfoSeller is about to be installed, click **OK**.

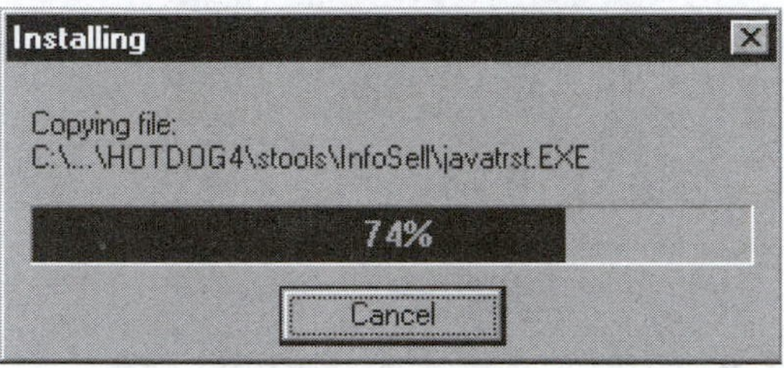

Figure 17. The **Installing** dialog box tells you the status of the **InfoSeller** SuperTool installation.

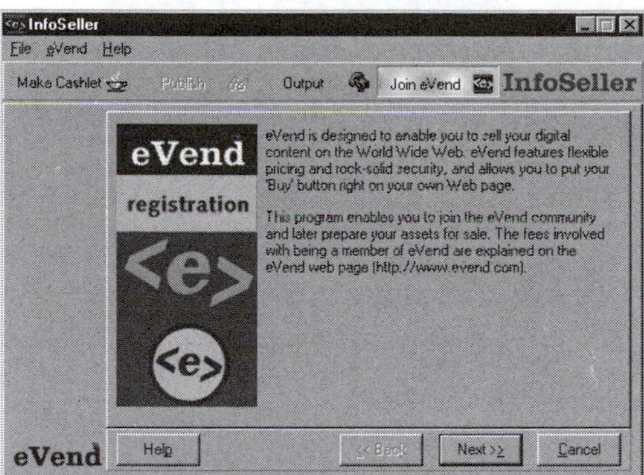

Figure 18. The **InfoSeller** guides you through the process of registering with eVend and creating Java applet "cashlets" for selling files from your Web page.

5. The **Installing** dialog box appears, as shown in Figure 17, and tells you the status of the installation. When the **InfoSeller** finishes installing, you can register with eVend and create your cashlets.

To sign up with eVend and create cashlets with the InfoSeller

1. Go online.
2. Select **InfoSeller** from the **SuperToolz** menu.
3. When the **InfoSeller** application window appears, as shown in Figure 18, click the **Next** button, and follow the instructions. The InfoSeller guides you through the steps of registering with eVend so you can create and sell online cashlets.

Once you register with eVend, the **InfoSeller** guides you through the process of creating cashlets and generates the HTML code and Java CLASS files for you. You can create additional cashlets at any time by launching the **InfoSeller**.

Link Exchange

Get the word out about your site—join the Link Exchange. Link Exchange members display banner advertisements on each others' Web sites in exchange for free advertising on other members' Web sites. Once you insert the Link Exchange's special banner code in your HTML document, the Link Exchange automatically displays banner advertisements on your page. First, you visit the Link Exchange's Web site at *www.linkexchange.com*, read their information, and register with them. They'll also give you tips and hints on creating a banner advertisement for your Web site. Then you launch the **Link Exchange** SuperTool to insert the Link Exchange's banner code on your home page.

Figure 19. You can register with the Link Exchange from their home page at **www.linkexchange.com.** The **Link Exchange** SuperTool then helps you generate the required banner advertisement code.

To exchange banner ads

1. Create a banner ad that is 400 pixels wide by 40 pixels high (you can make a simple one in your Windows Paint accessory, and convert it to a GIF or JPEG with the **Button Editor** SuperTool).
2. Visit the Link Exchange's home page, as shown in Figure 19, read their information, and fill out their registration form.
3. Return to HotDog Pro, open the document you plan to feature banner advertisements on, and place your cursor at the insertion point of the document.
4. Select **Link Exchange** from the **SuperToolz** menu.
5. When the **Link Exchange** dialog box appears, select the **Existing User** radio button.
6. When the second **Link Exchange** dialog box appears, enter your LinkExchange account number (this is generated when you register with them), and click the **Finish** button.

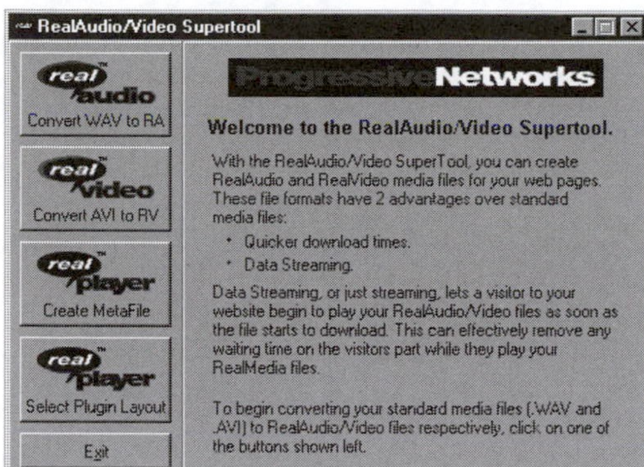

Figure 20. The **RealAudio/Video SuperTool** helps you convert your large WAV and AVI movies to RealAudio and RealVideo multimedia that streams quickly to your visitors' browsers.

RealAudio/Video

Video and audio can make Web sites more exciting and interactive. Instead of just showing pictures from your band's last gig, your visitors can download actual video and sound clips. Or you can highlight the sights and sounds from your last vacation, or demonstrate your company's products. So why doesn't everyone display multimedia on their Web site? Because sound and video files are enormous and take a long time to download.

Now, the **RealAudio/Video** SuperTool gives you an edge. It converts your WAV sound files and AVI movies to RealAudio and RealVideo multimedia files, and generates the code for embedding the files in your Web page. If your users have the Progressive Network's RealMedia Player plug-in, your files start playing back right away. The user never has to wait for the entire file to download. The technology that makes this possible is called *real time streaming*. You and your users can get the latest version of the RealMedia Player from Progressive Networks' home page at *www.realplayer.com*.

To convert WAV and AVI files to RealAudio and RealVideo files

1. Select **RealAudio/Video** from the **SuperToolz** menu.

2. When the **RealAudio/Video SuperTool** application window appears, as shown in Figure 20, click the **Convert WAV to RA** to convert a WAV sound file, or click **Convert AVI to RA** to convert an AVI movie (RealAudio and Video are saved with the **.RA** file name extension). When the conversion options appear, browse for your multimedia files and pick a directory for the converted files.

3. Click the **Create MetaFile** button to create a **MetaFile** with the **.RM** file name extension. The MetaFile contains file information that the RealPlayer plug-in needs to play your sound track or movie. You can also create a "play list" with multiple files. When the **MetaFile** dialog box displays, click the **Next** button and follow the dialog box's instructions for entering a URL and listing your RA file.

4. Click the **Select Plug-in Layout** button to specify options for how the RealPlayer plug-in displays on your Web page.

Index

M

N

P

R

S

T

U

V

W